T0271234

Conversations with
Dana Gioia

Literary Conversations Series
Monika Gehlawat
General Editor

Conversations with
Dana Gioia

Edited by John Zheng

University Press of Mississippi / Jackson

The University Press of Mississippi is the scholarly publishing agency of the Mississippi Institutions of Higher Learning: Alcorn State University, Delta State University, Jackson State University, Mississippi State University, Mississippi University for Women, Mississippi Valley State University, University of Mississippi, and University of Southern Mississippi.

www.upress.state.ms.us

The University Press of Mississippi is a member of the Association of University Presses.

Manufactured in the United States of America
First printing 2021
∞

Library of Congress Cataloging-in-Publication Data

Names: Gioia, Dana, interviewee. | Zheng, Jianqing, editor.
Title: Conversations with Dana Gioia / edited by John Zheng.
Description: Jackson: University Press of Mississippi, 2021. | Series:
  Literary Conversations series | Includes bibliographical references and index.
Identifiers: LCCN 2020028472 (print) | LCCN 2020028473 (ebook) | ISBN
  978-1-4968-3203-0 (hardback) | ISBN 978-1-4968-3204-7 (trade paperback) | ISBN
  978-1-4968-3206-1 (epub) | ISBN 978-1-4968-3205-4 (epub) | ISBN 978-1-4968-3208-5
  (pdf) | ISBN 978-1-4968-3207-8 (pdf)
Subjects: LCSH: Gioia, Dana—Interviews. | Poets, American—21st
  century—Interviews.
Classification: LCC PS3557.I5215 Z46 2021 (print) | LCC PS3557.I5215
  (ebook) | DDC 811/.54—dc23
LC record available at https://lccn.loc.gov/2020028472
LC ebook record available at https://lccn.loc.gov/2020028473

British Library Cataloging-in-Publication Data available

Works by Dana Gioia

Poetry

Daily Horoscope. Graywolf Press, 1986.
The Gods of Winter. Graywolf Press, 1991.
Interrogations at Noon. Graywolf Press, 2001.
Pity the Beautiful. Graywolf Press, 2012.
99 Poems: New & Selected. Graywolf Press, 2016.

Criticism

Can Poetry Matter?: Essays on Poetry and American Culture. Graywolf Press, 1992.
    Revised Tenth Anniversary Edition, 2002.
Barrier of a Common Language: An American Looks at Contemporary British Poetry.
    University of Michigan Press, 2003.
Disappearing Ink: Poetry at the End of Print Culture. Graywolf Press, 2004.
The Catholic Writer Today. Wiseblood Books, 2014.
Poetry as Enchantment. Wiseblood Books, 2016.
The Catholic Writer Today: and Other Essays. Wiseblood Books, 2019.

Fine Press Editions

Daily Horoscope. Windhover Press, 1982.
Two Poems. Bowery Press, 1982.
Letter to the Bahamas. Abattoir Editions, 1983.
Summer. Aralia Press, 1983.
Journeys in Sunlight. Ex Ophidia Press, 1986.
Words for Music. Parallel Editions, 1987.
Two Poems/Due Poesie. Stamperia Ampersand, 1987.
Planting a Sequoia. Aralia Press, 1991.
The Litany. Aralia Press, 1999.
On Being a California Poet. Southern Methodist University Library, 2003.

Lonely Impulse of Delight: One Reader's Childhood. Artichoke Editions, 2007.
Homage to Valerio Magrelli. Stamperia Ampersand, 2009.
The Living and the Dead: Translations of Mario Luzi. Aralia Press, 2012.
Film Noir, Aralia Press, 2014.
The Ballad of Jesús Ortiz. Providence Press, 2018
Two Epitaphs. Aralia Press, 2019.

Volumes in Translation

La ce bun poezia?: Două eseuri despre poezia şi cultura americană (Translated into
  Romanian). Translated by Mirella Balţşand Gabriel Stănescu. Bucharest, Romania:
  Criterion Publishing, 1998.
Interrogations at Noon: Selected Poems and Essays (Translated into Russian). Edited by
  Nikolai Paltsev. Translated by Paltsev et al. Moscow: Rosspen, 2007.
The Voice at Noon: Selected Poems and Essays by Dana Gioia (Translated into Russian).
  Rossiyskaya Politicheskaya Entsiklopediya, 2007.
La Escala Ardiente. Seguida Del Ensayo ¿Importa la Poesia? (Translated into Spanish).
  Translated by José Emilio Pacheco, Elsa Cross, Hernán Bravo Varela, Zulai Marcela
  Funetes, Jennifer Clement, and Víctor Manual Mendiola. Mexico City: Ediciones el
  Tucán de Virginia, 2010.
Planting a Sequoia and Other Poems (Translated into Greek). Translated by Kostas
  Zotopoulos. Athens, Greece: Society of (de)Kata, 2019.
La oscuridad intacta. Poemas escogidos (Translated into Spanish). Edited and translated
  by Gustavo Solórzano-Alfaro. Valencia, Spain: Colección La Cruz del Sur, Editorial
  Pre-Textos, 2020.

Operas and Libretti

Nosferatu (2004), music by Alva Henderson. Libretto published by Graywolf Press,
  2001. Recorded by Albany Records, 2005. Audio CD with libretto.
Tony Caruso's Final Broadcast (2008), music by Paul Salerni. Recorded by Naxos
  Records, 2010. Audio CD with libretto.
The Three Feathers (2014), music by Lori Laitman.
Haunted (2019), music by Paul Salerni.

Other Musical Collaborations

Counting the Children (1994), dance theater with music by Robert Lindner and choreography by Mark Ruhala.

Never Broken (2003), song cycles with music composed by Stefania De Kenessey. Recorded by Center Stage Records, 2003.

Speaking of Love (2016), songs and song cycles composed by Paul Salerni. Recorded by Troy records. Audio CD with lyrics.

Sung with Words (2015), jazz songs composed by Helen Sung. Recorded by Stricker Street Records, 2018. Audio CD with lyrics.

Edited Books

The Ceremony and Other Stories by Weldon Kees. Abattoir Editions, 1983.

The Ceremony and Other Stories by Weldon Kees. Expanded edition. Graywolf Press, 1984.

Formal Introductions: An Investigative Anthology. Aralia Press, 1994.

Certain Solitudes: Essays on the Poetry of Donald Justice, coedited with William Logan. University of Arkansas Press, 1998.

Selected Short Stories of Weldon Kees. University of Nebraska Press, 2002.

This Man's Army: A War in Fifty-Odd Sonnets by John Allan Wyeth. University of South Carolina Press, 2008.

Sacred and Profane Love: The Poetry of John Donne. Trinity Forum, 2010.

God's Grandeur: The Poems of Gerard Manley Hopkins. Trinity Forum, 2016.

Jack Foley's Unmanageable Masterpiece, coedited with Peter Whitfield. Monongahela Books, 2019.

Selected Edited Anthologies and Handbooks

Poems from Italy, coedited with William Jay Smith. New Rivers Press, 1985.

New Italian Poets, coedited with Michael Palma. Story Line Press, 1991.

The Longman Anthology of Short Fiction: Stories and Authors in Context, coedited with R.S. Gwynn. Longman, 2001.

The Longman Masters of Short Fiction, coedited with R.S. Gwynn. Longman, 2001.

The Misread City: New Literary Los Angeles, coedited with Scott Timberg. Red Hen Press, 2003.

California Poetry: From the Gold Rush to the Present, coedited with Chryss Yost and Jack Hicks. Heyday Books, 2003.

Twentieth-Century American Poetics: Poets on the Art of Poetry, coedited with David Mason and Meg Schoerke. McGraw-Hill, 2004.

Twentieth-Century American Poetry, coedited with David Mason and Meg Schoerke. McGraw-Hill, 2004.

100 Great Poets of the English Language. Longman, 2004.

The Art of the Short Story: 52 Great Authors, Their Best Short Fiction, and Their Insights on Writing, coedited with R.S. Gwynn. Longman, 2005.

Handbook of Literary Terms: Literature, Language, Theory, coedited with X. J. Kennedy and Mark Bauerlein. Longman, 2008.

An Introduction to Fiction, coedited with X. J. Kennedy. Longman, 2010.

An Introduction to Poetry, coedited with X. J. Kennedy. Longman, 2010.

Literature for Life, coedited with X. J. Kennedy and Nina Revoyr. Pearson, 2012.

Backpack Literature: An Introduction to Fiction, Poetry, Drama, and Writing. Pearson, 2016.

The Best American Poetry: 2018. Scribner Poetry, 2018.

Literature: An Introduction to Fiction, Poetry, Drama, and Writing, 14th edition, coedited with X. J. Kennedy and Dan Stone. Pearson, 2020.

Translations

Mottetti: Poems of Love by Eugenio Montale. Graywolf Press, 1990.

Juno Plots Her Revenge by Seneca. Aralia Press, 1993.

The Madness of Hercules (*Hercules Furens*) by Seneca. Included in *Seneca: The Tragedies*, Volume 2, edited by David Slavitt. Johns Hopkins Press, 1995. 43–104.

Key Government Reports (developed, introduced, and coauthored by Gioia)

Reading at Risk: A Survey of Reading America. National Endowment for the Arts, 2004.

To Read or Not to Read: A Question of National Consequences. National Endowment for the Arts, 2007.

How the United States Funds the Arts. With Tyler Cowen. National Endowment for the Arts, 2004; 2nd ed. 2007.

Reading on the Rise. National Endowment for the Arts, 2009.

Contents

Acknowledgments

For a project as challenging and complex as *Conversations with Dana Gioia*, I owe a list of debts. First, I am indebted to my editors, Katie Keene and Mary Heath, for their patience; to the series general editor, Monika Gehlawat, for reviewing the manuscript; and to all UPM staff, including Craig Gill, UPM Director, for their support and help behind the scenes. I am also indebted to the interviewers and the copyright holders for granting me permissions. Next I owe a debt of gratitude to Theodore Haddin for reading the introduction. Finally I am grateful beyond measure to Dana Gioia for his generous support and encouragement. Without his confidence in me, this project would still be a dream. I hope you will enjoy reading this book as much as I have enjoyed editing it.

Introduction

Dana Gioia—poet, critic, and cultural leader—has been internationally acclaimed as a unique voice in contemporary American poetry and literary criticism. The publication of his controversial essay "Can Poetry Matter?" in the *Atlantic* in 1991 (followed the next year by his influential collection *Can Poetry Matter?: Essays on Poetry and American Culture*) triggered a heated debate about the diminishing role of the poet in contemporary culture. The poet's forthright question alerted readers to the diminished state of American poetry, and his thought-provoking essay has continued to resonate. Gioia's positions were frequently attacked, especially by members of the creative writing establishment, but he called that censure "a small price to pay for the freedom to write honestly" (Davis).

Honesty and skepticism have been notable qualities of Gioia's literary criticism. He states what he believes clearly, often from the perspective of a serious writer outside the university. As a public intellectual, he holds that the "best criticism tends to come from dissenters" (Davis). After the success of *Can Poetry Matter?*, Gioia published *Barrier of a Common Language: An American Looks at Contemporary British Poetry* (2003), *Disappearing Ink: Poetry at the End of Print Culture* (2004); and *Catholic Writer Today and Other Essays* (2019) as well as editing over twenty literary anthologies. A creative visionary, forthright critic, and pioneering poet, he has played a pivotal role in contemporary American poetry similar in some ways to that of Ezra Pound in early Modernism. Like Pound, Gioia's goal has been to change literary opinion and expand the possibilities for poetry. He recognized the end of Modernism and the moribundity of the institutionalized avant-garde; he argued for more honest and intelligent reviewing; he questioned the isolated state of American poetry; he advocated the return to form and narrative. What's more, he had "a knack for seeing the talents of [new or neglected writers] and promoting them when no one else would do so" because he has "something in short supply in the literary world—integrity" (Mason 135).

Gioia has gained fame as a literary critic and public intellectual, and his achievements as Chairman of the National Endowment for the Arts made notable contributions to American culture. But poetry has always been the center of his literary identity. He has followed an independent course as a poet. He created a distinctive lyric style, mixing elements from high and popular culture, and exploring both formal and free verse. His five collections of verse have established him as a major contemporary poet. *Daily Horoscope* (1986) garnered unusual attention for a first book. Critics commended or condemned the book for its use of rhyme and meter. *The Gods of Winter* (1991), which commemorated the death of his first son, was praised on both sides of the Atlantic, and Gioia shared (with Adrienne Rich) the Poets' Prize that year. *Interrogations at Noon* (2001) won the American Book Award. After a long break occasioned by Gioia's public service, *Pity the Beautiful* (2012) appeared, and soon thereafter Gioia won the Aiken Taylor Award for lifetime achievement in modern poetry. When *99 Poems: New & Selected* (2016) appeared, reviewers treated Gioia's poetic stature as self-evident, and the volume earned the author a second Poets' Prize.

In regard to the general aesthetic of his poetry, Gioia asserts, "Mine is essentially postmodernist in that it tries to combine the intensity and integrity of Modernist poetry with the sensual appeal and musical power of meter and rhyme" (Johnson). Gioia sees his poetic work as an alternative to the intellectuality of academic postmodernism. He seeks to reconcile the intensity of Modernist poetry with vital elements drawn from popular culture. His style did not originate in an aversion to Modernism. Gioia locates his poetic mentors as key modern figures such as T. S. Eliot, Wallace Stevens, Ezra Pound, Rainer Maria Rilke, Eugenio Montale, and Paul Valéry, but as a young poet, he felt the creative possibilities of Modernist enterprise had already been exhausted. Surviving mostly in the university, the once vital movement had become remote and cerebral. Meanwhile the free verse confessional style of the 1970s seemed to him slack and self-indulgent. He felt that poetry needed a vital connection with the musical and narrative energy found in popular culture, especially film, rock, jazz, and later hip-hop. Gioia has identified W. H. Auden, Weldon Kees, and Philip Larkin as precursors in this synthesis between high and popular culture.

To revitalize American poetry, Gioia helped create a new style and sensibility among young poets of his generation. Advocating the revival of form and narrative, he became a central figure of the New Formalism. This influential movement, he claimed, "connected literary poetry to the energy of the popular culture—which had remained rooted in auditory forms like song and storytelling. In this sense the revival was both populist and democratic, though deeply informed by literary tradition. It also helped reconcile Modernist poetic practice with the possibilities of traditional techniques. It moved poetry forward while also reconnecting it to its primal roots in orality and performance" (Johnson).

Conversations with Dana Gioia is a collection of interviews over a span of almost thirty years, selected from more than one hundred published interviews and arranged chronologically. Presenting Gioia's thoughts about literature, music, culture, Catholicism, aesthetics, and life, the book covers the different aspects of Gioia's broad-ranging career. The interviews also explore his childhood and family background, his education from parochial school through graduate school at Stanford and Harvard, as well as his decision to leave a doctorate program in Comparative Literature for business. He describes both his fifteen years at General Foods when he wrote only at night and on weekends, and explains his decision to quit his job to write full-time. He also discusses the sudden death of his first son and its difficult aftermath. Other interviews examine his later public service as Chairman of the National Endowment for the Arts and his return to California where he became both the Judge Widney Professor of Poetry and Public Culture at the University of Southern California and the state poet laureate. Across the many different phases of his life, one senses an underlying integrity. When asked about his most satisfying literary achievement, he responds: "In general terms, I'm proud to have engaged and expanded the audience for poetry. I tried to do this as an artist, a critic, and a cultural leader" (Cusatis).

Significantly for this book, Gioia takes the interview seriously as a literary form. Some writers have a casual attitude toward interviews. Gioia looks on the interview as a powerful vernacular form of literary criticism—a contemporary version of the classical form of dialogue. He uses the interview to communicate his ideas and aesthetics to a nonacademic audience. Many of the interviews were done in written form with the reporters submitting questions, and Gioia offering careful written answers. The conversations cover numerous topics, but they consistently engage issues of literary history and poetic theory. Committed to the role of the public intellectual, Gioia avoids academic jargon. He cultivates an intelligent but accessible public style that addresses both the intelligent common readers and the literati.

Likewise, Gioia emphasizes the importance of serious and engaged criticism to the health of literary culture. He repeatedly speaks of himself as a poet-critic working in the tradition of Eliot, Pound, Auden, Jarrell, and Rexroth, who considered criticism an integral part of their poetic vocation. These critics also wrote for a general non-specialist audience as public intellectuals. Gioia takes pride in his conviction that poet-critics often note changes in literary culture earlier than their academic counterparts. As working writers, they feel the pulse of literature. In an interview with Garrick Davis, Gioia presents his visionary sense of the role of the poet-critic: "The poet-critic plays a crucial role in modern literary life, especially during times of artistic innovation or cultural stagnation. The critic creates the perspectives and standards by which new work can be understood and judged. . . . They observe changes in the art, the audience, and the culture before non-artists do. They also write about their art with the passion of personal commitment."

In other interviews, Gioia laments the decline of honest and engaged criticism. He points out that today "most poets have abandoned criticism" (McPhillips). Few take the risk of writing negative reviews. One of the major themes of "Can Poetry Matter?" is the negative impact of creative writing programs on American poetry. "Once poets begin to think of themselves as academic professionals, their rules of behavior begin to diverge from the rules an artist would follow. In America, the problem is the professionalization of poetry." He continues to remark, "There are, consequently, two types of poetry criticism being written in America; one is theoretical and ideological and the other is subjective and, alas, blandly descriptive, rather than evaluative" (Cartwright). Specifically, Gioia refers to the professional conflicts of interest that undermine honest reviewing: "In America, one teaching poet rarely gives a bad review to another teaching poet, no matter how dull or dreadful the book is. Most book reviews are blandly approving, and poetry criticism has become rife with euphemism and empty compliments" (Cartwright). Untrustworthy reviews impede the course of literary criticism. They distance readers from approaching poetry willingly and further encapsulate poetry in the small world of academia. Observing the decline of reviewing, Gioia reminds us that "criticism creates the conversation about literature that informs and enlarges the audience. When criticism is healthy, literature becomes more relevant and vital. Reviews give us the news of literature. These reviews matter greatly when they are intelligent, well-written, and honest" (Passafiume).

Gioia's interviews also illuminate his poetry and poetics. Since the interviews are so consciously done, they represent an extension of his critical thinking. His remarks about New Formalism in certain interviews complement his essays such as "Notes on the New Formalism" and "The Poet in an

Age of Prose." Here, for example, Gioia comments on his notion of "pseudo-formal poetry," a term he coined to define a type of slack contemporary poem:

> It is a poem that employs formal principles so sloppily that they have no integrity. The lines appear roughly similar but lack the energy that regular rhythm gives. Pseudo-formal poems may be arranged in regular stanzas, but on close examination the visual form has no integral relation to the sound. A good poem rewards scrutiny. The closer one looks at any formal element in a pseudo-formal poem, the more arbitrary or imperfect it appears. Nothing survives close examination. It's just language chopped up into a vaguely regular shape without sufficient attention to sound or structure. It is neither good formal verse nor good free verse—just superficial pretense. (Brame)

This passage provides an expanded commentary on the fifth section of "Notes on the New Formalism." It recapitulates his analysis of a stylistic trend that emerged in the 1980s, concerning the style's incompetence, incongruity, and confusion shown in structure, rhythm, form, and line lengths.

Convinced of the human importance of poetry, Gioia maintains his hope for the art in an age when poetry is generally considered a marginal and declining medium. Insisting on its cultural relevance as a central literary form, Gioia reminds his interlocutors that poetry is the most ancient mode of human imagination. He is never apologetic about the art. Instead, he celebrates the physical immediacy of poetry. The art is "embodied truth created for creatures with bodies. A poem doesn't communicate primarily through ideas. It expresses itself in sound, images, rhythms, and emotions. We experience poems holistically. They speak to us simultaneously through our minds, our hearts, our imaginations, and our physical bodies. They speak to us, in other words, as incarnated beings" (Koss).

Throughout the various interviews, Gioia also recalls his own literary influences. He praises the intellectual force and independence of Eliot and Pound, notes Frost's ability to create a poem that argues with itself, and admires Auden's moral seriousness. He envies W. B. Yeats's verse technique and praises Robinson Jeffers's visionary naturalism. He also fondly remembers his teachers, Elizabeth Bishop, Donald Davie, and Robert Fitzgerald, who served as early role models. Though he recognizes writers who influenced him, Gioia also understands that "influence is a fluid thing. Sometimes a poet teaches you one small but useful trick, sometimes they change your life" (Paul). This fluidity of influence nevertheless came first in his childhood from his mother, who recited beloved poems from memory.

She helped him understand that "poetry is an art for all of humanity . . . poetry is primarily an aural art . . . poetry is a way of communicating things that are otherwise not easily said" (Lindner 38).

Further, Gioia talks about his public service as Chairman of the National Endowment for the Arts from 2003–2009. As a federal cultural leader, Gioia championed a clear and simple vision of bringing the best art and arts education to the broadest audience possible. He stated, "America is the wealthiest and most powerful nation in the history of the world. But the measure of a nation's greatness isn't wealth or power. It is the civilization it creates, fosters, and promotes. What I hope to accomplish here, in the broad sense, is to help foster the public culture that America deserves" (Bandler). At the NEA, he was an innovative leader who helped launch large national initiatives, including the Big Read, Shakespeare in American Communities, Jazz Masters, Operation Homecoming: Writing the Wartime Experience, and Poetry Out Loud. These public programs successfully drew millions of people, especially young adults, into writing, reading, performing, and reciting. Gioia's effort in establishing these national programs cost him years of his writing life, but he felt content, saying, "It gave me deep personal satisfaction. It also demonstrated that our country doesn't have to accept the notion of cultural decline. Of all the public programs, my favorite is Poetry Out Loud, the national high-school poetry recitation competition . . . [which] has brought a new generation of Americans into poetry" (Cusatis).

The focal point of Gioia's interviews, however, is inevitably poetry. The interviews are especially useful because his practice and poetics differs from most of his contemporaries in a number of important ways. First, Gioia's poetics emphasizes poetry's ancient and inherent connection to music and song. He sees poetry as primarily an auditory art that has a physical impact on the listener who experiences the poem mostly in non-intellectual ways. He believes that "a poet can arrange the words into shapes that simultaneously emphasize both the music and the sense" (Brame) and that poetry communicates in ways that the reader may not initially understand but feels physically, emotionally and intuitively. This conviction has manifested itself in Gioia's many musical collaborations in opera, song, jazz, and dance. No other major poet of his generation has been so deeply involved with music and musicians.

Second, Gioia's poetics insists on the permanent importance of form and narrative in poetry. Although he writes in both free and metrical verse, Gioia sees form as essential to all poetry. Some formal principle—traditional or innovative—is necessary to shape and thereby intensify ordinary

language into poetry. He sees meter as the most ancient and universal formal principle. Likewise, he feels storytelling is a human universal that is
always an available option to poets. He sees New Formalism as a movement
dedicated to reconnecting poetry to a broader audience by reviving these
primal and popular elements of poetic technique.

Third, Gioia's poetics is grounded in spirituality. He is fascinated by
poetry's ability to suggest meanings that lie beyond words. The art's metaphysical dimensions have special meanings for him as a Catholic alert to
the theological traditions of his faith. Believing that a poet must reconcile
realistic and metaphysical insights in literary creation, Gioia maintains that
"it's the poet's job to redeem the ordinary world around us for the imagination and the spirit. . . . One must see the world for what it is. One must
present all of the burdens and miseries of this common life and still see
the value in it. This spiritual challenge is at the root of my notion of poetic
tension" (McPhillips). His poetry explores spiritual dimensions of human
existence—an instinct reinforced by his belief of poetry's primal origins
in myth and ritual. To Gioia, the art's spiritual connection has never been
entirely broken, even in the modern era.

Fourth, Gioia insists on the continuing importance of place and region
in literary culture. As literary culture becomes increasingly global and
American poetry grows homogenized and placeless, Gioia believes that
the poet can be nourished by a deep and longstanding relationship with
local landscape, culture, and social reality. People live in actual places. The
natural world articulates itself differently in different places. Although cos-
mopolitan in his outlook, Gioia also sees himself as a California poet whose
imagination is shaped by the state's landscape, culture, and history. In his
eyes California is "a fantastic place for a poet to be born" (Paul).

Finally, Gioia sees poetry as a basic human art, not a specialized intellectual activity. He insists that intelligent and alert readers across society
respond to poetry. He claims no poet need condescend to address a mixed
audience. As a poet, Gioia aims for inclusivity. He does not write "for readers of any particular faith, politics, or aesthetic" (Koss). He believes that
poetry can arouse the sense of beauty, because "even the poorest people—
perhaps especially the poor—need beauty and the transcendent. Beauty is
not a luxury. It is humanity's natural response to the splendor and mystery
of creation. To assume that some group doesn't need beauty is to deny their
full humanity" (Koss). His democratic vision of poetry's audience rests on
the assumption that the appetite for poetry is widespread.

Despite his Stanford and Harvard education, Gioia rejects the elitism of much academic culture. He grounds this belief in his own early life experience among working-class people who had little formal education but nonetheless enjoyed poetry. As he recounts in many interviews, Gioia was born in an immigrant family of Italian and Mexican descent in Hawthorne, California. He recalls, "My dad's family spoke a Sicilian dialect. My mother knew no Italian, so we spoke English at home—not always grammatically. The neighborhood spoke Spanish. The schools taught in English. And the Church still worshipped in Latin" (Paul). Gioia's polyglot childhood was doubtlessly good training for his writing as was his early training in music.

From editing this volume and from reading his poetry and criticism, I realize how much contemporary American literature owes Gioia for crafting a personal poetic style suited to the age; for leading the revival of rhyme, meter, and narrative through New Formalism; for walloping the "intellectual ghetto" of American poetry through his epochal article "Can Poetry Matter?" (Gioia 24); for helping American poetry move forward by organizing influential conferences; for providing public service and initiating nationwide arts projects through his leadership of the National Endowment for the Arts; and for editing twenty best-selling literary anthologies widely used in American colleges.

This volume will also clarify the details of Gioia's background, biography, and beliefs. His career has been so varied and unusual that it has often been presented in confused and conflicting accounts. For example, newspaper articles often report that Gioia was raised speaking either Spanish or Italian. Neither assertion is true. Although raised in a polyglot environment, he spoke English at home. Likewise, sources label Gioia's mother as a Mexican immigrant. She was, in fact, born in Los Angeles's large Mexican community. In reading through these interviews, a reader will notice that Gioia's seemingly complicated career has a simple underlying narrative. Gioia has always been a poet. His singularity lies in that he decided not to be a professor. He pursued other careers to support himself and his family, but he has always kept writing seriously as a poet and public intellectual.

Since this book provides a strong context for reading the actual conversations, introductions in a few interviews, which existed to introduce the writer to readers who might not have known anything about him, have been omitted since they have minimal documentary value. Further, since Gioia was often asked similar or even identical questions, the interviews have occasionally been edited slightly to avoid conspicuous repetition. This volume also contains a chronology of the author's life to provide further factual context.

Conversations with Dana Gioia has been a challenging project because it tries to portray a complex and original writer who is not only still alive but fully active. At every stage of his busy polymathic career, Gioia has articulated his unique vision of American culture and poetry. His interviews not only increase our understanding of his poetry and poetics; they also offer aesthetic pleasure in themselves. This book provides an informal, intimate, and personal encounter with a writer who has made poetry matter. In short, it presents the actual voice of Dana Gioia who speaks of his personal and creative life page by page.

JOHN ZHENG

AUGUST 2019

Works Cited

Gioia, Dana. *Can Poetry Matter?: Essays on Poetry and American Culture.* Graywolf Press, 1992.

Lindner, April. "Interview with Dana Gioia." *The Edgar Allan Poe Review* 6.1 (Spring 2005): 37–46.

Mason, David. "The State of Letters: The Inner Exile of Dana Gioia." *Sewanee Review* 123.1 (Winter 2015): 133–46.

Chronology

1950	Born Michael Dana Gioia on December 24 in Hawthorne, California, to Michael Gioia and Dorothy Ortiz.
1957	Begins twelve years of Catholic education at St. Joseph's parish school in Hawthorne and Junipero Serra High School in Gardena, California.
1969	Enters Stanford University.
1970	Studies in Vienna, Austria; discerns his vocation as a poet.
1973	Receives a Bachelor of Arts, winning English department honors for best essay; serves as editor of *Sequoia*, Stanford's literary magazine (1971–1973) and later as its poetry editor (1975–1977).
1975	Receives a Master of Arts in Comparative Literature from Harvard University where he studies with the poets Robert Fitzgerald and Elizabeth Bishop; decides to leave graduate school.
1977	Receives a Master of Business Administration from Stanford University; joins General Foods Corporation, eventually becoming Vice President for Marketing.
1980	Marries Mary Elizabeth Hiecke.
1984	Edits *The Ceremony and Other Stories* by Weldon Kees with Graywolf Press, which is chosen as one of the "Notable Books of the Year" by the *New York Times*; featured in *Esquire's* first list of "Men and Women Under Forty Who Are Changing America," which makes him nationally known as the "businessman-poet."
1986	Publishes *Daily Horoscope* with Graywolf Press; wins the Frederick Bock Award for Poetry.
1987	Birth of his first son, Michael Jasper Gioia, in August. Death of son from Sudden Infant Death Syndrome in December.
1988	Birth of second son, culture critic Theodore Jasper Gioia, in November.
1991	Publishes *The Gods of Winter* with Graywolf Press and simultaneously

with Peterloo Poets in Britain; essay "Can Poetry Matter?" published in the May issue of *Atlantic* generates international attention; resigns from General Foods to become a full-time writer.

1992   Publishes *Can Poetry Matter?: Essays on Poetry and American Culture* with Graywolf Press, a finalist for the National Book Critics Circle Award; shares the 1992 Poets' Prize with Adrienne Rich; begins writing and broadcasting for BBC Radio.

1993   Birth of third son, filmmaker Michael Frederick Gioia, in January.

1994   Publishes new edition of *An Introduction to Poetry* with X. J. Kennedy, the first of over a dozen best-selling college textbooks he will coedit with numerous other writers. *Counting the Children* staged by choreographer Mark Ruhala.

1995   Cofounds and codirects with Michael Peich the West Chester University Poetry Conference, which becomes the nation's largest annual all-poetry writing conference; translation of Seneca's *The Madness of Hercules* is performed in New York.

1996   Returns to California to live in Sonoma County.

1997   Serves as music critic for *San Francisco Magazine*; serves as Distinguished Visiting Writer at Colorado College.

1998   Completes first opera libretto *Nosferatu* for composer Alva Henderson; work-in-progress is showcased at the Western Slope Music Festival in Colorado.

2001   Publishes *Interrogations at Noon* and *Nosferatu: An Opera Libretto* with Graywolf Press; founds the Teaching Poetry Conference dedicated to improving high-school teaching of poetry.

2002   *Interrogations at Noon* wins the American Book Award; nominated by President George W. Bush to serve as Chairman of the National Endowment for the Arts; moves to Washington, DC.

2003   Unanimously confirmed by US Senate and serves as NEA Chairman until 2009; publishes *Barrier of a Common Language: An American Looks at Contemporary British Poetry* with University of Michigan Press; launches the NEA Shakespeare in American Communities national initiative; receives honorary degree from St. Andrews University, the first of eleven honorary doctorates.

2004   Publishes *Disappearing Ink: Poetry at the End of Print Culture* with Graywolf Press; *Nosferatu* is premiered by Rimrock Opera and Opera Idaho; expands the NEA Jazz Masters Awards; launches the NEA Operation Homecoming: Writing the Wartime Experience program.

2005   Initiates NEA's Poetry Out Loud, a national high school poetry recitation contest in partnership with the Poetry Foundation; releases *Nosferatu* with Albany Records; receives the John Ciardi Award for Lifetime Achievement in Poetry.

2006   Profiled as "The Man Who Saved the NEA" in *Business Week*; launches another NEA national initiative, The Big Read, in response to the NEA research publication *Reading at Risk: A Survey of Literary Reading in America* which details a twenty-year decline in literary reading.

2007   Delivers the commencement speech at his alma mater, Stanford University.

2008   Second opera, *Tony Caruso's Final Broadcast*, with music by Paul Salerni, wins the National Opera Association award for best new chamber opera and is premiered in Los Angeles; receives the Presidential Citizens Medal; inducted into the College of Fellows of the Dominican School of Philosophy and Theology.

2009   Leaves his position as Chairman of NEA; serves as the first director of the Harman-Eisner Program in the Arts at the Aspen Institute; receives Lifetime Achievement Award from The Conference on Christianity and Literature.

2010   Releases *Tony Caruso's Final Broadcast* with Naxos Records; receives the Laetare Medal from the University of Notre Dame for outstanding service to the Church and society.

2011   Named the Judge Widney Professor of Poetry and Public Culture at the University of Southern California. Premiere of "Prayer" with music by Morten Lauridsen.

2012   Publishes *Pity the Beautiful* with Graywolf Press.

2014   Receives the Aiken Taylor Award for Lifetime Achievement in American Poetry; *The Three Feathers*, with music by Lori Laitman, is premiered by Virginia Technical University and Opera Roanoke; Stanford address listed by National Public Radio as one of "The Best Commencement Speeches, Ever."

2015   Creates the first "The Future of the Catholic Literary Imagination" national conference; appointed California State Poet Laureate by Governor Jerry Brown.

2016   Publishes *99 Poems: New & Selected* with Graywolf Press and *Poetry as Enchantment* with Wiseblood Books; receives the Denise Levertov Award.

2018   Receives the Poets' Prize for *99 Poems*; publishes *The Ballad of*

Jesús Ortiz with Providence Press; Helen Sung releases album *Sung with Words,* a jazz song cycle inspired by Gioia's poetry; edits *The Best American Poetry 2018* with Scribner.

2019   Premiere of dance-opera *Haunted* with music by composer Paul Salerni at Lehigh University; publishes *The Catholic Writer Today and Other Essays* with Wiseblood Books. Resigns chair at University of Southern California to return to full-time writing.

Conversations with
Dana Gioia

Dana Gioia: An Interview

Robert McPhillips / 1992

From *Verse* 9.2 (Summer 1992): 9–27. Reprinted by permission of Dana Gioia.

Robert McPhillips: What was it like to grow up in Los Angeles in the 1950s and 1960s?

Dana Gioia: I was born and raised in Hawthorne, California—a working-class town set in the middle of Los Angeles's megalopolitan sprawl. The town was a mix of Mexicans and Okies with a few Irish to run the police and politics. Most people worked in the airplane factories for Hughes and Northrop. Hawthorne was extraordinarily ugly in the cluttered, haphazard way of factory towns, but it did have gorgeous Southern Californian weather, and the beach was only twenty minutes away. We were poor but the weather was free. Since no one we knew had much money, we never considered ourselves underprivileged.

RM: What was your childhood like?

DG: I had a happy, solitary childhood. Both of my parents worked. My father was a cab driver and later a chauffeur. My mother worked as an operator for the phone company. I was left alone a great deal. I was raised in a tightly-knit Sicilian family. We lived in a triplex next to another triplex. Five of these six apartments were occupied by relatives. Sicilians are clannish folk. They trust no one but family. My grandparents rarely socialized with anyone who wasn't related. My mother (who had been born in Hawthorne from mainly Mexican stock) had to become more Italian than the Italians to fit in. All of the older people had been born in Sicily. Many of them spoke little or no English. Conversations among adults were usually in their Sicilian dialect. It was an odd childhood by mainstream American standards but probably not too unusual among immigrant families.

Living in New York now, I often hear people describe Southern California in the typical Hollywood clichés. These popular images of glitz and glamour have little to do with the working-class Los Angeles of my childhood, which was quite old-fashioned, very European, and deeply Catholic. No, "European" is the wrong word. Very *Latin*. The Sicilians blended very easily into the existing Mexican culture.

RM: Was Catholicism important to you?
DG: Catholicism was everything to me. Growing up in a Latin community of Sicilians and Mexicans, one didn't feel the Roman Catholic Church as an abstraction. It was a living culture which permeated our lives. In parochial school, we attended Latin Mass every weekday morning, in addition to the obligatory Mass on Sunday; so for eight early years I went to Mass six days a week. The hymns we sang were still the classics of Medieval Latin liturgy. As altar boys, we learned all the ceremonial responses by heart. Our nuns scrupulously drilled us in liturgy, ritual, and dogma—which we tolerated—and recounted the flamboyant folklore of saints and martyrs—which we adored.

This world seems so distant now. The Second Vatican Council unintentionally killed it. Working-class kids in Los Angeles today do not have the benefit of this sectarian but nonetheless broadening and oddly international education. In my Catholic high school the Marianist brothers drilled us relentlessly in Latin and Theology. We worked our way through most of St. Augustine and St. Thomas Aquinas's arguments. We also read Horace, Catullus, Virgil, and Ovid. We even translated the bawdy and beautiful songs of the Wandering Scholars. I was in the last generation that experienced Latin as a living language. Some of my teachers had attended ecclesiastical colleges in which all instruction was done in Latin. This cultural heritage opened new worlds to kids like us whose everyday lives were otherwise so narrow.

RM: What was it like to go from this working-class, ethnic background to an elite university like Stanford?
DG: Going to Stanford was a great shock. I had never been around people my own age whose parents had gone to college. At Stanford I experienced the shock of meeting the children of America's ruling class. It took me years to sort out my own reactions. I was simultaneously impressed and repelled by the social privilege my fellow students enjoyed. I was also naively astonished at how little their education meant to them. I felt then, as I do now, that in the circle of my friends in a working-class Catholic high school there

were more serious intellectuals than among my contemporaries at Stanford. Of course, I was then—and continue to be now—most naive of all in thinking that being an intellectual has some value.

RM: And yet you fit in fairly well as an undergraduate. Weren't you chosen as editor for *Sequoia*, the literary magazine?
DG: I did well at Stanford because I was so hungry to learn. I often took six courses a quarter rather than the recommended four. I was also hungry after my own kind. I wanted friends who were interested in the arts. I joined the staff of *Sequoia*, Stanford's literary magazine. As a junior I became the editor of this tottering enterprise. I took the magazine from bankruptcy to become the largest small magazine—pardon the oxymoron—on the West Coast.

RM: What did you do on *Sequoia*? I know your association with the magazine was extensive.
DG: I had two stints on *Sequoia*. As I said before, I served as editor-in-chief for my last two years as an undergraduate. Then, a few years later, when I returned to Stanford for business school, I became poetry editor and did literary interviews. While in business school, I also began writing book reviews for the *Stanford Daily*. They let me do long pieces about whatever new books interested me. In retrospect, I'm amazed by the freedom they gave me. I was able to write at length about authors like Pound, Cavafy, Eliot, Montale, Nabokov, Rich, Burgess, as well as younger poets. I wrote a review every other week for two years. I probably learned more about writing by reviewing for the *Stanford Daily* and by editing *Sequoia* than I did in my English classes. Writing for publication makes you very serious about what you are doing. Learning to put sentences together, to develop a line of thought, to select one good poem from a hundred mediocre submissions teaches you a great deal about literature. That sort of practical experience is invaluable to a young writer.

RM: What kind of courses did you take? What literary figures interested you most as an undergraduate?
DG: Although I was a voracious reader, literature mattered less to me at first than music. I came to Stanford planning to be a composer. After a short time with the Stanford Music Department, however, my passion for music was frustrated. I wanted to compose tonal music, but my teachers believed that tonality was a dead tradition. They ridiculed or dismissed as minor most of the living composers I admired—figures like Samuel Barber,

Benjamin Britten, Michael Tippett, Walter Piston, William Walton, and Ned Rorem. I spent my sophomore year in Vienna studying music and German. I escaped to Europe because I was so disappointed intellectually in Stanford. I wanted to try something else. Luckily, the California State Scholarship which helped pay my way through college, was also applicable to the Vienna program because it was administered by Stanford.

In Austria my primary interest gradually shifted from music to poetry. By the time I returned to California, I wanted to be nothing else than a poet. I had this change of heart in Austria for two reasons. First, I began recognizing the limits of my musical ability. Second, speaking German so much of the time somehow changed my relationship to English. I found myself writing poems in English and spending much of my time reading poetry in English and German.

RM: What literary courses did you take after returning from Europe?
DG: My formal coursework at Stanford was less important to me than the books I read on my own, the private passions I fostered without any sensible academic supervision. My course curriculum seems to me, in retrospect, quite haphazard. I was terribly naive as a student. I had the mistaken impression that one took the courses that interested one most. What I soon discovered was that the only way to get an education was to seek out the best professors, regardless of what they were teaching. I was lucky as an undergraduate to have a couple of terrific teachers, most prominently Herbert Lindenberger, who headed the Comparative Literature program at Stanford, and Diane Middlebrook, who has since achieved fame as the biographer of Anne Sexton.

RM: Did you study a great deal of contemporary literature as an undergraduate?
DG: I attended college in Northern California from 1969 to 1973, and I don't think that my development as a poet can be separated from this particular period of American literary history. For example, my freshman English composition teacher assigned us the following books: *Notes of a Native Son* by James Baldwin, *Soul on Ice* by Eldridge Cleaver, *A Clockwork Orange* by Anthony Burgess, *Native Son* by Richard Wright, *Trout Fishing in America* by Richard Brautigan, and *The Plum Plum Pickers* by Eugene Barrio, a Chicano labor novel. A curious list for a class in composition. My first survey course in American literature assigned Robert Creeley, Robert Bly, Allen Ginsberg, Lawrence Ferlinghetti, Gregory Corso, and Amiri Baraka. So I

was never able to think of Beat poetry as nonacademic or revolutionary. By 1971, it was already canonized as part of Stanford's approved version of American Literature. Coming to maturity as a writer in the California of Haight Ashbury, one was engulfed in waves of fashion. I found myself resisting. My literary sensibility tends to be contrarian. Had I grown up in a period when people wrote sonnets and villanelles, I would probably have gone off to Black Mountain College.

RM: How did you move from studying contemporary American literature to reading earlier writers?

DG: Before college, I had what, in one sense, was a very bad literary education. I never had a historical survey of either English or American literature. I had not read most of the major British or American poets. I was, however, fortunate to have had teachers who communicated both the pleasure and personal value of literature. Although my education was academically inadequate and historically lopsided, it was psychically valid. When I came to college, I discovered Ezra Pound's *ABC of Reading*. That book filled me with determination to learn as much as possible about poetry in English and foreign languages. I systematically tried to fill in my gaps as an undergraduate. But going to college in the early '70s, one was always hit with the notion of relevance—"relevance" usually being defined as what one's teacher felt was morally correct and timely. The situation seems farcical in retrospect. I wanted to read the classics, and my teachers encouraged me to pursue the latest trends. Being up to date, to misquote Oscar Wilde, is America's oldest tradition.

RM: When did you read the *ABC of Reading*?

DG: I had never heard of Ezra Pound before I came to Stanford. Pound was not allowed in the American high school anthologies of the '50s and '60s because of his indictment for treason. My best friend from high school, Jim Laffan, who knew much more about literature than I did, showed up at Stanford one weekend with a paperback copy of Pound's *ABC of Reading*. I remember noticing the serious, bearded author on the cover, and I listened to Jim spout all sorts of fascinating generalizations about literature that he had discovered in this book. I asked to borrow it. I read and reread that book for the next two years and started reading through all of Pound's work. Pound shamed me into learning French, which I immediately started when I returned from Vienna, as well as teaching myself standard Italian, and keeping my Latin more or less current. Pound did American literature an invaluable service by reminding us that poetry is an international art.

RM: Did reading Pound's *ABC of Reading* change your personal reading list or did it make you seek out different types of courses to take beyond contemporary literature?

DG: It did both. I consciously took courses in earlier periods to broaden my education with writers like Chaucer or the Elizabethans because of Pound's suggestions. I also audited a Dante course. I've always been comfortable learning on my own, and even when I was taking five or more classes in a single quarter, I still found time to do outside reading. This ability to work on my own proved my salvation in later years.

RM: Did Pound influence you to study comparative literature in graduate school?

DG: My Poundian bias made me feel, possibly unjustly, that comparative literature was the only adequate way to study literature. When I applied to graduate school, I applied only to comparative literature programs. At that point I planned to be a professor of literature who also wrote poetry. The few living poets I had seen—Edgar Bowers, Kenneth Rexroth, Christopher Middleton, Donald Davie—had all been professors. I had never really known a poet, only caught passing glimpses at a reading or lecture.

RM: Did you take any poetry writing courses as an undergraduate?

DG: I did not take creative writing classes as an undergraduate. In fact, I had a certain unfair prejudice against creative writing. The writing majors at Stanford didn't seem to me as serious as the literature students. I looked on writing courses as a kind of self-indulgence. It never occurred to me that one needed classroom instruction to write poetry. I concentrated on learning literature and foreign languages while writing poems on my own.

RM: Journalists and critics often compare you to Wallace Stevens. Has Stevens influenced you as a poet?

DG: Stevens's importance to me has been two-fold. First, he demonstrated that it was possible to work in business and develop as a serious writer. You have no idea how important—psychologically and spiritually—Stevens and Eliot were to me in my midtwenties. I had left the university for business. I knew few writers, and those few were all based in the academy. I didn't even know of a living writer who worked in business. I felt immensely isolated. Coming home each night after ten or twelve hours at the office, I had to find not only the energy to write but also the conviction that it was possible. One needs a great deal of faith to work for years without any external encouragement. Stevens and Eliot became my patron saints. I'm sorry to phrase it in such Catholic terms, but that's the way my mind works. Second, Stevens has represented a standard of artistic integrity to me. Stevens wrote only what he believed in. He stayed away from the literary marketplace. He never courted fame or popularity. He trusted poetry absolutely. He achieved this absolute integrity at great human cost. I don't envy or admire that side of him, but his personal isolation doesn't diminish the value of his artistic example.

RM: But did Stevens influence you stylistically or thematically?
DG: Not all literary influences are best measured by comparing texts. Stevens has profoundly shaped my poetry in ways that are mostly invisible on the page. He reminded me that a poet is free to do what interests or delights him or her—no matter what the literary or ideological fashions of the times. In that sense, perhaps, Stevens contributed paradoxically to my conviction that form and narrative needed to be brought back into American poetry. His influence was more spiritual than stylistic or intellectual. I have, however, always admired Stevens's sheer verbal extravagance—exactly those features which Donald Davie can't abide. Stevens's over-abundant diction and quirky elegance have encouraged me to exploit the possibilities of the language. Stevens reminds us that poetry should not be ashamed of being magnificent.

RM: Who are the poets who have most influenced you?
DG: There are several kinds of influence, and it is important to distinguish among them. First, there are the writers whom one imitates at the beginning. Nowadays, many young poets—at least in America—begin by imitating their teachers. That isn't altogether bad if your teacher is Theodore Roethke, Elizabeth Bishop, or John Crowe Ransom. But with a mediocre master, such imitation may stunt a young poet's growth. My early models all came from books. I have been reading poetry as long as I have been reading, but I'm not sure the enthusiasms of my childhood like Poe and Kipling have influenced me as much as the writers I embraced in late adolescence when I was beginning to think of myself consciously as an artist. Those early "singing masters of my soul" were Auden, Eliot, Pound, Rilke, and Graves. I often think, however, that a young poet isn't influenced so much by poets as by individual poems. In that sense, I was fascinated with particular poems by many other writers such as Wilfred Owen, Archibald MacLeish, Elizabeth Bishop, E. E. Cummings, and Randall Jarrell.

There is another kind of influence, however—namely writers whose ideas and examples shape one's sense of what it means to be a poet. At different stages of my life there have been poets to whom I have looked as spiritual examples. They have helped me lead my life. Stevens, Eliot, Rilke, Auden, and Jeffers have all been important as spiritual guides at particular times in my life.

RM: Did any poets influence your technique?
DG: I have consciously studied the verse technique of many poets, especially Yeats, Eliot, Auden, and Frost. But the single most influential experience I had was in my early twenties when—God help me, I'm not kidding—I scanned every line in half a dozen major plays by Marlowe, Shakespeare, and Webster. I wanted to learn the secrets of blank verse from the poets for whom it was a living *spoken* art rather than a codified *written* form. I learned some valuable lessons about how poetry is heard from those masters, observations I have never seen in any book on prosody. I patterned much of my own verse technique on those poets. I was amused when a conservative critic attacked my prosody as too loose. Augustan critics made the same complaints about Elizabethan dramatists.

RM: I presume you hadn't been to the East Coast before studying at Harvard. Was Harvard a different type of experience for you from being at Stanford?
DG: The most important thing to remember about my earlier years was how naive I was. I had virtually never been outside of California except for my brief stint in Vienna. (Even when living in Vienna, I didn't have enough money to travel much and see Europe.) I had never been to New England before I arrived at Harvard. I had imagined Cambridge to be an idyllic New England town. You can imagine my horror when I arrived in Harvard Square expecting a tranquil village green only to discover a subway stop in the middle of a traffic circle. Yet Harvard was the most exciting intellectual experience I've had in my life. Harvard was the first time I had ever been in a milieu of serious writers and intellectuals.

But my two years at Harvard were also extraordinarily lonely. I was quite poor. My first year I lived in a dilapidated basement studio on a dead-end alley. The squalor was unbelievable. My life became like something out of Dostoyevsky's *Notes from the Underground*. I also suffered a serious back injury and fractured a vertebra of my spine. I didn't receive proper treatment, so during most of my time at Harvard I was in constant pain. I wasn't psychologically strong enough to deal with this protracted injury. There was a point when I grew suicidal. But, as awful as they are to live through, suffering and isolation do clarify your life. I clung to poetry as a means of sanity.

RM: You've published a memoir of Elizabeth Bishop with whom you studied at Harvard. You and she became friends, then corresponded afterwards. What kind of influence did Bishop have on you?

DG: My first year at Harvard I took standard academic courses in French, German, and English literature. I learned a great deal. But I knew no other writers and had few close friends. During my second year, however, I was fortunate to meet Elizabeth Bishop and Robert Fitzgerald as well as two younger writers, Alexander Theroux and Robert Shaw. These individuals were extraordinarily important to me. They were the first dedicated imaginative artists I had ever really known. Bishop was less important to me as a writer than as a friend. When I studied with her at Harvard, her reputation was in eclipse. My advisor, a noted literary theorist, scoffed at the notion of my taking her class. He told me bluntly that her course would be a waste of time. Luckily, I ignored his counsel.

There were only five of us in Bishop's course on modern poetry. Harvard students did not consider her a literary celebrity like Robert Lowell or William Alfred. Almost immediately, Bishop and I struck up a relaxed and rather intimate friendship. We would go off to tea after class. Our talk was almost never about poetry, but about other things that we liked in common—music, novels, cats, flowers, travel. Bishop was a remarkably strict, indeed often discouraging teacher. She covered any work we submitted with corrections and suggestions, but she was extraordinarily encouraging to me. She believed in me both as an aspiring critic and a poet to a degree which no one had before. Her encouragement was entirely private. I never asked her for any help in the literary world, but her unsolicited personal endorsement came at a crucial time since I had just made the decision to leave academia for business.

RM: Your relationship to Bishop seems a bit like hers with Marianne Moore, who was notorious both for her generosity in reading her early drafts but also with a kind of real strictness in suggesting revisions. Do you see any parallel between that relationship and yours with Bishop?

DG: My relationship with Elizabeth Bishop was neither as longstanding nor as intimate as hers with Marianne Moore. But she did hammer into me the notion that every line one writes must be relentlessly considered, revised, and perfected. Every essay or translation I gave to her—because hers was not a course in creative writing—she would return to me scrupulously copyedited and covered with suggestions for revisions, expansions, and deletions.

Her example came at a crucial time because I, like all graduate students, was being encouraged by my other professors to write in a formal academic style. Bishop insisted that I write clearly, intelligently, and unpretentiously. I quickly realized that one had to make a choice between writing for the academic profession or writing for the common reader. I have chosen to write for the common reader. But the common reader, as both Samuel Johnson and Virginia Woolf remind us, does not mean an unintelligent reader.

RM: You also studied with Robert Fitzgerald, the classicist and poet. What type of influence did he have on you?
DG: Robert Fitzgerald was the single most important influence I had as a poet. Once again, his influence was not so much encouragement to write in a particular style or about particular subjects. Rather, Fitzgerald's influence was of writing to the highest standards with a knowledge of tradition and a respect for the craft of poetry. Quite by accident, I ended up taking two courses with him simultaneously my second year at Harvard. The first was a class called, in the inimitable Harvard way, "Studies in Narrative Poetry." We read Homer, Virgil, and Dante. In order to be admitted you had to be able to read at least two of these writers in the original. Everyone in the class but me was an expert philologist. I squeaked by with reasonably good Latin and minimal standard Italian. It was a wonderfully intimate and enthusiastically learned course. We did close textual analyses of selected passages from each author and tried to build a general notion of the epic tradition that bound the poems together.

At the same time, I took another graduate course from Fitzgerald called "The History of English Versification." I enrolled assuming it was a class in historical prosody. To my astonishment, I discovered that, in addition to the historical and theoretical reading, we were also expected to write a verse exercise each week in whatever meter we were studying. Fitzgerald did not ask us to write a poem—only to produce verse which scanned and made sense. These exercises were the most valuable learning I had as a young poet. I had always written in both free and metered verse, but my formal work was halting and uncertain. Versification is a craft which one can learn more quickly and better from a master than by oneself.

Under Fitzgerald's tutelage I learned in practical terms how the traditional meters worked. Fitzgerald also provided an important personal example. He had come to teaching later in life. He had worked as a journalist, had served in the Navy during the Second World War, and had spent years as a writer in Italy where he first translated Homer's *Odyssey*.

I saw in him a representative man of letters, a person who had dedicated his life to poetry.

RM: You dedicated the title sequence of your first book *Daily Horoscope* to Robert Fitzgerald. I take it that the poem is not directly based on your relationship with him. It's one of your most sophisticated works, and yet it has gotten very little critical attention.

DG: I consider "Daily Horoscope" one of my best poems, but I suspect that many people find it intimidating. The two critics who have written on it at length tried to interpret it as an elegy for Robert Fitzgerald. The sequence, however, was published while Robert was still alive, so it certainly was not intended as an elegy. I dedicated it to him because he was my most valuable teacher as a poet. I had come across a wonderful passage in the *Inferno* in which Dante saluted Virgil as his master and teacher in poetry. I put those lines as an epigraph under the dedication to Robert, not realizing that by quoting the *Inferno*, some critics would then read the sequence as a Dantescan poem about the afterlife. Perhaps it can be adequately read that way. That was not, however, the way I intended it.

RM: How did you intend the sequence to be read?

DG: I don't believe that poets are the best judge or interpreter of their own work. A poet knows things that aren't in the text and, blinded by his or her own intentions, often misses things which are there. I know, or think I know, my intentions in writing "Daily Horoscope." How well those ambitions are realized in the final text is not for me to judge.

The only observation I would make about the poem is to explain its title. I borrowed both the title and the style of the sequence from the horoscope columns you find in most daily newspapers. I was fascinated by the way astrologers addressed their readers in the second person and used the most intimate tone possible to tell what will happen to "you" each day. I also loved the way these columns create a brooding sense of mystery and danger. They tell you what to do and what to avoid. I decided to use that style in a lyric poem, and slowly it grew into a sequence. It was my intention that all of the poems were spoken to a single protagonist in the course of a single day from morning to night, but that intention may not be apparent to anyone but the author in the actual printed text.

RM: When I first read the poem, it reminded me of John Ashbery's work. I know another poet who feels the same way. I've always admired the sequence, but it remains pleasingly elusive, like much of Stevens's or Ashbery's poetry. Do you want to comment on the resemblance?

DG: "Daily Horoscope" may remind some readers of Ashbery's work, but I had read virtually nothing of Ashbery's when I wrote it. I suspect the elements in "Daily Horoscope" you noticed come from my debt to European Modernist poetry, a tradition Ashbery and I share. My own poetry draws on two somewhat contradictory traditions. One part comes out of the heritage of Anglo-American writers like Auden, Hardy, Jarrell, Larkin, and Kees, a sort of novelistic type of poetry. The critics who have written about my work with the greatest enthusiasm usually respond more deeply to this side of my sensibility. But there is another side to my work which comes out of European High Modernism. "Daily Horoscope," to the degree that it is written in any tradition, comes out of the Modernist lyric as exemplified by Montale, Rilke, and Valéry. Perhaps this European heritage makes the poem puzzling to critics who are more attracted by the Anglo-American aspects of my work.

RM: It seems to me that the other work closest in tone to "Daily Horoscope" is your translation of Montale's *Mottetti*. I have been struck by how different the poetry that you translate from the Italian is from most of the poetry that you write in English.

DG: Surely the great joy of translation comes from making a beautiful but alien poem your own. Why translate an author similar to yourself? As a translator, I am drawn to poets with whom I feel a deep imaginative sympathy but who also seem mysteriously foreign. Translation is a way of reconciling those opposite reactions. The period of literature which exercises the greatest fascination on me is European Modernism—not just in Italian but also in German and French (which I can read) as well as in Russian, Greek, and Spanish (which I don't know). I have been besotted with Modernist poetry since my teens. My own poetry is permeated with Modernist elements, but they are not the conventional ones, so readers don't necessarily recognize them as such.

I consider the first half of the twentieth century the greatest period of American poetry. Modernist poetry may even be the high point of *all* American literature. The incredible cluster of talent, which began with E. A. Robinson and ran through Frost, Jeffers, Eliot, Pound, Moore, Cummings, Williams, Stevens, and up through Crane, Ransom, and Tate seems unrivalled in American literature.

RM: But some critics would argue that your poetry rejects Modernism.

DG: My poetry is shaped by Modernism but not imprisoned by it. I have tried to assimilate what is still useful to an artist, but I am writing poems for today, not for Paris in 1913. Modernism is dead. Its historical moment has passed. Although it still influences what any serious American poet hopes to do, it is no longer a viable tradition. Of course, there is a group of poets and critics who pretend Modernism is still the vital mainstream. They desperately try to perpetuate the theory that the avant-garde remains a living force. To me, being avant-garde in the 1990s is a kind of antiquarianism. The central task for poets in my generation is the perennial challenge of reinventing poetry for the present moment. We must find a way to reconcile the achievements of Modernism with the necessity of creating a more inclusive and accessible kind of poetry.

RM: That brings us around to the question of the New Formalism. You've been identified with a movement in American poetry called the New Formalism. Would you care to give a definition of the New Formalism?
DG: One can't define New Formalism without discussing the origin of its name. New Formalism was a term given by unfriendly critics in the mid '80s to young poets who had begun writing in forbidden techniques—rhyme, meter, and narrative. The name was intentionally reductive and uncomplimentary because these critics felt American poets should not write in rhyme or meter. The term "New Formalism" inadequately describes a movement by a group of poets of my generation. Our work has several similarities. We write in rhyme and meter, though not usually exclusively in rhyme and meter. At least half of my poetry, for instance, is written in free verse. Second, many of us are interested in reviving narrative poetry—not autobiographical stories, but stories about other people. Third, we differ from what one might call the New Critical poets, the post-war academic formalists, in that we consciously borrow elements from popular culture. We often appropriate style, subject matter, and even whole genres from popular culture. And our work is less self-consciously intellectual and academic than some of those earlier writers. We believe that writing can be intelligent without being pedantic. We are trying to regain for poetry both a variety of techniques, which had been forgotten in the free verse era, and a kind of public voice which in some ways has been lost since Modernism.

RM: What other poets share this aesthetic with you?
DG: There are a number of poets whom one might classify as New Formalists. My short list would include R. S. Gwynn, Charles Martin, Gjertrud Schnackenberg, and Timothy Steele. Each of these poets is different, but what they have in common is an impressive sense of formal accomplishment.

They have created a new kind of music by mixing contemporary speech and formal meters. These poets are consciously using the line and the stanza as musical elements in their poetry. R. S. Gwynn, who is a Southerner, writes very much out of popular literature. He has a poem called "Among Philistines" which retells, brilliantly, the Samson story from a suburban American perspective. Charles Martin is very conscious of his Modernist roots and his poetry plays with Modernist paradigms with verve and ingenuity. Gjertrud Schnackenberg bears the strongest resemblance to a formalist of the older generation, but her poetry has an emotional accessibility and gorgeous musicality which seem both personal and new. Timothy Steele is an accomplished lyric poet, who writes in the plain style, but in a direct and memorable way, which I greatly admire. There are other poets one might mention like Paul Lake, Robert Shaw, Mary Jo Salter, and William Logan or narrative poets like Robert McDowell and Andrew Hudgins. These poets share a sense of concentration and musicality. They write with a sense of tradition, but without being burdened by tradition.

RM: Recently I've read a book by a young academic critic on postmodernist poetry which concluded with an attack on New Formalism. Specifically, he attacked Gjertrud Schnackenberg's poem "Supernatural Love"—which I think is an exquisite poem—by comparing it to a poem by Allen Tate. He said both poems were filled with certain determinate images and that once you figure out those images, the poems' meanings are exhausted. Poems not self-consciously composed in "open" forms are denied canonic postmodern status.

DG: This critic looks at poetry as a puzzle, and he esteems only those puzzles he cannot solve. The major problem of contemporary poetry is that it has become the slave of contemporary criticism. Criticism values texts that generate critical discussion. I, however, subscribe to the quaint and discredited opinion that poetry is an art which is not created primarily for critics. There are enduring masterpieces of poetry about which very little can be said. Critics have a tendency to overpraise what they can talk about and to ignore wonderful works about which not much can be said. For years, Thomas Hardy's reputation as a poet languished because he wasn't very interesting for critics of a certain generation to discuss. It is not coincidental that Hardy's reputation was revived largely by poets—by Auden, Larkin, Davie, Ransom, and Reeves. The most influential Anglo-American criticism now concerns itself mainly with theoretical issues. If it addresses contemporary poetry at all, it is often to make an ideological analysis. Consequently, one often finds voluminous discussions of contemporary poems of minimal artistic merit. Some of this current criticism is interesting, but it does not have a great deal to do with what matters to me as a poet or as a reader.

RM: This leads us around to your own criticism. The first piece I ever read by you was a critical piece on John Cheever. What attracted to me about the article was that it was written in a clear and personal style. I read it at a time when I was finishing an extremely academic dissertation. It came as a revelation to me that there were young critics writing seriously about literature in a nonacademic way. I subsequently discovered that you had written a series of critical essays not from within the academy but while a business-man at General Foods.

DG: One of the major problems of American poetry today is that most poets have abandoned criticism. If one goes back several generations to the early Modernists, most of them were also accomplished critics. Even if they wrote criticism as irregularly as Frost or Jeffers, they could still write compellingly about poetry. And the central poet-critics—Eliot and Pound—rank among the greatest critics in the English language. The next generation—Blackmur, Winters, Ransom, Tate—not only continued this tradition but also helped transform the academic study of literature, as did their students, the generation of Jarrell, Berryman, Schwartz, and Shapiro. Ironically, once poets entered the academy to teach creative writing, they began to write less criticism. Donald Justice once commented that while teaching literature develops a critical mind, teaching creative writing somehow does not. He has bemoaned the failure of his generation to produce many distinguished poet-critics.

In my own generation, there are few poets of note who take writing criticism seriously. Consequently, for the first time in this century, American poets have conceded critical discourse on contemporary poetry to literary theorists and academics. I don't mean to belittle academic scholarship or criticism. I only insist on making a distinction. The concerns of an academic will by definition be different from the concerns of an imaginative writer. Academic critics write for their professional colleagues. Poets write for their real and potential readers. Academic criticism arises out of studying the past whereas criticism by artists emerges from a vision of the future. Criticism by poets has historically educated and nourished a broader audience.

I have taken my role as a critic seriously. I have worked hard to find the right tone to discuss poetry responsibly, intelligently, but accessibly. One does not compromise a critical essay by writing it for general readers. I have probably impeded my reputation as a critic by writing in a public idiom and by discussing figures outside of the contemporary canon. A young critic can make a reputation much more quickly by writing conventionally on well-known figures than by becoming an advocate for worthy but forgotten writers. But what's the point of writing another essay saying the same things on the same writer? Why write unless one has something new to say? I'm not interested in writing on major figures unless I have a dissenting opinion.

Since I have made my living in business, I have the freedom to write only about what interests me. Consequently, I've devoted a great deal of critical energy and research to some forgotten or misunderstood figures, like Weldon Kees or Robinson Jeffers. I believe Kees is a major poet, although he appears in no literary histories and few anthologies.

RM: You've been the primary advocate of Weldon Kees of our generation. You've written several essays on his work and edited the selected stories. What attracts you to Kees? His work seems so different from yours.

DG: What is the use of art if we can't admire writers different from ourselves? From the moment I read Kees's work, I felt that I had come across a master. There were so many things to admire in Kees's work. First, he was able to get all kinds of heterogeneous material into his verse. His poetry was equally informed by Shakespeare and the movies, by jazz and Joyce, and yet he put them together in an exciting and satisfying whole. Second, Kees was a relentless experimentalist. He invented at least a dozen new poetic forms, most of which he used only once or twice. Usually when we talk of experimental poets, we talk about poets who leave us interesting messes, poems which are more satisfying to talk about than to read. But Kees's experiments are almost uniformly successful. They get sensibilities and subjects into poetry that were never successfully assimilated before. Kees was an accomplished visual artist. He exhibited with the Abstract Expressionists. It wasn't until I knew his work for many years that I understood the connection between these two sides of his sensibility. His central visual medium was the Modernist collage. He does the same things in verse. He combines surprising and unlikely material to illuminate the arcane connections between dissimilar things. Isn't that the way poetic metaphor operates? Kees fits as much of American experience into poetry as any post-War American poet has managed.

RM: Many would argue that John Ashbery is also doing that. Certainly he's notably influenced by the Abstract Expressionist painters and the collage method. You yourself once pointed out that Kees was an unacknowledged influence on the New York School poets.

DG: Kees is never classified as a New York School poet, and yet he seems the very model of a modern New York School poet. He was the first poet to integrate the techniques of Abstract Expressionism into verse. When I compare Kees's work with Ashbery's, however, I feel Kees is more concise, emotionally direct, and accessible than Ashbery. I know when I use the word "accessible," I sound like a Philistine to some people, but ultimately one must judge art by a subjective reaction. Art either registers on one's imagination or it doesn't. And so by "accessible," I don't mean "simple." Kees is a complex, challenging poet. He is probably the bleakest, most apocalyptic poet in American literature. He is also among the most allusive. But the sheer emotional desolation of his work is redeemed by his imaginative brilliance. The closest counterpart to Kees in American poetry is Hart Crane.

RM: Let me return to an earlier subject. Why did you leave Harvard graduate school in 1975 to make a career in business?
DG: I'm not sure that anyone understands entirely why one makes important decisions in life. Decisions are always complex. They involve both rational and emotional factors. I believe that I left Harvard for two reasons—the first economic, the second literary. I was the oldest son in a large working-class family. I had absolutely no money, and I felt a great deal of responsibility to provide an economic basis for the rest of the family. So, in one sense, I entered business because I needed to make a living and wanted some modest control over my life. The other reason I left academics was to become a poet. That sounds paradoxical, but I felt that I was becoming a worse writer with each passing year in academia. My poetry was becoming too studied and self-conscious. I was writing poems to be interpreted rather than to register on the imagination and emotions. As a critic, I felt I was being—I didn't feel, I *knew* I was being—encouraged to write for other specialists versus a wider audience. Why write in a style that your most intelligent friends outside the university can't follow, when you can say everything with as much accuracy in a more accessible way? My writing was changing for the worse.

Perhaps the reason I had to leave the university was because I liked it so much. I was too susceptible to its intellectual blandishments. I found the intense atmosphere of Harvard too interesting. I couldn't shield myself from the influences as well as somebody who didn't like the scholarly environment. Watching my friends who stayed in academics, I notice that they are under constant, external pressure, because they're surrounded by so many intelligent, self-conscious, critical people. It's hard for innovative or unconventional ideas to have the time and privacy to gestate under those circumstances. It's like living in a fish tank.

RM: How far along were you at Harvard when you left?
DG: I left Harvard after having completed all the course work for my doctorate and most of the language requirements in French, German, Italian, and Latin. On departing I was awarded something appropriately called a "terminal" master's.

RM: Your departure from Harvard seemed to coincide with the rise of literary theory in the universities. In 1975 was literary theory already a presence there?
DG: In comparative literature, literary theory was already gaining dominance in the early '70s. At Harvard, one of my pro-seminars was conducted by Edward Said. For Said, we read books by Foucault and Barthes in French before they had been translated into English. We also read Lukacs, Goldmann, Hirsch, and other theorists who since have become influential. Most were already prominent in Europe. The two theorists who influenced me most were an unlikely pair, Georg Lukacs (especially his *History of Class Consciousness*), and E. D. Hirsch (for his *Validity in Interpretation*). That was before Hirsch achieved national fame with *Cultural Literacy*. In other words, the areas which interested me most in literary theory were Marxist dialectics and hermeneutics. As a critic, I seem to have a very Germanic imagination.

RM: It's somewhat ironic, then, for you to move from Marxist theory to business. Isn't the type of criticism that you are doing now the antithesis to the type of literary criticism that is being done in the universities?
DG: Is it ironic for a poet who later became a businessman to have been influenced by Marxism? I don't think so. Marxism would not have dominated a great deal of European thought if it did not have some basis in truth. As an analytical technique, Marxism gets at certain social realities better than any other philosophical school. I have never agreed with the *prescriptive* political conclusions of Marxism, nor its claims at being a *scientific* political methodology. But, as an analytical tool, Marxist dialectic can be profound. One of the things that Lukacs taught me was how institutions work, and by institutions I mean not only political or economic institutions like the government or industry, but institutions such as the legal profession or academic literary studies.

One of Lukacs's major *apercus* was that there comes a point when an institution becomes so inwardly focused on perfecting its own methodology that it loses touch with its original social function. Academic literary study has fallen into what Lukacs would have called a contradiction. It has become so obsessed with its own methodology that it no longer serves its primary educational purpose. So I would, ironically, use Marxist analysis to criticize many university theorists who themselves are Marxists.

The general audience for serious literature in America is dying, even as the academic profession thrives. Much of the country is sinking into illiteracy. Literature means less every year to the educated classes. And what is the response of the academy? To burrow more deeply into intricate and arcane theory incomprehensible to anyone outside the profession. I deplore this smug parochialism. I naively believe that poetry still has value for a society.

RM: I was surprised to hear you speak so eloquently on behalf of literary theory. As a critic, you often seem to be battering the dominance of theory.
DG: I have, in principle, a high regard for literary theory. Literary theory is an essential branch of humanistic study. But one must recognize what theory can and cannot do. It's important to understand where literary theory fits into an academic curriculum. In America the academy grossly overemphasizes literary theory in its curriculum. I personally regret the shift in literary study from reading primary texts to reading critical and theoretical texts. The major problem today among students is that they simply have not read enough literature. Consequently they do not have the necessary background to take a critical attitude towards literary theory. One needs to test every abstraction against experience.

RM: Literary theory's other sin is that it has placed a layer of critical jargon between a literary text and the critics' own emotional and intellectual responses to it. Critics who try to speak clearly to a general audience are dismissed as journalists or failed academics.
DG: In America, there is an unprecedented cultural situation. Academic critics and imaginative writers not only possess no common set of concerns, but they no longer even share a common language. Neither side respects or even fully understands the other's language. Consequently, American literature is suffering the effects of an enervating bifurcation. At least one reason the poetry audience has declined in the United States is that there are no longer many first-class critics writing in a public idiom. One can point to only a handful of writers (ironically, often very scholarly ones like Hugh

Kenner or Guy Davenport) who still write seriously in an accessible manner. Bruce Bawer is one of the few strong young critics who has continued the tradition of the public intellectual. Not surprisingly, he has had to make his career outside of the university.

What we now possess is an impoverished public culture. If mass circulation journals cover poetry at all they do so only in short journalistic pieces dumbed down to reach the lowest common denominator. Meanwhile, the many academic journals and presses publish work written in a kind of professional jargon. That sort of criticism, as far as I can tell, is frequently written not to be read but to be weighed by a promotion committee.

Isn't it interesting that in the entire history of the world, there have never been so many people paid to profess poetry as in America today? We have tens of thousands of poetry professionals. And yet there's never been a culture in which poetry has played so small a role, in which poetry has been so alienated from the common educated reader. Surely that cultural paradox must reveal something about the failure of our literary enterprises.

RM: Surely working outside of the university has been important to you. How has working in business affected your writing?

DG: I am not sure I can answer that question accurately. Our professions mold us gradually in many ways that we ourselves can't see. Whenever I get together with old friends who have become teachers or lawyers, I marvel at how their work has accentuated some parts of their personalities while allowing other parts to atrophy. I would offer only two observations about the impact my job has had. First, unlike most university poets, I spend all day working with adults—most of whom are smart, mature, and practical. That experience differs from spending your days teaching the young. I think that the experience of working with peers rather than my juniors has shaped the concerns of my poetry in many ways that I only half understand. Second, by making a living outside of literature, I have been able to be quixotic about poetry. I can spend (and, alas, sometimes *have* spent) years working on a poem or essay. I have been able to write about whatever subjects I want without worrying about the commercial consequences. I can send work to small magazines, including long prose pieces that took months to write. Poets who must support themselves as writers could never afford that luxury. They must write for the marketplace. Even though my work appears in mass circulation magazines like the *New Yorker* or the *Atlantic*, I feel more allegiance to smaller journals like the *Hudson Review* or *Verse* whose central mission is literature and the arts.

RM: What did you hope to get out of business?
DG: One attraction of business was the privacy it gave me as a writer. There are so many conflicting claims on young poets today that they develop very slowly. They have to sort through more possibilities, more influences than ever before. I felt that I needed anonymity to discover myself. I needed a time with no external pressures for publication.

After leaving Harvard, I did not send any poems out for nearly eight years. But I wrote virtually every night after work and on the weekends. Much of the time I spent revising. I would sometimes rewrite a particular poem off and on for years only to discard it. But the process of submerging myself utterly in my imagination and my medium was invaluable. I could never have borne the sheer loneliness of those years if I had not had an office full of people to go to each morning. Not worrying about publication gave me the freedom to make mistakes, to follow odd impulses. This period of public silence let me discover my own voice, develop my own set of concerns, without worrying about anyone outside approving or disapproving.

RM: Did your colleagues at work know that you wrote poetry?
DG: Of course not! I kept my writing a secret from them as long as I could. I felt that being known as a poet could only hurt my reputation inside the company. I also didn't want the people I worked with every day—good but very conventional middle-class folk—to know what I was writing. Offices are just like villages. People poke their noses into each other's affairs. For years I never sent work to the *New Yorker* because I was afraid someone at the office might see my poetry there. I wanted the freedom to write about whatever I wanted, and that required absolute privacy.

RM: Was that a difficult time for you?
DG: Absolutely. All young writers crave praise and recognition. I was no exception. I felt, however, that isolation and anonymity were the necessary price for self-discovery. I had to shut off the distractions in my life. I had published many poems as an undergraduate and graduate student, but I found, at this beginning stage, that editors did not publish my "best" work. They would often select the poems in which I imitated some other writer. To an editor, those poems were more obviously accomplished than the clumsy, inchoate musings in which I was struggling to define my own material. When I had these early exercises in other people's styles accepted, I found myself encouraged to write more in those borrowed mainstream styles rather than to work out my own murky destiny. Consequently, I felt I

needed *not* to publish. I was not strong enough to resist the unintentional influence of editors. I also knew that I was not yet strong enough to make a career in business while writing and publishing. One of those things had to go, and it was publishing.

RM: Could you be more specific in terms of characterizing those early poems? What poets influenced you? What type of poetry were you writing as a graduate student and in your early days as a businessman?
DG: My strongest early influences were Eliot, Auden, Pound, Roethke, Rilke and sometimes anyone I happened to be reading at the time. By the time I completed my first quarter in business school, I had made the decision to stop publishing. So what I'm describing is my early work.

RM: How many, if any, of those early poems made it into *Daily Horoscope*?
DG: The earliest poem in *Daily Horoscope* is "The Burning Ladder," the first draft of which was written when I was studying with Robert Fitzgerald. There are only one or two other early poems which made it into that book. "Four Speeches for Pygmalion," for instance, is based on a long dramatic monologue I wrote for Fitzgerald. All of the other poems were written after I had gone into business. Virtually none of my early work has been collected.

RM: Didn't you take one poetry writing seminar as a business student at Stanford?
DG: Yes, paradoxically, the only creative writing I ever took was while I was in business school. I took Donald Davie's graduate poetry writing seminar, which was officially open only to the master's candidates in creative writing, but Donald bent the rules and let in two outsiders—myself and an Indian student from the Food Research Institute named Vikram Seth. Donald's seminar was one of the most interesting intellectual experiences I've ever had. It was full of bright people—like Vikram, John Gery, and Vickie Hearne. It was a first-rate course in practical criticism.

I felt, however, that Donald's course was extraordinarily damaging for me as a poet because the work I was trying to write was at odds with the sort of poetry that he wanted. He had strong preconceptions of the traditions an American poet should follow. Perhaps the work we brought him was still half-formed, but too much deviation from the schools of either Pound or Winters was not encouraged. In retrospect, I am grateful to Donald for being so discouraging. It toughened us up. It let us know that, if we were going to do something different, we had to expect the worst from critics.

RM: It's odd that the type of poetry that Davie would encourage was not the type of poetry that you were writing. A number of the poets you mention—Seth, Gery, and yourself—were later associated with New Formalism. I am struck by the parallels between New Formalism and Davie's early allegiance, The Movement. Davie ended up reacting against The Movement. Was he going through a phase when he was very influenced by Pound?

DG: Donald is one of the great living literary critics. But he was so English that he approached—half correctly, I think—American poetry as a foreign tradition. At that stage, Donald did not believe that Americans should be writing metrical poetry or narrative poetry. He also rejected any stylistic elegance or overt musicality. He encouraged us to write free verse about what he considered authentic American experience. I still remember the poem he praised most generously during the entire term was a formless memoir of Midwestern childhood. This poem had no redeeming quality except its Americanness. But, once again, when you have a poet-critic as strong as Donald Davie for a teacher, you must recognize that he will have his own agenda. What interests him may not interest you.

One fine thing that came out of this class, however, was that several of us established our own informal writing group. John Gery, Vikram Seth, Vickie Hearne, Gail Lynch, and I formed a weekly poetry group. We would get together at someone's house or a bar and show each other our poems. John, Gail, and I were the most loyal members. Vikram and Vickie were more irregular. But that experience of nonacademic writing group, which was entirely new to me then, helped me a great deal.

RM: When you left Stanford, didn't you work for a year in Minneapolis?

DG: No, I worked for a large company in Minneapolis the summer of 1976 between my two years in business school. I had never been in the Midwest before. I knew no one in Minneapolis, and it was an extraordinarily lonely period for me. I spent my days analyzing trade budgets and charting trends. I found the work and the environment most unsympathetic, and living in isolation, I spent most of my free time reading, writing, walking, and fretting. It was my first experience working for a large corporation. It made me a nervous wreck.

RM: Did you write much poetry at that time?

DG: I wrote a great deal of poetry in Minneapolis. Several poems in *Daily Horoscope* came out of that brief sojourn, such as "My Secret Life" and "An Elegy for Vladimir de Pachmann." In Minneapolis I also began a long poem called "Pornotopia," which was a kind of sexual nightmare in the tradition of

Eliot and Thomson. I discarded most of this poem, but a few sections survived in *Daily Horoscope*—"Pornotopia," "The Memory," and "Speech from a Novella." "My Secret Life" was a parallel poem I wrote at the same time. I wanted to explore the fantasy worlds which some people use to escape life. The most important experience for me in Minneapolis, beside the unbroken solitude of my summer there, was discovering Weldon Kees.

RM: Both "Pornotopia" and "My Secret Life" seem quite different from the domestic themes in the first section of *Daily Horoscope* or the love lyrics there and in *The Gods of Winter*.

DG: I don't think of myself as a domestic poet. I have written very few autobiographical poems about family life. When I read the reviews of my first book, I was surprised at the difference between how the critics saw me and how I saw myself as a poet. *Daily Horoscope* is a diverse book of poems. I consider diversity a virtue in a poet, though not everyone will agree. But most critics focused on only one part of my writing, the narrative or semi-narrative poems about everyday life. They linked me to the tradition of Larkin, Frost, and Hardy. I consider that a great and perhaps undeserved compliment.

There's another side of my work, which is more private, more apocalyptic that is also central to my sensibility. In addition to lyric and narrative poetry, I am interested in an exploratory kind of cultural and political poetry. Poems like "A Short History of Tobacco," "My Secret Life," "An Elegy for Vladimir de Pachmann," "The Lives of the Great Composers," "My Confessional Sestina," "News from 1984" represent an equally central part of my sensibility. I also believe that poems which have a lyric element, such as "In Cheever Country," "In Chandler Country," and "The Next Poem," are not simply lyrics, even if that is sometimes the easiest way to approach them critically. But an author always has grandiose visions of his or her own work! I'm interested in creating a lyric poetry which operates ambitiously, which reflects the aesthetics of concentration, allusiveness, and even the impersonality of the Modernist lyric, but which nonetheless doesn't borrow the style of Modernism.

RM: Perhaps I used the term "domestic" too quickly. I used it with reference to what I perceive to be the narrative movement, if there can be said to be one in the first section of *Daily Horoscope*, which concludes with a vision in "In Cheever Country" of suburbia as a type of paradise. Certainly some

earlier poems in the section, like "Insomnia," demonstrate that a suburban home doesn't necessarily provide a sense of security.
DG: Wouldn't that make it anti-domestic?

RM: Well, no, it seems to me that there's a tension in the poems between being a poet and living in the modern world, between being a businessman and a poet. There is also a sense of psychological tension in poems like "The Man in the Open Doorway" and "Men After Work" that business life can be unfulfilling for many people—balanced by the final poem, "In Cheever Country," where you write: "If there is an afterlife, let it be a small town / gentle as this spot at just this instant" that suggests at least a temporary sense of solace, resolution.
DG: A poet must be honest to experience. Whatever I write must somehow be grounded in my actual life. Contemporary American poetry does not have nymphs and shepherds, but it has its equivalent clichés. Most American poetry takes place in prefabricated literary landscapes, be they redwood forests or working-class bars—conventionally poetic places where poets have poetic experiences. I have tried to write out of the range of my actual experience, which means the suburbs as well as nature, which means books and music as well as the family. If some of that subject matter is domestic, it's usually a kind of imperiled, precarious domesticity.

My practical theory of poetry is based on tension. Any poem I write that moves comfortably along in one direction doesn't satisfy me. Good poems have unexpected leaps and turns. In the same way the language of a poem should stretch against whatever form one lays out. There should be lines and turns of phrase that surprise the reader. Unless a poem contains some surprising contradiction between its subject and its form, between its departure point and its destination, it doesn't interest me much.

RM: If one can identify, however problematically, one persona, connected with all of the poems in the opening section of *Daily Horoscope*, this persona achieves, especially at the end of "In Cheever Country," "a momentary stay against confusion," which is what Frost thought a poem should do.
DG: I believe the poet's job is to redeem the ordinary world around us for the imagination and the spirit—even if that world is the suburbs and office life. But the poet cannot attempt this redemption at the price of simplifying or distorting it. One must see the world for what it is. One must present all of the burdens and miseries of this common life and still see the value in it.

This spiritual challenge is at the root of my notion of poetic tension. It's hard for me to see beauty without somehow acknowledging the fragility of it. If I am a transcendentalist, it is of an austere and unillusioned sort.

RM: Has Frost influenced your poetry?

DG: I consider Frost a pivotal figure in American poetry. He redefined the possibilities of our literature. Whitman and Williams created an authentic American voice only by discarding the past. That led to a very narrow definition of American art, one that was progressive and yet oddly provincial. But Frost found a way to be American without rejecting tradition. He quietly and masterfully transformed it to suit new purposes. He was our secret Modernist. He reinvented formal prosody to fit modern American speech. He used traditional genres like the narrative poem and the pastoral in startlingly innovative ways. But, because he stressed his continuity with tradition, the novelty of his efforts was not recognized during his lifetime. No later poets pursued the rich possibilities his work opened up. That neglect is why Frost is so attractive to me.

In the mid-1970s when I tried to write narrative poetry seriously for the first time, I found no contemporary models. Modernism had declared narrative poetry defunct. Poets still wrestled with the epic—the massive culture poem in the tradition of Pound or Crane. There were lots of poets writing anecdotal, autobiographical poems in the confessional vein. But no one seemed to be exploring narratives about other people's lives.

I wanted to write what I once called in my essay "The Dilemma of the Long Poem," "poems of middle length," verse narratives that were equivalent in scope to a short story. After discarding a few aborted poems, I began searching for a usable tradition to draw on. Browning seemed too remote; Tennyson lovely but inert. Early Eliot was attractive but too idiosyncratic. Robinson came close, but his language and manner were too severe for my sensibility. Then I looked at Frost, and all sorts of possibilities occurred to me. He had found just the balance between lyric tension and narrative credibility. He had created a style whose full potential had not yet been realized.

RM: You have extended your range as a narrative poet in your second collection. The tension between lyric epiphany and violence is even more emphatic in "Counting the Children" than "The Room Upstairs" from *Daily Horoscope*, and in "The Homecoming" it is most emphatic of all. Are you consciously invading the territory of prose in these longer poems?

DG: Absolutely. By the end of the 1970s American poetry had been reduced to a few lyric genres. The potential of the art had been diminished. The main contribution of the so-called New Formalists has not been the reintroduction of rhyme and meter. That was only a manifestation of a deeper change in sensibility. Their most important accomplishment was the reinvention of traditional genres in a viable and unpedantic contemporary form. We wanted workable forms that went beyond the autobiographical and surrealist lyric. Some poets like Charles Martin, Tom Disch, and R. S. Gwynn have focused mainly on satiric and discursive genres. They want to steal some of the energy and flexibility of prose without necessarily giving up the formal strength of poetry. My own interests have been largely focused on finding a way to tell stories memorably in verse, to create something that works both as a compelling narrative and a forceful poem. That hasn't been easy. It requires a different kind of poetic language from what the lyric needs. The reinvention of the narrative poem seems to me the most important thing now happening in American poetry. It is also the clearest signal that Modernism is dead, and that poets are creating a new aesthetic.

RM: Did the death of your first son alter your development as a poet?
DG: It utterly transformed my life. How could it not also transform my consciousness as a writer? Tragedy simplifies your vision. It sweeps everything away that isn't essential. Losing my first son made me realize how little most things in my life mattered to me—and how desperately important the few remaining things were. There was a searing clarity to the grief. I stopped writing for a year. It took all of my energy to get myself and my wife through each day. When I gradually began writing again, I saw poetry differently. Writing took on a spiritual urgency I had never experienced before—at least in so sustained and emphatic a way.

RM: How was writing these new poems different for you?
DG: I was no longer concerned with what the reader would think about the poems. I wrote them for myself. I trusted my intuition and emotions. In one sense this made the poems more difficult. I didn't worry about explaining an image or situation if it had a private resonance to me. But, in a different sense, it also made the poems more emotionally accessible. I admitted my obsessions and allowed myself to be vulnerable. I no longer cared if critics thought I was morose or sentimental. Perhaps all I am saying is that I wrote the poems that my life dictated without trying to turn them into something else.

RM: Most of the poems in *The Gods of Winter* are directly or indirectly about death, including some poems written before your son's death. How do you account for that eerie coincidence?

DG: Some of the poems were composed earlier. "The Gods of Winter," for instance, was written for my wife after she had recovered from some potentially serious surgery. But some of the poems were reconceived and recomposed after my son's death. When I began writing again, I grew dissatisfied with some of the poems I had written after *Daily Horoscope*. I no longer felt the impulse that had created them. Since I normally work on poems for years before publishing them, it was natural for me to revise these poems-in-progress into something which spoke to my new situation. I could never have finished them in their original form. My Rilke translation, "The Song," for example, seemed elegant but evasive. I rewrote it into something quite personal. When I looked at "The Homecoming" (which was then titled "The Killer"), I suddenly saw the theme of the poem differently. It wasn't about religion but about family. I rewrote it from beginning to end. I took the narrative poem I had been working on the night before my son died— "Counting the Children"—and turned it into a longer, darker poem which eventually resolved itself into a vision. The episode I had originally planned as the ending became instead a turning point at the middle. That poem especially became a kind of spiritual self-examination for me. There was no other way for me to finish it except to transform it into something new.

RM: Has the immense public response to your essay—"Can Poetry Matter?"—had any effect on you as a writer?

DG: Yes, for several months it kept me too busy to write. I knew it would prove a controversial piece. I was prepared for criticism, but I was utterly defenseless for praise. Hundreds of letters arrived. Reporters called at the office. Radio and television producers booked interviews. Critical rebuttals and endorsements poured in. I made the mistake of trying to deal with the publicity responsibly. I answered a great many of the letters personally. I spent countless hours talking with reporters who knew very little about poetry. I wanted them to understand why the issues at stake were important. Meanwhile I had to maintain my normal business schedule. The whole experience drained me. I should have run for cover.

RM: What are your plans for the near future?

DG: To write poems again, if the Muse will still have me.

Dana Gioia: Interview

Isabelle Cartwright / 1994

From *The Irish Review* 16 (Autumn-Winter 1994): 109–22. Reprinted by permission of Isabelle Cartwright.

Isabelle Cartwright: Does poetry matter?

Dana Gioia: Of course, it matters. Poetry remains our most concise, affecting, and memorable way of speaking. It allows us to say the things that move us most deeply and stay most fixed in our minds. Poetry comes from a point in our past when we understood our own experience without separating our mind from our bodies, our logic from intuition and imagination. The subsequent history of mankind has been the ever-increasing specialization of ways to speak about ourselves and describe ourselves. You can see this in the departments of a university—psychology, sociology, religion, literature, history, anthropology, biology, all of these specialized methodologies for understanding ourselves. The poet's role remains primitive—namely to reflect existence truthfully as we experience it individually, which is to say, holistically. If we lose that faculty, as a race, a society, a culture, then we've lost something that is essential to our humanity.

IC: So it's a faculty, an impetus, and a need. Is it unique?

DG: The medium closest to poetry is song. It affects us in the same mysterious, emotive way. In fact, in our society, popular music now occupies most of the cultural space that poetry has given up. That's not altogether bad, but poetry as an art made up solely of words does certain things better than song can. Song is a mixture of words and music, and the words can be rather lazy. Clichés, for example, can work quite well in song if the music is powerful enough. As wonderful as it is in other ways, song does not always clarify our experience in the ways that poetry can.

31

IC: But is song not more communal and democratic reflecting more common experience between persons?

DG: There are also intimate kinds of song. Music is extraordinarily diverse. Poetry should ideally have the same range. On one side there's communal, public poetry. You can see this historically in writers like Tennyson or Longfellow. On the other hand there is a more private kind of poetry—Emily Dickinson and Wallace Stevens, for example. Part of the problem in our culture today is that we have greatly narrowed the range of poetry.

What worries me most about the state of poetry today is not that it isn't read by the common person, but that it's not read even by literary intellectuals, people for whom literature is a primary interest. In America at least, poetry has a small audience that consists mainly of poets, would-be poets, and their captive students. Those are wonderful people, but they are not an audience diverse enough to nourish a healthy art.

IC: There are many reasons why poetry is in this state; but, has there ever been a time when poetry hasn't had to struggle?

DG: The good news is that it has always been a bad time for poetry. That being said, I'm not sure that we've ever had a worse time than the present moment. Poetry today is caught between the seductive competition of popular culture (films, television, pop music, video games, comic books) and the overly analytical and self-conscious environment of academia. The university is not a bad place for poets to be, but it's a bad place for *all* poets to be. Once poets begin to think of themselves as academic professionals, their rules of behavior begin to diverge from the rules an artist would follow. In America, the problem is the professionalization of poetry. Over the past half century the American poet has changed from an individual artist who works as an independent cultural agent to an educational specialist who works in large, mainly state-run institutions as part of an elite, trained corps.

IC: Your essay "Can Poetry Matter?" is critical of poets confined to the university. Is it because you think their poetry grows out of a narrower range of experience than the work of poets in the past such as T. S. Eliot, Wallace Stevens, and William Carlos Williams who worked in the unrelated fields of banking, insurance, and medicine respectively?

DG: The advantage that Eliot and the others had in having their various professions was that their daily engagements separated them from the mainstream of literati in their lifetime. I would never say that the daily work of an insurance lawyer was necessarily more nourishing than the daily work of a creative writing teacher. The real problem is twofold. First, in America, by 1990, the vast majority of poets were creative writing teachers at a college level, and indeed most young people had begun to believe that the creative writing teacher was the social role of the poet. That situation is bad because it defines the poet, not as an artist, but as a type of professional. Second, it's bad for a culture whenever all its poets have such social homogeneity.

When you work in a large institution that's part of a larger set of institutions that constitute a profession or industry, then those institutions begin to determine the ways that you think and live. In America, once most poets began working as writing teachers, they began behaving more like college administrations than as intellectuals. I'll give you an example: Intellectuals believe as one of their cardinal principles in the value of truth, of candid speech. If they review a book, it is their duty to tell what they think of it truthfully. A professional, however, often believes that one should display "professional courtesy." One doctor or lawyer rarely badmouths another, at least in public. Too much honesty hurts the whole profession. In America, one teaching poet rarely gives a bad review to another teaching poet, no matter how dull or dreadful the book is. Most book reviews are blandly approving, and poetry criticism has become rife with euphemism and empty compliments. Consequently, the average reader no longer trusts poetry reviews. They are almost indistinguishable from dust jacket blurbs.

IC: How consciously has your work as a critic cleared away a place for your own poetry and did that criticism begin as a response to the work of poets whose work you have admired, Larkin, Stevens, and Auden perhaps?
DG: Never underestimate the importance of negative influences. At least part of the reason I began writing criticism early, even though I thought of myself primarily as a poet, was because I was living in a confused time. I saw bad poetry praised, good poetry ignored, and valuable poets being praised for their worst tendency. I felt that in order to clear some space in my own mind, I needed to grapple with some of the problems facing poets of my own generation. Criticism, like poetry, became an act of spiritual self-preservation.

IC: Do you ever write in direct response to other poems?
DG: Literature is always a conversation. Poems reflect—overtly or implicitly—other poems that have preceded them. Almost anyone who is writing about painting in contemporary poetry, for example, has Auden looking over

his or her shoulder. "Musée de Beaux Arts" is the only poem that Auden ever wrote about a specific painting, and yet it is such a masterpiece that it has cast a spell over the genre. Auden has always been one of my favorite poets and so directly or indirectly, there's a great deal of him in my work.

I've sometimes consciously taken another literary work and used it either as the raw material for a poem or as the ground base to counterpoint a poem. "In Chandler Country" and "In Cheever Country" both incorporate prose quotations from Raymond Chandler and John Cheever. In both cases they are homages to those writers. Raymond Chandler wrote about Los Angeles, the city I was born in, and John Cheever wrote about Westchester County where I lived for the last eighteen years. I found a way of talking about my native or adopted landscape refracted through a rather eccentric literary tradition. I like doing that, but it has to be done so that someone who doesn't know the sources can still read the poem. I like writing poems that have a surface which executes one shape and a subtext which executes another. Those are the poems which give me most pleasure.

IC: What is the connection between the current revival of formal and narrative poetry and the broader shift of sensibility in the arts?
DG: Modernism was the greatest period of American poetry. But Modernism as a viable avenue for young American poets has been dead for at least thirty years, perhaps longer. Yet, Modernism remains the institutionalized style of the Academy and the State. If a piece of public sculpture is to be commissioned in America, it will be an abstract construction; if an academic talks about the direction of contemporary poetry, it will inevitably be seen as some sort of linear development out of Modernism. That's not surprising. Academic institutions always define contemporary art by looking backwards. We saw that in nineteenth-century France, in Renaissance Italy. The artist, however, as Ezra Pound noted, is the antennae of the race. The artist perceives what is happening in society around him or her earlier than a scholar.

My generation faced a complicated question: What was the direction of poetry in the aftermath of Modernism, in an academic culture which, though it talked about poetry, was increasingly separated from the experience of poetry, and in general from a society which no longer cared about poetry? Depending on your perspective, you could either find this a terribly depressing situation or a uniquely liberating one. Since nobody cared, you were free to do whatever you wished although as soon as you got noticed you would undoubtedly be attacked by the powers that be.

It seemed to me that there were at least two large issues at stake. The first was to reconcile serious art with popular art. Most people, including most intellectuals, have a deep abiding engagement with contemporary popular art, especially film and music. It seemed important—rather than looking on popular art as something that is antithetical to high culture—to try to learn something from popular art without necessarily trying to bring one's writing down to that level. Popular art reminded us that all art must somehow be rooted in pleasure.

IC: How has your life changed since you opted out of business to become a professional writer?

DG: My life is both simpler and more complicated now. I'm making a living as a writer, but that means anything but leading a simple life. I write reviews and essays. I do translations. I'm writing an opera libretto, I've written song lyrics. I also travel giving readings and lectures. I'm editing textbooks. And, yes, I even write poetry! It is a given in our society that a poet must do something else for his or her living. I work hard to avoid full-time teaching. Having worked for nearly two decades as part of a business institution, I'm in no hurry to become the employee of another institution. It's important that some poets remain unaffiliated. We need a few independent, skeptical perspectives on literary life.

IC: As a writer, what are your own special needs?

DG: What I need as a writer is solitude and time for random meditation. I like to think about things before I begin writing. My favorite exercise both physically and intellectually is to take long walks. I will walk for miles composing a stanza in my head, saying it aloud, revising it slightly, composing it again and again. Or I will walk for an hour to mull over a sentence or two in an essay, to wrestle with an idea. I find this disorganized speculation is extremely nourishing.

IC: I'm especially interested in your religious sense, more specifically, your Catholicism. Do you consciously strive to illuminate that ethos?

DG: I've always been suspicious of poetry that follows an external social or political agenda. Why? Because that sort of poetry tends to use other people's words or employ secondhand slogans and principles instead of originating in the experience of the individual. I'm surprised that you view my poetry as religious, although I consider myself a religious poet. I am—and I have no choice about it—a Catholic poet. I am unconcerned with addressing the dogmas or teachings of Catholicism, but my spirituality has been shaped by the intellectual disciplines and ethical worldview of Catholicism, the habitual self-examination of conscience.

The basic donnée of the Catholic writer is to examine the consequences of living in a fallen world, to explore the distance between what we would like to be and what we are, the world we should have created and the world that we inhabit. The dissonance between those two realms of experience, the real and the imaginary, the visible and the invisible, is the fundamental tension of Catholic poetry. That's true even for Dante although he embodied that drama in a supernatural setting.

IC: Being a Catholic has been used against you by some of your critics to support their view that you are a "conservative" writer/critic. They suggest that you and other New Formalists advocate an absolute and final return to formal poetry.

DG: I have been denounced by all sides. I am condemned by members of the free verse mainstream as a slave to fixed forms, even though about half of my work is in free verse. Indeed, when I use regular metrical forms, I usually avoid fixed schemes. I have always been attacked by traditionalists as too experimental and progressive. I have been condemned for writing sonnets and villanelles although I have never published an original sonnet and have only written a single villanelle which has never appeared in my books. It's hard to take such overtly partisan criticism seriously.

American intellectual life remains very anti-Catholic. Anti-Catholicism is the one permissible bigotry. Part of that is a class bias, the old WASP prejudices against poor European immigrants. My father's family were Sicilian immigrants, my mother's family were Mexican. I was acutely aware at Stanford and Harvard that despite their overtly democratic principles, these institutions were relentlessly snobbish and elitist enterprises.

IC: How critics continue to deal with your attitude to poetic form is instructive. It tells us much of how form is and has been perceived. Perhaps form helps to produce resonance that can take a reader to a place that is prelinguistic, or, in your words, a place of "irrational musical shape above and beyond the sense of the language." How do you understand its relationship to content?

DG: The New Critics rightly insisted that there is no such thing as a separation between form and content in poetry. The way one says something is part of the meaning. All poetry is formal even if the form can only be apprehended retrospectively. My own feeling is that the more rich and arresting you make the surface form, the greater part of a reader or auditor's attention you engage and the more powerfully you are able to speak to his or her subconscious. Poetry does not recognize a difference between the mind and the body, the emotions and the intellect. Form is one of the integrating elements of poetry.

Critics who ten years ago condemned regular form as elitist were not only wrong, they were radically wrong because form is the most primitive, popular, and democratic aspect of poetry. The more consistently formal and apprehensible the rules by which a poem behaves, usually the more the unsophisticated reader understands it. All popular art is formal. If you listen to a pop song, the rhythm is usually regular, the chord progressions are regular, the language is rhythmically regular, the diction is formal, the themes are generic. Those conventions not only allow the listener to engage with the song, but also ironically they highlight what makes an individual song different.

I've always been struck with the similarity between poetry and sports. In sports, there are complex and precise rules. Once you understand those rules, they allow you to observe in this frenzy of physical activity, minute and individual characteristics. Form is a way of heightening our perception. What literary art does is make us listen to language more intensely and more permanently than we ever do with ordinary speech. In the same way in sport, it makes us observe physical activity more precisely than we ever could if it happened in an unstructured way.

IC: In the same controversial essay "Can Poetry Matter?" you have identified the need for "a new bohemia." How would you safeguard that kind of institution from the dangers you have identified within the academic subculture?

DG: Yes, recently I have been discussing the growth of a new bohemia—a non-institutional, intellectual and artistic subculture where writers, critics, and readers can meet in an egalitarian and largely unstructured way. But it is not an institution I am describing—it is a decentralized, cultural network. The new bohemia is already emerging in the United States. In the last ten years, the rise of independent presses, bookstores, lecture series, community-based art centers combined with the ease of electronic publishing has expanded literary culture beyond the university. I have no illusions that this bohemia will be any more perfect than the academy. It has its own inherent biases and weaknesses. What I believe is that literary life will be healthier, more diverse by having competition. Traditionally, bohemia keeps academia honest and vice versa. The problem with American literary culture is not that there are so many poets in the academy but that there have been no nonacademic institutions powerful enough to offset the university's monopoly on American literary life.

IC: You're speaking a business language.

DG: As a student of business and economics, I can assure you that all monopolies, be they private or governmental, abuse their power. Monopolies tend to exploit their constituents. They lack innovation. They're not responsive to changing conditions nor are they morally responsible. In the long run the university will behave no better than an oil company. Competition, however, forces you to address problems that you yourself don't want to bother with. If you have a literary culture, as we do in America, where most poets have been in school since the age of six, they begin to think, as John Barth's joke runs in *Giles Goat-Boy*, that the university is the universe. They unthinkingly identify literary life with academic life. That insularity is the problem, not the university itself. What needs to happen—and is happening—is the creation of a vital and serious bohemian life.

IC: Then success of that life depends on critical methodology. If criticism continues to be primarily analytical, then the universities will have no serious competition.

DG: A beautiful opportunity awaits any serious, nonacademic critic right now. Academic criticism has grown so parochial, so ideological, so dull that there are vast continents for the independent critic to explore. Intelligent, engaged, accessible but serious criticism is the lifeblood of a literary culture. Good artists need good critics. Part of the reason why American poetry has gone so bad in the last quarter-century is the lack of responsible criticism that engages anyone outside of the academic profession.

IC: Has your critical work encouraged others to write more honestly?

DG: I hope so. After the success of "Can Poetry Matter?" a number of poet-critics wrote to me and said that they felt they had been too soft in their reviews and they understood why it was important to give bad reviews. There is an assumption in America that since poetry receives so little public coverage that we should take those few opportunities to celebrate it. I believe that one of the reasons why poetry receives so little public space is that, whenever poets write about their art, they do so in adulatory terms. Both editors and readers find that unqualified praise not only dull but very much at odds with their own experience with new poetry, most of which is mediocre or worse.

The assumption among poets seems to be that the art is so sick that a few bad reviews might kill it. If that's the case, then the art of poetry deserves to die. No movie critic worries that Paramount will go bankrupt if they give a bad review to a crummy movie; no music critic believes that Nashville will collapse if they say the latest album from a country and western singer isn't very good. To say that criticism is a life-support system is an admission that the art is in the terminal ward.

IC: What are your impressions of Irish poetry?

DG: There are so many Irish in the United States that Americans have always had a special place in their hearts for Irish literature. In fact, today Americans read virtually no contemporary British poetry but almost everyone who reads poetry knows the work of Seamus Heaney. William Butler Yeats is probably the most popular non-American poet of the century. I worry, however, that in America we customarily anoint one Irish poet whom we worship at the expense of all other poets. For example, I've always thought it sadly ironic that while celebrating Seamus Heaney, we ignore Derek Mahon who seems to me one of the best living poets in English. Mention Mahon's name to American poets, and you usually see a physical question mark appear on your interlocutor's face. If you made a list of the best Irish poets of the century you will see that Americans don't read them. A poet who I have always loved is Louis MacNeice; he's virtually unread in the States as are John Montague, Patrick Kavanagh, and Thomas Kinsella.

IC: You've written long dramatic monologues, although I've only read three of them, and they are quite disturbing. Does that form allow you more nearly to explore fear?

DG: I've only published three long narrative poems. I wrote more but threw them away. I'm most interested in telling stories that have mortal stakes. When a poet tells a story, he or she usually brings it one step closer to myth than a novelist would. As Geoffrey Hill said, "no bloodless myth will hold." Myth is about primal fears that can only be conquered through some sort of blood sacrifice, and I'm interested in darker subject matter to begin with. There are some truths that we can only tell as stories. The more uncomfortable and frightening the truth the more necessary it often is to approach it as a story if you want to keep people from turning away. Although I myself did not always realize it until after they were completed, my narratives are also very Catholic. "The Homecoming" began as a much shorter narrative poem, but it didn't work. As I began revising it, I understood that it needed to become a theological poem as much as a psychological poem. What it was really about was a Catholic critique of a certain type of American Protestant worldview. The other two poems struck me in the same way but not until they were done. In retrospect, their spiritual origins became patently clear.

IC: Your poetry carefully avoids making simple resolutions. There are all kinds of undertones, but you respect certain privacies, I think.
DG: A poem is often more true to life by leaving some element unresolved. It's so easy to classify individuals and circumstances with preexisting labels. Surely, at least one of the purposes of fiction (in prose or verse) is to demonstrate the importance of seeing people in all their complex particularity rather than to view them through preexisting categories.

One critic complained that the language and perceptions of "Counting the Children" could not possibly have been experienced or articulated by a Chinese American accountant. I think that says more about the critic's stereotype both of Asians and of businesspeople than it does about the poem. One thing I learned in business, as I did in the many manual labor jobs I had growing up, is the depths of feeling and perception of nonliterary people. When I hear English professors say, either implicitly or explicitly, that no one can approach or experience a work of literature without substantial training, I want to vomit. What elitist nonsense! That is not to say that education doesn't refine your perceptions and allow you to articulate them more clearly. But endorsing literary education is not the same as saying that people have no ability to perceive and experience the complexity of both life and art without that training. I reserve the right to be both elitist and democratic but not in the way that the university currently practices either of those religions.

IC: Your poem "Counting the Children" has been made into a ballet theater piece.
DG: Yes, it has been done by the Mark Ruhala Company, which commissioned an original score, created an environmental set and had a cast of about twenty dancers as well as a small children's choir. It was a relentlessly serious production in an avant-garde tradition that incorporated the entire text of the poem and made no compromises to the audience. To my astonishment, it was wildly successful. It sold out every performance and went into an extended run. Eventually, the production stopped only because

some of the dancers had other engagements. The audience was mostly non-literary people, and even though the poem is a long challenging poem, they wanted to read it again. In every performance there were people weeping in the audience. Its diverse, nonacademic audience reminded me that these were the people that contemporary poetry had lost. Given a serious poem in a context that they could engage with imaginatively, they not only enjoyed it but wanted more. Many people came back to see the production again.

IC: Do you plan to write original verse drama?

DG: I am interested in exploring the possibilities of poetry beyond the lyric mode. Modernism concentrated so intensely on the lyric that there are vast and tantalizingly unexplored areas awaiting the contemporary poet in the narrative and dramatic modes. Poetic drama is the siren's song for English language poets. Who can read Shakespeare, Marlowe, Webster, and Jonson without being lured towards those dangerous breakers? Look at the history of Romanticism. The best poets of the nineteenth century were obsessed with recreating poetic drama—Shelley, Byron, Wordsworth, Coleridge, Keats, Browning, Arnold, Tennyson, Longfellow, Swinburne—because they saw the cultural power of combining drama with poetry. They were especially fascinated by the dream of recreating poetic tragedy—the most existentially penetrating dramatic genre. And what do we have to show for their immense expenditures of genius? *Manfred, The Cenci, Empedocles on Etna, The New England Tragedy.*

Will I succumb to this self-deluding and wasteful fantasy? Probably. But if I try my hand, I think I will follow Yeats's example and investigate new dramatic forms. The only way verse drama can be revived—even temporarily—is by reimagining the genre, probably in collaboration with another art. That requires luck as well as talent. One needs to meet the right composer, director, or choreographer—as Auden did in the 1930s with his collaboration with Christopher Isherwood, Benjamin Britten, and Rupert Doone. Given the right set of circumstances, I would gladly scribble away at a verse play, wouldn't you?

Paradigms Lost: Interview with Dana Gioia

Gloria Glickstein Brame / 1995

From *ELF* 5.1 (Spring 1995): 34–40 and *ELF* 5.2 (Summer 1995): 34–38.
Reprinted by permission of Gloria Glickstein Brame.

Gloria Glickstein Brame: The title essay of your first book of critical essays, *Can Poetry Matter?*, argued that poetry has become "the specialized occupation of a relatively small and isolated group." To reclaim its rightfully essential place in our culture, poetry must be liberated from the bureaucracy of academia. What has been the reaction to your arguments among poets and critics?

Dana Gioia: *Can Poetry Matter?* has generated more discussion than I had ever imagined possible. The original essay and the subsequent book provoked hundreds of essays, articles, editorials, symposia, and reviews as well as television, radio, and information-network commentary. Curiously, the responses have not been limited to America but also came from England, Ireland, Canada, and beyond. The astonishing thing is that most of the reactions have been favorable. I feel that I should stay out of the discussion and get on with my other work. If an author is fortunate enough to have his or her ideas enter public discourse in a meaningful way, they should remember that their original ideas were only the starting point. The culture itself is now having a conversation, and the writer is now only one voice among many in that ongoing discourse. To instigate a serious discussion on an important subject is the real purpose of criticism. The culture will take the discussion where it needs to go.

If the reception of *Can Poetry Matter?* taught me anything, it was to appreciate the complexity of literary culture, which is a collective enterprise involving thousands of writers, teachers, critics, editors, publishers, librarians, booksellers, and arts administrators—as well as innumerable readers. The failure of contemporary academic criticism and literary theory originates in its assumption that literary culture centers on the university. Culture is not an institution; it is an ecosystem, composed of many independent but interrelated entities. The university's self-absorption has ultimately led to all sorts of blind spots and distortions, most notably the curious cultural paradox I described in my *Atlantic* essay—America's thriving, institutionalized poetry subculture that is increasingly removed both from the society around it and the art it professes to serve.

GGB: Off the record, you've commented that you have been criticized by reviewers for statements you never made and ideas you never advanced. Would you comment for the record?
DG: Whenever a book attracts as much attention as *Can Poetry Matter?*, there are bound to be distortions. Once the public picks up on a particular set of ideas, it naturally turns them to its own end. I would be naive to complain about the predictable consequences of notoriety. One may dislike being misrepresented, but as Oscar Wilde observed, "There is only one thing in the world worse than being talked about, and that is not being talked about." All artists are vain—even poet-critics. I do, however, insist that my views are better represented by what I have published in books and essays than by what a reviewer, columnist, or feature writer claims I believe.

I am astonished by some of the things people mistakenly assume I have said—such as "Poetry is now a dead art," "Free verse is a bankrupt technique," "No one reads contemporary poetry," or "All Creative Writing Programs should be shut down." I admit that last dictum is tempting, but I have always suggested reforming these programs, not destroying them. I suspect many critics project their own fears and desires onto their image of me. It is easier to declare me a demon than address the points I raise.

GGB: Can you give a specific example of an incorrect claim?
DG: One consistent misreading of *Can Poetry Matter?*—by both its defenders and detractors—is that I crave a mass audience for contemporary poetry. I have even been cited as equating the size of a poet's readership with his or her literary merit. Not only have I never said such a thing, I explicitly reject these notions in the book. Of course, I wish that poetry had a larger audience in the United States. What poet, critic, or educator does not share that desire? But, for the record, let me restate my own beliefs as clearly and succinctly as possible.

The size of American poetry's audience matters less than the intelligence, engagement, and diversity of its readership. The problem with contemporary American "high-art" poetry is not so much that its audience is small (which, alas, it is) but that its core readership is distressingly homogeneous. The voluntary audience of serious contemporary poetry consists mainly of poets, would-be poets, and a few critics. Additionally, there is a slightly larger involuntary and ephemeral audience consisting of students who read contemporary poetry as assigned coursework. In sociological terms, it is surely significant that most members of the poetry subculture are literally *paid* to read poetry: most established poets and critics now work for large educational institutions. Over the last half-century literary bohemia has been replaced by an academic bureaucracy.

The main problem with the audience for American poetry originates in the uniformity and professional inbreeding of this coterie audience. Now, it is important that I explain this last point carefully since it can easily be misunderstood. There is nothing wrong with a poet teaching. What better teacher of literature can there be than an engaged writer? The problem starts when *all* the poets and critics in a culture teach—when, in other words, they all belong to the same professional network, when, in fact, they are mostly state or municipal employees—like police or postal workers. The pressures of institutional life gradually undermine their intellectual and artistic independence. Or, to state the problem in another way, we live in a society where not only do ordinary people not read poetry, but even most novelists, dramatists, and literary critics no longer read it. An art that speaks only to its own practitioners is a diminished enterprise.

GGB: "Can Poetry Matter?" set off lively, at times vitriolic, debate nationwide, particularly in the MFA programs whose mediocrity and insularity you decry. Is Dana Gioia popular on campus?
DG: I am mostly a *persona non grata* on campus. The university is an institution, and one thing institutions hate—be they academic, military, or industrial—is criticism from the outside. I have been amused by how wildly rancorous and passionately loony some of the professorial attacks on me have been. They remind me of nothing so much as 1950s Southern Baptist preachers denouncing rock 'n roll. Unfortunately, these cultural ministers don't know much more about the real content of my work than their predecessors knew about Little Richard. They just know listening to us is dangerous to their flocks.

I have also found many eloquent defenders on campus. The university is not a monolith. There are still many independent-minded teachers and writers who keenly understand how troubled both creative writing and the academic study of literature have become. They appreciated that *Can Poetry Matter?* is not an anti-university tirade. It is a book that critiques some specific problems in current academic literary study, especially in creative writing programs, anthologies, and poetry reviewing, and then suggests— rather tentatively, in fact—some basic reforms. For all its legendary ferocity, *Can Poetry Matter?* is really a rather gentle and openhanded book. Candid and pointed, yes, but never cruel.

GGB: Mona Van Duyn, in a 1993 lecture delivered at the Library of Congress, takes issue with your thesis that poetry is a captive of university writing programs and argues that poetry is evident everywhere in the mainstream of culture. She goes on to say that the question you should have asked is "why, in America, poetry matters so much to so many people, particularly their own poetry." *Should* you have asked this question, or is yours the right one?

DG: Mona Van Duyn has raised an interesting issue. In America today the only poetry that matters to many writers is their own. Like subsidized farming that grows food no one wants, the poetry is written and published for the benefit of the author not the reader. Van Duyn's observation reflects both the narcissism of our culture and the failure of contemporary literary education. Imagine someone trying to become a composer without hearing any music but his or her own. It would be ludicrous. And yet in many creative writing courses an analogous situation often exists. Students are asked to write out of their own experience without any disciplined study of first-rate models.

Learning to write poetry is no less difficult than mastering any art. You can't write well without reading widely and deeply. A person who reads only his or her own work—and we all know individuals like this—does not deserve the title poet. Such a person is, at best, a diarist, at worst, a *poseur.* So, I disagree with Van Duyn. I don't consider people concerned with their own personal effusions proof of poetry's importance to America. I consider it more evidence of our society's growing ignorance and narcissism.

GGB: In "Can Poetry Matter?" you propose an agenda for change in the form of "six modest proposals" which poets, teachers, and arts administrators should implement to renew public interest in poetry as a vital and thriving art form. Are you a crusader seeking to convert or a teacher seeking to enlighten? And if you are a teacher, why aren't you in academia?

DG: Am I hopelessly old-fashioned to believe that not all teaching is done in the classroom? I consider my essays, reviews, and anthologies as a type of teaching—an engaged and open conversation with a reader. I occasionally teach in universities on a visiting basis, but I have decided to make a living as a writer rather than an academic. Teaching is both a great pleasure and a great privilege, but it is easier to be candid and independent if one is an outsider.

As for whether I am "a crusader seeking to convert," I think not. What would I convert people to? Poetry is not a creed or dogma. It is a special way of speaking and listening. Poetry is an art that stretches back to the origins of human civilization, a primal and essential art that is endangered in the modern world. I'm not ashamed to admit that I love poetry. The art has given me immeasurable pleasure, consolation, and enlightenment. Nor am I ashamed to say that I consider poetry important enough to argue over passionately and to defend. A society that loses its ability to hear and value poetry is a diminished thing, a culture that has lost part of its full human potential. My role as a critic has been mostly to insist that poetry still deserves a role in public culture. If that conviction constitutes a crusade, then I am guilty of tilting at a few windmills.

GGB: You have described Longfellow as "the most popular American poet who ever lived." Yet you also note that he, along with Whittier and others, has become a poet one must know of but not one to read; critics do not simply neglect him, but dismiss his entire aesthetic enterprise. The villain is Modernism, which you say "by prizing compression, intensity, complexity, and ellipsis . . . cultivated an often hermetic aesthetic inimical to narrative poetry." What is the importance of the narrative form to contemporary verse?

DG: When poets stopped telling stories, they not only lost a substantial portion of their audience; they also considerably narrowed the imaginative possibilities of their art. As long as there have been poets, those poets told stories. These stories were rarely about their own lives but about imagined lives—drawn from myth, legend, history, or current events. The source scarcely mattered as long as the poet vividly reimagined them for the reader. From Homer, Virgil, Ovid, Attar, Firdausi, Dante, Boccaccio, Chaucer, Camões, Spenser, LaFontaine, Milton, Goethe, Pope, Pushkin, Byron, Longfellow, Mickiewicz up to Frost and Jeffers, the history of poetry was inextricably bound with the history of narrative—until, that is, about seventy years ago.

Modernism, which grew out of Symbolism, was primarily interested in exploring the expressive possibilities of the lyric mode. American Modernism especially prized compression, intensity, indirection, and allusion. Not surprisingly, the movement had little use for the expansive and mostly linear nature of narrative. That mode was best left to middlebrow novelists and the movies. I won't condemn Modernism's rejection of narrative because the movement produced some of the greatest poetry written in our language. All artistic movements make decisions on what to explore and what to ignore. If they produce great art, one must concede they made the proper choices.

Now that Modernism is dead, however, the problems with its bias toward the lyric mode have become obvious. No Modernist masterpieces have been produced for decades. The avant-garde is moribund. But the American arts establishment, especially in the visual and literary arts, still passively accepts most of Modernism's tenets. Even in the 1960s when contemporary poets first returned to the narrative mode, they made a crucial mistake under the influence of Modernism. They tried to recreate poetic narrative out of an autobiographical lyric "I" rather than the invented third person. The Confessional aesthetic that resulted exhausted itself artistically within five years, but it continued to be the mainstream style of American poetry for the next three decades. The recent return to narrative is one of the crucial changes now transforming American poetry. This broadscale shift in sensibility represents perhaps the surest evidence that Modernism is now an irretrievably dead period style, despite the cosmetic expertise of the embalmers of academe like poor Marjorie Perloff who naively believe in an eternal avant-garde.

GGB: Is there any way to escape the artistic claustrophobia of the poetry subculture?

DG: There must be an escape for poetry to survive as a meaningful public art. I would maintain that the history of post-war American poetry has been a series of escape attempts from its internment in the English Department. What seemingly dissimilar literary movements like the Beats, Feminists, Confessionals, Anti-Vietnam writers, Black Consciousness poets, New Formalists, New Narrative, and Men's Movement all have in common is their determination to reestablish poetry's link with the broader culture. Whatever one thinks of each movement's artistic success, they are united in their initial eschewal of critical fashion—even if almost every group was soon tamed and brought back into the academy.

GGB: In the conclusion to "Can Poetry Matter?" you assert that it's "time to restore a vulgar vitality to poetry." Exactly what do you mean? Aren't we vulgar enough?

DG: When I asked for more "vulgar vitality" in our poetry, I used the word *vulgar* in its root sense, which means "of the people." The best American poetry of the last few decades has too often been paralyzed by its own sophistication. There is nothing wrong about academics and intellectuals writing poetry. The problems begin when they start writing primarily for one another. Academic art has the tendency to become too knowing and self-conscious. Poetry is not a branch of analytical philosophy. It is a primal, holistic kind of human communication. A poet needs innocence as much as knowledge, emotion as much as intelligence, vulnerability as much as rigor. A poet can become too smart for his or her own good and forget the child-like pleasures of sound and story, sense, and sensuality that poetry should provide. The challenge for a writer is to master the medium of poetry without losing that inner innocence.

Do you remember the early Italian Renaissance when academic poets wrote in an artificially reconstructed classical Latin rather than the vulgar Italian of the streets? (They didn't even write in the Church Latin that monks and schoolmasters spoke—it was too *déclassé*.) None of that carefully contrived work survived. What we read today is the poetry of the vulgate by Dante, Boccaccio, Cavalcanti, and Petrarch, which we now realize was more truly sophisticated than the verse of the sophisticates. It created an imaginative dialectic that embraced the high, the middle, and the low in its aesthetic. Isn't that range one reason why we consider Shakespeare our greatest author in English? I'm not asking for poetry of the commonplace. I'm asking for art powerful and comprehensive enough to reflect the full range of human experience and desires.

GGB: In your essay "Tradition and an Individual Talent," you align yourself with T. S. Eliot on the dynamic interrelation between the contemporary poet and his antecedents. You use the work of Donald Justice to demonstrate how tradition plays a crucial role in achieved modern verse. You say Justice "understands the sustaining power of tradition without seeking to stifle innovation and experiment."

DG: *Tradition* has become such a loaded word that one can hardly use it today without being misunderstood. One hears it employed mostly as a code word to signal a reactionary defense or radical attack on some body of work. But, as an artist, I see tradition as something quite different from a fixed or oppressive canon. It is neither static nor prescriptive. Tradition is a vast, living landscape we have inherited—so rich and varied that not only do we constantly discover new aspects of it but the places we revisit always seem slightly different.

In art, there is no absolute break between the past and present. One grows naturally out of the other. Moreover, once a new work is written, it exists in an eternal present tense with all the works of the past; and by finding its own place, each new work slightly changes everything around it. The heroic bluster of Romanticism and early Modernism makes it easy to forget that no artist exists in isolation. Art is a collective enterprise embracing past and present, artists and audience. There is also no single past. Artists choose their own predecessors, and great artists reconfigure the traditions to which they belong.

Postmodernism looks on tradition as a huge library in which the contemporary artist roams borrowing things from this source or that. All of the past is available, but none of it needs to be taken too seriously. Art becomes collage—all intertextuality and allusion—and the artist is less a creator than an editor. Needless to say, such a theory could only have been promoted by professors. What the postmodernist aesthetic misses is the utter necessity for art to have integrity and authenticity. Whatever the artist borrows from the past must be completely integrated into a new whole, and the artist can only create that new entity by assimilating the material inside his or her own psyche. The process of assimilation transforms the past into something different. Virgil scrupulously modeled his *Aeneid* on Homer but nonetheless created an extraordinarily original poem—because every borrowing was transformed by his sensibility.

Tradition is not, as postmodernists maintain, a library or museum the artist plunders. It is the endless conversation between the living and the dead. Young artists enter into this conversation passionately—not merely intellectually, though study and analysis play a part. They live and breathe it. Tradition is not a public building. It is a love affair.

GGB: Critically, you are considered a champion of formal verse and poetically, a chief figure in the "New Formalist" movement. Yet unlike many formalists, you make quite clear that this is merely a descriptive term and does not imply a value judgment of any particular work. What are the criteria for good formal verse?

DG: The form of a poem—be it in meter or free verse—must grow naturally out of its substance. The form and meaning are not merely inseparable; the form is an essential (if often ineffable) part of a poem's meaning. If the form seems mere decoration, if it appears arbitrary or excessive, if it calls attention to itself in ways that do not deepen the overall impact of the work, then the form is being used badly. The formal elements have not been successfully integrated into the totality of the work. This disjunction is not only a problem with bad poetry in traditional forms; it is a common failing of avant-garde art where technique often either becomes an end in itself or—more commonly—extreme styles are employed to mask banal content.

Poetry is an art form that demands heightened attention and retention. It both invites and rewards more intense involvement than we normally give to other kinds of speech. Poetic technique, therefore, is never esoteric but eminently practical. It serves at least two purposes. First, it announces that a poem differs from other kinds of speech, that it requires the audience's special attention. A poem begins by attracting our attention through its sound, shape, typography, syntax, texture, or tone. Second, the technique maintains the audience's involvement. All poetic form is a way of keeping the audience's attention beyond what ordinary language requires. Meter, for example, creates a gentle trance state in the auditor. Since poetry is more intense, condensed, and expressive than ordinary language, it needs these techniques to carry the burden of its message.

The form of any poem is an *ad hoc* contract between author and audience. The poet sets down the principles by which the work will unfold and asks the reader or auditor to pay special attention. For that reason, a poet must keep up his or her side of the contract. To change the rules midway for no compelling reason, to fudge the form when it becomes too demanding, to merely approximate the terms of the contact, is intolerable when the audience is giving each word heightened attention. If a poet asks the audience to surrender to the terms of a poem, the author cannot abuse that trust. A poem that meaninglessly disregards those principles is a bad formal poem.

GGB: How does that differ from what you term "pseudo-formal" poetry?
DG: "Pseudo-formal" verse is a term that I coined to describe a common type of bad contemporary poem. It is a poem that employs formal principles so sloppily that they have no integrity. The lines appear roughly similar but lack the energy that regular rhythm gives. Pseudo-formal poems may be arranged in regular stanzas, but on close examination the visual form has no integral relation to the sound. A good poem rewards scrutiny. The closer one looks at any formal element in a pseudo-formal poem, the more arbitrary or imperfect it appears. Nothing survives close examination. It's just language chopped up into a vaguely regular shape without sufficient attention to sound or structure. It is neither good formal verse nor good free verse— just superficial pretense. And isn't one of the big problems with so much contemporary poetry that it's carelessly written and pretentiously presented?

GGB: You have said that formalism is only one response to the troubling situation of contemporary poetry. What are some other major trends?

DG: Over the last fifteen years American poetry has changed from a visual to an auditory art. This shift is of paramount importance because it ultimately determines both how the author shapes a literary work and how an audience perceives it. The change is apparent throughout the poetry world, although few mainstream critics seem to have noticed it yet. It should be obvious to anyone, for example, that the primary means of publication for new American verse is now oral—namely the poetry reading. Poets reach many more people through readings than they do through books, and their direct experience with the audience affects how they write. Meanwhile there has been a reemergence of popular poetry—like rap, cowboy poetry, slam poetry, and performance poetry—that is primarily oral. Some of it is even quasi-improvisatory. It exists only as oral performance. These new poetries do not necessarily contain individual works of great artistic significance. But collectively they reveal huge change in literary sensibility.

There has also been the revival of formal and narrative poetry. Rhyme, meter, and storytelling all have evident appeal to the ear. The recent resurgence reflects the broader shift in our culture away from the printed word and back to the spoken word. Although many aspects of this change should rightly worry literary intellectuals, the shift is not an entirely bad thing for poets. Poetry, after all, is an art form that pre-dates literacy. It is not impossible to imagine that it will outlive mass literacy as well.

GGB: Do you have a vision for the role of poetry in the twenty-first century?

DG: My vision for the future of American poetry is of an art that is rooted in the great literature of the past, but understands that tradition is necessarily a dynamic process—the past enriches the present, but does not restrict it. I want a poetry that can learn as much from popular culture as from serious culture. A poetry that seeks the pleasure and emotionality of the popular arts without losing the precision, concentration, and depth that characterize high art. I want a literature that addresses a diverse audience distinguished for its intelligence, curiosity, and imagination rather than its professional credentials. I want a poetry that risks speaking to the fullness of our humanity, to our emotions as well as to our intellect, to our senses as well as our imagination and intuition. Finally I hope for a more sensual and physical art—closer to music, film, and painting than to philosophy or literary theory.

Contemporary American literary culture has privileged the mind over the body. The soul has become embarrassed by the senses. Responding to poetry has become mostly an exercise in interpretation and analysis. Although poetry contains some of the most complex and sophisticated perceptions ever written down, it remains an essentially physical art tied to our senses of sound and sight. Intelligence is an irreplaceable element of poetry, but it needs to be vividly embodied in the physicality of language. We must—as artists, critics, and teachers—reclaim the essential sensuality of poetry. The art does not belong to apes or angels, but to us. We deserve art that speaks to us as complete human beings. Why settle for anything less?

GGB: *The Gods of Winter* is dedicated to the memory of your son, Michael Jasper. Has your son's death redirected your artistic vision?

DG: The sudden death of my first son not only changed my life initially, but it still influences me daily in ways both large and small. Losing him brutally clarified my life. It made me recognize what mattered and what did not. I more or less stopped writing for a year. I no longer saw the point of working towards anything. Until then I had always found solace in writing. During my first ten years in business, I had managed to write almost every night, even after spending twelve hours in the office. I worked every weekend. I gave up a great many things to carve out this time, but this nightly routine sustained me spiritually and creatively. It made my daytime life possible.

Then suddenly the world I had so carefully constructed collapsed. My will had snapped. I have never regained the patient discipline or quiet certitude of those years. As I slowly emerged from my pain, I resolved to reshape my life—to build my daily existence on the things I valued most. I proceeded slowly because I wasn't always sure what I wanted. I made many changes. The most obvious one was leaving a business career I had invested seventeen hard years in building.

How did these changes affect my writing? You may see the influences better than I do. My work has always been dark, but it now became more emotionally direct. Rightly or wrongly, I became impatient with poems that could not bear a certain spiritual weight. I also gradually realized that all lyric poetry is directly or indirectly about mortality. The reason we feel the overwhelming force of a particular moment is that our lives are finite. As Wallace Stevens said, "Death is the mother of beauty."

GGB: One of the book's more remarkable qualities is the tranquility and understatement of its poetic meditations. As a poet, and a father who experienced a fatal loss, where does the dividing line fall in your work between the personal and the confessional? Should a poet respect his form over his feelings?

DG: In a good poem there is no division between form and feeling. The form embodies the feeling just as the emotion animates the form. Pure form is lifeless and abstract, pure emotion subjective and incoherent. A madwoman screaming on a street corner has emotions enough for an epic, but she lacks the form to express her interior life clearly to anyone else. I believe that emotion is most keenly felt when it is partially held in check. A poem need not shout to be heard.

As for the poems in *The Gods of Winter*, there was an additional private concern. I did not want my son remembered by uncontrolled howls of pain. My wife and I suffered more than I can express, but to make poems merely out of the agony would have been self-pitying and dishonest. My son had been my greatest joy. His birth had left me awe-struck and humble before life. He turned me from a son into a father—and allowed me to understand my own father clearly for the first time. If I mourned him, I also wanted to preserve the joyful mystery of his existence. The sorrow could not be adequately appreciated without also expressing the joy and wonder. I wonder if what you perceive as tranquility isn't actually two strong and conflicting emotions momentarily holding one another in check.

GGB: [Quotes poem]:

I saw beyond my daughter to all children,
And, though elated, still I felt confused
Because I wondered why I never sensed

That thrill of joy when looking at adults
No matter how refined or beautiful,
Why lust or envy always intervened.

(From "Counting the Children")

I'd like to know if the narrator ever found the answer to this question. Are children innocents in your work? Are adults corrupt?
DG: I'm probably the wrong person to ask. Once an author finishes a poem, he or she becomes merely another reader. I may remember what I intended to put into a text, but what matters is what a reader actually finds there—which is usually something both more and less than the poet planned. Each reader of "Counting the Children" will have to decide whether the poem adequately answers the father's quandary. I have never subscribed to the sentimental romantic notion that children are innocents. I am a Catholic and consider

man's fallen nature an article of faith. If children are in some sense innocent, they are also greedy, cruel, domineering, self-centered, and temperamental as well as curious, tender, loving, loyal, and ingenious. In other words, children are just like adults, although they have not yet learned to disguise their less attractive impulses. Likewise adults are not necessarily corrupt, but they are almost inevitably weak—sometimes fatally so. Human nature isn't doomed, but it is nervously balanced between contradictory impulses.

GGB: There are chilling undercurrents (and sometimes vivid descriptions, as in "The Homecoming") of violence in your narrative poems. Why? Is there something about the narrative form which unleashes your violent impulses?

DG: "The Homecoming" is the longest poem I've ever written. It took years to finish. "Counting the Children" and "The Room Upstairs" were only slightly less difficult to complete. Writing extended narrative poems is a different proposition than writing shorter lyric poems. A memorable idea is not enough for a narrative poem. Style and sensibility are not enough. A lyric poem articulates the impulse of a moment, but a narrative brings all sorts of other matters to bear. Something crucially important needs to be at stake. Otherwise the story becomes merely anecdotal. A story too boring to tell in prose doesn't become more interesting told in verse. I could not have worked on "The Homecoming" for so long had it not dealt with actions of mortal consequence.

Why is "The Homecoming" so violent? There was no other way to tell that story truthfully. It is a poem about the power of evil. Violence has become an unavoidable subject for American poets. Too much contemporary poetry is platitudinous, full of blandly uplifting and usually self-congratulatory sentiments. We need darker, more dangerous poetry—not sensational but willing to probe uncomfortable areas.

GGB: "Counting the Children" is one of several poems which attempt to reconcile life, death, and immortality. In this poem you wrote about immortality: " . . . we do not possess it in ourselves. / We die, and it abides, and we are one / With all our ancestors, while it divides // Over and over, common to us all . . ." Your view on immortality somewhat resembles your aesthetic position on poetic tradition as an eternal cycle in which contemporary poets and their antecedents are immortally engaged. Is poetry itself an immortal engagement or an existential dilemma?

DG: Genuine poetry always grows out of our basic existential dilemma—our mortality. Our minds have the ability to reach across time to scan the past and ponder the future, but our bodies die. "Counting the Children" is spoken by a Chinese American narrator. Although born in America, he understands instinctively how deeply his life is rooted in the past—of his family, his heritage, his race. The vision he has at the climax of the poem may seem odd to someone raised in the American traditions of progress and individualism; he sees his destiny as historically determined and collective. For him, immortality is not merely about the future; it is a concept that unites the past, present, and future. His vision is tribal rather than individual. The present is a pivot turning between the past and future.

GGB: How do you balance the self-consciousness of writing poetry which emerges from the existential dilemma with the detachment that craft requires?
DG: I've always considered my work fairly unselfconscious. In fact, I often don't know what a poem is *really* about until years later. I try to keep myself busy with the surface of the poem, so that my unconscious has free play to write the rest. I think of my poems mostly in musical and sensory terms. I want them to be physically arresting—like music or painting. I work obsessively to point and balance the language of my poems. In revising, I consciously shape the rhythm, tone, and texture. I also deliberately look for things to cut out. I rarely know where a poem is going until it is finished. In fact, if I know initially how a poem will end, I lose the impulse to write it.

GGB: [Quotes poem]

Where will it end? This grim cycle of workshops
churning out poems for little magazines
no one honestly finds to their taste?
This ever-lengthening column of contributors
scavenging the land for more students,
teaching them to write their boot-camp sestinas?

(From "My Confessional Sestina")

This witty poem—a sestina which satirizes sestinas—reiterates some of the points you have made in your criticism about contemporary poetry as an industry, and a banal one at that. Does your awareness of this dismal state of affairs weigh on you when you write poetry?

DG: Absolutely not. The current state of literature is always dismal, and yet literature gloriously survives. Genuine poetry is both more timeless and more timely than the fashions of the moment. Compared to the excitement earlier this century, American poetry does now seem to be in a *fin-de-siè-cle* slump. I can't imagine that even the most indiscriminate cheerleaders of creative writing would pretend that we have anything happening at the moment comparable to the twenties when Frost, Stevens, Eliot, Williams, Moore, Millay, Pound, Jeffers, Ransom, Cummings, MacLeish, Hughes, Crane, and H. D. redefined the art. There had never been a moment like that earlier in American poetry, so it's probably not surprising that it isn't recurring now. We have some superb poets writing today, but we no longer have the conviction that our best new writing is also our most innovative.

How does this sense of the cultural moment affect my writing? It depends. When I am writing an essay or review, I consider its current context. My opinions and approach grow out of the critical discourse surrounding the subject. Critical prose is necessarily timely and pragmatic. But poetry—at least in my experience—originates and develops differently. When I'm writing a poem, I hardly consider its contemporary context. I'm not conversing with current opinion; I'm talking with the language and its history. That's why I can work on a poem for years without feeling it is losing anything essential whereas a critical piece might easily lose its edge. Very few literary essays are readable after a century, but the best poetry still feels fresh.

GGB: You seem to feel that contemporary poetry is doomed to mediocrity.

DG: No, just the opposite. I can't tell you how happy I am when I come across a really splendid new poem in a journal—a poem I know I will reread for the rest of my life. I'm especially pleased if it is by an unfamiliar author. I get a physical thrill of excitement and delight. I remember when I heard my first poem by Philip Larkin. It was "Poetry of Departures." I had no idea who Larkin was then, but I knew immediately that he was the writer I had been looking for—not merely a master but a confidante. Likewise, I vividly recall coming across a set of poems, including "The Garden of Medusa" by Radcliffe Squires in the *Sewanee Review* twenty years ago at Stanford. I reread them every day for a month. This electrifying feeling of discovery and kinship reminds me of Larkin's description of his passion for New Orleans jazz, "On me your voice falls as they say love should, / Like an enormous yes." I felt that "enormous yes" the first time I read particular poems by Weldon

Kees, Ted Kooser, Charles Martin, Gjertrud Schnackenberg, James Fenton, Edward Field, and R. S. Gwynn. It doesn't happen often. It doesn't have to. Good poems don't wear out.

GGB: Having proclaimed the death of Modernism in your criticism, what do you, as a poet, do now that Modernism is dead?
DG: It would not only be pompous to represent myself in an historical context, it would also be misleading. I never think of literary trends when I'm writing poetry. I didn't begin working in formal meters as a student twenty years ago because it was fashionable. At the time, rhyme and meter were almost universally despised. I explored meter because it seemed the right way to compose the poems that were haunting my imagination. The same was true of narrative. I wanted to describe certain things that could only be said as stories.

The British poet-critic Donald Davie, who was my unofficial mentor at that time, actively discouraged me from working in both form and narrative. Donald was a Modernist. Americans, he told me, should work in free verse; that was our vital tradition. But the older generation can never teach the young how to write. Every poet must undertake that slow, difficult task on his or her own. And young poets can't expect that the older generation will necessarily like their solutions. Every new movement in poetry will inevitably meet some opposition. If an artist isn't strong enough to keep his or her vision intact while meeting that opposition, he or she probably shouldn't be writing.

GGB: Who are your poetic heroes? What example have they set which you follow in your work?
DG: There are so many ways in which I can answer your question. I admire a great many poets for different reasons. The poets who have influenced me most as an artist are probably W. H. Auden, Robert Frost, Rainer Maria Rilke, and Ezra Pound. Some of these influences have been very specific. Frost, for example, shaped my notions of the narrative poem. T. S. Eliot, George Orwell, and Randall Jarrell have influenced my criticism. Wallace Stevens and Eliot, both of whom worked outside academia, became important models for my spiritual life, as in different ways did Orwell and Thomas Merton. It's all fairly complicated and subjective. I have read voraciously since childhood, and hundreds of writers shaped my opinions and sensibility. I love E. E. Cummings's poetry—an unpopular enthusiasm nowadays—but, I can't point to a single poem of mine that was directly

influenced by his work (except perhaps "The Gods of Winter"). The sheer extravagance of Cummings's poetic language, however, is often before me as a reminder of how lyric poetry should work. I feel the same admiration for the language of Hart Crane, and early Stevens. They are touchstones.

Philip Larkin and Elizabeth Bishop have also been important influences in a different way. They reinforced my sense that poets should be slow to publish. It is not how much work a poet publishes, but how good that work is. I sometimes keep a poem back for ten years because a single line doesn't seem good enough. Or I will revise a poem fifty to a hundred times trying to get it exactly right. Some people consider that behavior neurotic. Larkin and Bishop, however, demonstrate that such a neurosis may not be altogether bad for a poet.

Let me mention one more thing. By the time an active writer reaches his or her forties, one's personal style has pretty much set. I can still learn some small trick from another author or be reminded of an important general principle, but I no longer feel another writer's sensibility actively shaping my work as I did at nineteen or twenty. Now, alas, I'm now stuck with myself. Self-improvement is now slow and difficult, and it must come from within.

GGB: You are fascinated by the art of translation—as evidenced by your book-length translations of Seneca and Montale, as well as the anthology of Italian verse which you coedited. If you could rewrite your own personal history, would you choose another native tongue in place of English? Which is the most perfect language for poetry? Are all languages perfect or are all inherently flawed?

DG: I can't imagine a more beautiful or supple language for poetry than English—especially American English. Just look at our vocabulary. It is as richly stocked as the British Museum. We have the sturdy Anglo-Saxon words and a suave overlay of Norman French. Then come borrowings from Italian, Latin, Greek and eventually Hindu, Spanish, and Yiddish. One can live in a house, home, villa, bungalow, cottage, cabin, manse, or condominium. The vocabulary of French seems low budget in comparison.

Of course, anyone who studies other languages learns that each offers its compensations. French has a clarity and purity that make all sorts of subtle effects possible that could never work *en anglais*. Since German is half-inflected, the word endings make it possible to use classical meters beyond the practical scope of English. When I hear Hölderlin, Goethe, or Rilke recreating the hypnotic beauty of dactylic hexameter or the elegiac couplet, I wish one could manage those rhythmic shapes in English. The sheer acoustic beauty of Italian—the language spoken around me in childhood—intoxicates the listener. It can either be as smooth as Petrarch or as spiky as Montale. And how easy it is to rhyme in French, German, or Italian! As a student in Austria, I wrote several poems in German, and the rhymes came effortlessly even for a foreigner. The effect I envy most, however, is the complete freedom of word order that Latin affords. A poet can arrange the words into shapes that simultaneously emphasize both the music and the sense. Latin can pack more meaning into fewer words than any language I know.

But what poet would willingly give up English—the mother tongue of Shakespeare, Milton, Mother Goose, Keats, and Dickinson? Or, to go back a hundred years ago, what other language could produce E. E. Cummings, Edna St. Vincent Millay, Wilfred Owen, Robert Graves, Hart Crane, Basil Bunting, Archibald MacLeish, and Langston Hughes—not to mention Noel Coward and Dr. Seuss—all within a single decade? Yes, I think I'll stay with English. I'm only just beginning to explore its possibilities.

On Writing *Nosferatu* and the Role of Poet as Librettist

LeQuita Vance-Watkins / 1998

From *Caesura* (Winter 1998). Reprinted by permission of LeQuita Vance-Watkins.

LeQuita Vance-Watkins: What is the leap from the poem to the libretto?
Dana Gioia: Ideally, there should be no leap—just a step. Opera began as a kind of poetic drama. The Renaissance Florentines who invented it were trying to recreate the ideal balance between poetry and music found in classical Greek drama. That balance between words and music should remain the artistic goal. I consider the libretto a significant poetic form whose literary potential has barely been realized in English.

LVW: The opera libretto isn't a particularly prestigious form—at least in literary circles. Why would a serious poet want to write one?
DG: To grow. It is exciting to explore a new form. In Shakespeare's time, poets took for granted that they could work in all three basic literary forms—the lyric, narrative, and drama. But nowadays poets are supposed to settle down and just write short lyric utterances. I want to try the larger forms of poetry that are now mostly neglected—the narrative and dramatic forms. There are some things a writer can only do in drama. Opera is the only branch of contemporary drama in which the poet remains an essential collaborator. Once you accept its special requirements, opera allows a writer to explore all sorts of material that doesn't easily work in other forms. It opens up extraordinary artistic possibilities.

LVW: What sort of possibilities?
DG: First of all, opera is the only living form of poetic drama. It is also the

only remaining form of tragic theater. If you want to write a verse tragedy today, you have to write it for the opera house.

LVW: How does a libretto differ from poetry?
DG: A verse libretto must work simultaneously as poetry and drama. The language must be memorable and expressive, but good words aren't enough. The libretto must create arresting characters and powerful situations that propel the action; otherwise, it is a failure. The great challenge is finding the right balance. The words must be emotionally direct and evocative but also extraordinarily concise. They must be richly poetic but not too dense or complex. The text must give the composer enough room to let the music take charge. The biggest difference between a poem and a libretto is its essentially collaborative nature. A libretto doesn't exist to be judged on its own literary quality. It exists to inspire a composer to create a compelling musical drama. The libretto ultimately justifies itself as the departure point for a collaborative work in which the poet is a minority partner.

LVW: How is a libretto similar to poetry?
DG: Good poetry is good poetry. Awkward language and stale images won't be redeemed by music. Writing lyrics requires arresting emotion, memorable phrasing, sharp images, and evocative compression. In *Nosferatu* I have set myself an additional challenge. I have tried to write a libretto that works both on the page as poetic drama and in performance as musical theater.

LVW: How did it happen that you and Alva Henderson worked together?
DG: My good luck. Fifteen years ago in New York I saw a production of Henderson's one-act opera, *The Last Leaf*. It both impressed and astonished me. *The Last Leaf* was the sort of new opera that isn't supposed to exist—dramatically powerful, stylistically distinctive, but radiantly melodic. It was also inherently vocal. So many modern operas focus on the orchestra rather than the human voice. After that evening, I made it a point to hear everything I could by him. I never thought we would be working together. For years the novelist-poet Janet Lewis had been his collaborator. But when Janet entered her nineties, Alva started looking for a new partner. We knew one another only slightly, but he set some of my poems to music. We both loved the results. When he suggested we work together on an opera, I immediately agreed. My only condition was that we chose a subject I could enter imaginatively.

LVW: How did you and Henderson pick *Nosferatu* as a subject?
DG: Sheer serendipity. Just as Alva and I started to discuss possible subjects, I happened to have lunch with the critic Gilberto Perez who told me he had just written an essay on F. W. Murnau's famous silent film. Reading his analysis of *Nosferatu*, I was struck by how much the film resembled a bel canto opera—like *Lucia di Lammermoor* or *I Puritani*. It depicted a strong and sensitive woman trapped by tragic circumstances beyond her control. It also occurred to me that there had never been a great vampire opera. Although the vampire is one of the central Romantic myths, and opera was the greatest Romantic art form, the two never came together. *Nosferatu* offered a great myth that was not only natural to opera but still untouched—an irresistible combination for a poet.

LVW: What did Henderson think about the idea?
DG: At first he was skeptical. He didn't see how he could create an opera with the vampire as its central character. I was then still living in New York. I flew out to California, and we spent an afternoon walking through Armstrong Redwood Grove—a natural masterpiece of Gothic Romanticism. I explained that I wanted to build *Nosferatu* around Ellen, the soprano role (just as Murnau had originally built his film around the heroine before it was cut for export). The opera would be a tragedy about a gifted woman caught in a supernatural trap. I didn't imagine a gothic thriller like Bram Stoker's *Dracula*. By the time we left the grove, not only was Alva convinced, but we had jointly created a rough scenario.

LVW: How did soprano Susan Gundunas get involved?
DG: She had sung in the Opera San Jose production of Alva's *West of Washington Square*. He loved her voice, and she loved his music. When Susan left the Hamburg Opera to return to California, she tried out Ellen's entrance aria from *Nosferatu*, which Alva had just composed. Alva then began writing the role with her voice in mind—just as Donizetti, Bellini, and Verdi wrote their finest roles for specific singers. Her voice is radiant and wonderfully emotive. A lot of contemporary composers write rather timidly for the voice since they don't know who will ultimately perform the role. With Susan at hand, Alva has been able to create powerfully virtuosic music. In both technical and dramatic terms, Ellen is a commanding *prima donna* role. The title role for baritone is almost equally virtuosic. It requires a singer with both a magnificent voice and immense stage presence—like Thomas Hampson.

LVW: What is new about *Nosferatu*?

DG: What is the most novel about *Nosferatu* is its traditional structure. The opera builds its story through arias, duets, trios, and ensembles. We have tried to reinvent these powerful forms of dramatic and musical expression. I've attempted to write real poems for these numbers, especially the major arias, to shape lyric language into traditional forms that convey contemporary psychology. These forms can focus huge amounts of energy as long as the composer finds fresh and authentic ways of using them. Arias, duets, and trios also elicit deep responses from singers. That is absolutely essential. Opera is a performing art. Unless it creates powerful expressive singing, it doesn't exist.

LVW: There is a long history of poetry and music collaborating. Do you find such collaboration as strong today as in the past?

DG: Most American poets don't take the idea of collaborative art seriously. They rarely write their best for musical setting. Our national tradition stresses the personal and indeed private side of poetry—the posture of an Emily Dickinson or Wallace Stevens. We have few modern models for either public or collaborative poetry. Working with another artist, one needs to find common ground, some area where both persons can work at their best. When artistic collaboration succeeds, it doesn't create compromise but a strangely intensifying transfiguration.

LVW: Did you find the process transfiguring?

DG: Absolutely. In writing the libretto for *Nosferatu*, I was able to make certain ideas work that I could never have brought off in other genres. Let me give you two examples. In Ellen's serenade, which opens the second act, I was able to write simple lyrics (albeit in an intricate metrical scheme borrowed from Tennyson) that work simultaneously on two levels—first as a love song for her absent husband and second as unwitting prophecy of the vampire's imminent arrival to claim her. Almost every phrase has a double meaning, but the dark irony only becomes evident as the scene unfolds. I love the idea of a direct and simple text that gradually reveals a complex and troubling subtext.

My other example is Ellen's prayer in the final scene. I wrote this aria in two languages. It is half Latin and half English. The aria might look obscure as a poem on the page, but it sounds utterly natural in operatic performance. Ellen begins the *Salve, Regina* in Latin. Then she breaks down and continues in English—mistranslating the prayer in ways that project her fears. Eventually the two versions become intermingled. The verbal effect is almost surreal. Alva created an overpowering aria—both exquisitely beautiful and genuinely terrifying. Having helped create that magnificent aria satisfies me as deeply as having written one of my own poems.

LVW: Is it only my perception or is it true that many people involved in the reading and writing of poetry do not venture far into the world of music?
DG: Most poets know very little about classical music, especially opera and lieder. This represents a great loss—in both individual and communal terms. The arts enrich each other. The poet who neglects music not only misses the pleasures it affords, he or she also misses the vast possibilities it opens to their art. The losses are especially great in two arts as closely related as poetry and art song.

LVW: You stand in a long line of poets involved in opera and lieder. Who stands out as a mentor or inspiration?
DG: There is no continuous tradition of the libretto in English, so there are few major examples for a poet starting out in the form. The one great exception is W. H. Auden, who wrote (mostly in collaboration with Chester Kallman) wonderful libretti for Igor Stravinsky, Benjamin Britten, Hans Werner Henze, and Nicholas Nabokov.

Auden has been a guiding light. I not only kept copies of his libretti on my desk but also his verse dramas. I also admire the libretto that Robert Graves and Alastair Reid wrote for Peggy Glanville-Hicks's *Nausicaa*, a feminist retelling of *The Odyssey*. Why is this beautiful work never performed? With all the current interest in women composers, it seems astonishing that no one has rediscovered this small masterpiece.

But most of my touchstones have been in Italian and German. I know both languages reasonably well. Felice Romani, who wrote many masterful libretti for Bellini and Donizetti, provided a model of creating powerful drama with elegant poetry. There is also, of course, Arrigo Boito who adapted Shakespeare for Verdi's *Otello* and *Falstaff*. (Boito helped create the only two Shakespearean operas that are greater works of art than the original plays.) I adore the lyrics that Bertolt Brecht wrote for Kurt Weill's *Threepenny Opera*. Brecht demonstrates how powerful verbal irony works in opera.

My patron saint, however, is ultimately Hugo von Hofmannsthal. His libretti for Richard Strauss are all significant imaginative works in their own right—gripping ideas brilliantly executed. *Ariadne auf Naxos, Die Frau ohne Schatten* and *Der Rosenkavalier* are literary as well as musical master-pieces. Hofmannsthal reminds a poet that the opera libretto need not be an inferior form.

LVW: Where are you and Alva headed with this new opera?
DG: To La Scala, Covent Garden, and the Met—we hope. We don't have a commission yet, but we haven't really gone looking for one. The opera is now about three-quarters finished. We recently had a sold-out showcase in Palo Alto. Next June the Western Slope Music Festival in Crested Butte, Colorado will present an expanded showcase. (They will pair *Nosferatu* with *The Magic Flute*—an ideal combination.) Then we will probably do another showcase in New York. By then, I trust we will have a commission. In the meantime we are premiering arias and scenes around the country. The music is so good I don't want to wait until we've finished it to present it.

LVW: At the moment I know of *A Bridge Too Far* being set for the Met in the near future and the commissioning of San Francisco Opera for Andre Previn to produce an opera based on *A Streetcar Named Desire*. Are there, to your knowledge, other productions of opera based on literature now in the works?
DG: Opera is now undergoing a rebirth in America, but the form still suffers from an inferiority complex. The composers too often feel that opera is not as good as absolute music. Contemporary librettists don't know whether to take the form seriously, so they too often turn out merely adequate texts. Many poets are handed a pre-selected literary property by a composer or impresario—usually a subject they would not have chosen on their own. The resulting libretto becomes a workmanlike affair rather than an imaginative enterprise in its own right. I find most new libretti unexciting as poetry and timid as theater. There is too much rehashed naturalism. The natural impulse is to take a well-known literary property—a famous novel or a play—adapt it and set it to music. The trouble is that few novels or plays translate naturally to musical theater. They need to be radically compressed and reimagined. Poets are just beginning to explore the possibilities.

Opera is more at home with myth than with naturalism. It also lends itself to symbolism and allegory. Look at *The Magic Flute, The Ring of the Nibelungen*, or *The Rake's Progress*. Even operatic language is mythic. Think about what they call a great soprano—a *diva*, which is to say, a *goddess*. Opera is closer to cinema than to novels or spoken theater. Opera and film are both bigger than life. One thing that drew me to *Nosferatu* was that

Murnau's original was silent. It had neither words nor music. But Murnau offered unforgettable characters, images, and situations all hovering around a great myth. The Italians invented opera by trying to recreate Greek tragic theater, which was the ritual reenactment of myth. If we are going to foster American opera, I think we had better not lose sight of myth and ritual.

LVW: Do you plan to write more libretti?

DG: For the right composer, of course. I am sure that Alva and I will do another opera together once *Nosferatu* is finished. I enjoy working with him immensely. In the meantime I will be writing a one-act libretto for the composer Paul Salerni. It is the first commission for a new opera house/concert hall in Bethlehem, Pennsylvania. I find the form fascinating. Why stop now?

An Interview with Dana Gioia

Kevin Bezner / 2000

From *Main Street Rag* 5.4 (Winter 2000): 35–42. Reprinted by permission of Kevin Bezner.

Kevin Bezner: *Interrogations at Noon* is your first new book of poems in ten years. Why has it taken you so long to publish your third full-length collection?

Dana Gioia: I have no good reason—only several bad ones. Perhaps the worst reason has been the mundane need to make a living. When I published *The Gods of Winter* in 1991, I still worked in business. Over the last decade I have supported my family solely as a writer. That has meant a huge amount of work. I have published seven large anthologies and countless essays, reviews, and articles during this time. Meanwhile, my poetic interests broadened. I translated a classical tragedy and wrote an opera libretto. Finally, silence is not necessarily a bad thing for a poet. I needed time to understand what I wanted to do as a poet. My last book came out of a terrible and transfiguring time in my life—the death of my first son. That loss changed my life in ways that it has taken me years to comprehend.

KB: You have an entire section of *Interrogations at Noon* devoted to poems in the form of songs. They range from the cuttingly satiric song, "The Archbishop," to the more serious songs from your opera, *Nosferatu*, to comic songs about a cat and a beggar. Have you felt a need to revive the song in poetry?

DG: Lyric poetry originally meant sung poetry. That tradition was maintained from Sappho to the Troubadours. Even after poems were no longer generally sung, lyric poetry evoked the song-like qualities inherent in language. I've always loved the songs of Herrick, Blake, Yeats, and Auden. It is such a natural way of writing poems. Poets did it for thousands of years, and then more or less stopped fifty years ago. I couldn't resist trying.

KB: Did you write your song poems knowing that you would accumulate them, or did you suddenly realize one day you had written more than you had realized?

DG: My experience was somewhere in between those two extremes. The songs came as real poems do—one at a time. I wrote them in the tight lyric form of songs because that was how the words wanted to be arranged. I saw the family resemblance between these poems and I wanted to publish them together. But it took years before I had enough to collect.

KB: Are you also interested in reviving the opera libretto among poets?

DG: I can't speak for other poets, but I am interested in the idea of poetic drama. Contemporary poetry has focused so much on the lyric that it has almost entirely abandoned the dramatic mode. Yet there are some stories that can only be told as dramas. Opera is currently the only living form of poetic theater. Why shouldn't poets give it a try? Writing *Nosferatu* let me explore things I had never dared touch before—mostly very dark subjects.

KB: *Interrogations at Noon* often has a somber tone. Several poems are literally about death or dying, and others deal with metaphorical deaths. Why is the new collection so dark?

DG: Those were the poems that came to me. I have never been able to choose what the Muse dictates. I also try to write truthfully. "The poets," Nietzsche warned, "lie too much." I try to avoid the small comforting lies that poetry makes seem plausible. I dislike inspirational poetry. So much of the new poetry I hear at readings or conferences is full of easy spiritual uplift. Audiences seem to love that sort of thing. But nothing depresses me more than uplift.

KB: Your new book opens with a poem that subordinates words—and by implication writing—to the natural world. Another poem is called "Failure," and a third poem ends with the phrase "our mutual defeat." Have you recently felt defeated by poetry?

DG: No, but I am more keenly aware of poetry's intoxicating deceptions. The more skillful one grows in writing verse the more one notices how easy it is to create elegant verbal fabrics that have nothing to do with reality. Of course, a deconstructionist would say that language never has anything to do with reality, and that poetry is a closed self-referential system. I don't agree with that, but the postmodernists have a point. Language has the natural tendency to slip into its own parallel universe. Some of my new poems ponder what can or can't be said with words. As you suggest, by implication they also ponder the nature and purpose of poetry.

KB: Five years ago you moved back to your home state of California after spending twenty years in New York. Has this move changed your poetry?
DG: I have always thought of myself as a Californian—although that identity was less problematic when I lived somewhere else. For the first year or two after I came back, I hardly wrote any poems at all. Then suddenly the poems came, and they were different from what I had been writing in New York. I not only found myself writing about the Western landscape but also about what was happening to it. I would never have written a visionary environmental poem like "A California Requiem" back East.

KB: You admire Robinson Jeffers. He has a dark vision of humanity and California. Do you agree with his bleak vision? Are your views similar to his?
DG: Robinson Jeffers is the greatest poet of the American West. He is also one of the two or three finest American nature poets. Literary critics often describe his vision as harsh and cruel. I find it quite sensible. Simply put, Jeffers believed that the world was not made for humanity alone. Mankind has a responsibility to live in harmony with the nonhuman world.

He was the first American poet to condemn the despoliation of the natural landscape and the devastating effects of overpopulation. He tried to see and celebrate the world from a viewpoint beyond humanity. He was the great visionary of twentieth-century American poetry. I rarely find much to disagree with him. I don't think it is bleak to note how things truly are, especially if you then work to improve matters. Reality is the only starting point for effective reform. Surely, the most pressing issue facing humanity today is our thoughtless destruction of the earth.

KB: You have helped bring attention to a variety of formalist poets, including Weldon Kees and E. A. Robinson. Are you working to bring attention to any others at this time?
DG: I have always gone out of my way to write about poets whom I felt were unjustly neglected, but I have never limited my advocacy to formal poets. Ted Kooser, Robinson Jeffers, and John Haines—to name just three poets I

have written about at some length—are not generally formal poets. I championed them for their excellence.

There are so many degrees of obscurity that I hardly know how to answer your question. I am immensely fond of poets like Norman Cameron, James Reeves, and Roy Campbell whom few people still read. I have also recently published a long two-part essay on the Cornish poet, Charles Causley, who seems to me a poet of real importance but has little readership in America.

I continue to write about Kees, who is a major poet in my book. I recently published an edition of a one-act play by Kees—his last work really. I also wrote an essay to introduce a selection of poems by Samuel Menashe. I wrote the first essay on Kay Ryan. It is extraordinarily important to explore and champion unfamiliar writers. Otherwise, the canon becomes too narrow.

KB: Aren't most of those writers formal poets? Have you championed many open form poets?

DG: Menashe doesn't typically write in form. He is a sort of visionary imagist. Ryan uses irregular rhyme, but she is not formal in any traditional sense. And Kees, to set the record straight, often wrote in free verse. I am especially drawn to poets who can work in both free and formal verse—like Anne Stevenson, Philip Larkin, Wallace Stevens, Donald Justice, or Kees.

But technique interests me much less than content. I recently wrote the introduction to a book by Jack Foley, a Bay Area experimentalist. I have also translated the work of Valerio Magrelli, a young Roman poet who writes only in free verse.

KB: You are connected with a wonderful Scottish magazine, *The Dark Horse*. You also have a new book of essays forthcoming from the University of Michigan entirely concerned with contemporary British poetry. No other American poet, it seems to me, has made such an effort at bringing current British and American poetry together. Why is the connection between British and American poetry so important to you?

DG: British and American poetry have grown so separate in the past half-century that they now seem like two foreign literatures written in the same language. Or rather in two overlapping languages. I have titled my forthcoming book of essays *The Barrier of a Common Language*, based on Dylan Thomas's remark (stolen from George Bernard Shaw who in turn stole it from Oscar Wilde) that England and America are two countries separated by "the barrier of a common language."

I am a Latin—a mix of Italian and Mexican. There is no English in my blood, but English is my native language and belongs to me as much as to any Londoner. I find it illuminating to see what these foreigners do with our mutual parlance.

My interest also rests on my deep love for the work of particular poets. Auden is perhaps my favorite poet except Shakespeare, and I love Larkin so much that I have much of his work by heart. Among living British poets, I especially admire the work of Charles Causley, James Fenton, Wendy Cope, Tony Harrison, and Anne Stevenson—to name only a few. (Stevenson, of course, is American, but she is ignored over here.) I also admire Thom Gunn and Dick Davis, two superb British poets who live in the US.

KB: In a conversation we had last year at the West Chester Writers Conference, you said, "We must cherish our minor poets." Which minor poets do you most cherish? And why should we cherish them in particular?

DG: Literature is not a short list of great books full of great ideas. It is a vast and various conversation between the writer and the reader, the living and the dead, the past and the present. The standard academic canon is full of wonderful writers, but it does not begin to exhaust the possibilities of poetry. What constitutes a major or minor poet is an interesting question that I don't want to get into here. I want only to insist that sometimes the poetry we need most is written on a modest human scale—the voice of one person talking intimately with another with no grand gestures or heroic sweep.

I could give you a long list of minor poets I adore. Let me start with a few Victorians—Coventry Patmore, James Thomson, and Robert Bridges. Each of them wrote poems that seem to me both perfect and unique. The interesting thing about minor poets is that usually one doesn't discover them in school. Someone recites a poem to you or sends you a copy. For example, I first heard Patmore recited to me by William Louis-Dreyfuss, a businessman who recently became President of the Poetry Society of America. William told me that Robert Frost had once recited "Magna est Veritas" to him. It was such a powerful poem that I started reading Patmore and discovered "The Toys," a small masterpiece, which I then learned was one of Sam Gwynn's favorite Victorian poems. I like those human connections to Patmore.

A few other minor poets I admire are Frances Cornford, James Reeves, Norman Cameron, John Betjeman, and Charlotte Mew. Is A. E. Housman a minor poet? Probably, but who would want to be without his work? To most people, Edwin Muir, Louis MacNeice, Wilfred Owen, and Robert Graves may be minor poets. To me, they seem very important writers.

KB: One of the sharpest edged poems in your collection is "The Archbishop," which skewers a pompous critic you don't name—so that readers, you say, can supply their own nominations. How has the state of poetry criticism changed since you brought its failings to our attention some ten years ago now?

DG: A great many things have changed in American poetry over the past ten years, but criticism hasn't been one of them. The state of reviewing remains dreadful, and academic criticism is still mostly remote and self-absorbed. I could hardly have believed it possible, but critical writing has actually grown duller.

One can read a long essay and not find a single interesting idea or even a memorable sentence. The opinions are bland and conventional, the mood is languidly upbeat. Few critics will risk a negative opinion of any book unless they can condemn it for prefabricated ideological reasons. No wonder most poets pay little attention to it.

On the positive side, a few strong new critics have emerged in the past ten years—not enough to change things in any significant way but at least enough to register the situation and articulate the issues. The three best new critics I have seen are Adam Kirsch, David Mason, and Christian Wiman. They differ from one another in several ways, but each is extremely intelligent, passionately serious, and prolific. And they all write extremely well.

KB: In a little but brilliant book called *The Craft of Verse*, which transcribes the lectures Jorge Borges gave at Harvard in 1967–68, but which was only published in 2000, Borges predicts the epic will make a comeback. I have seen no real evidence to date of such a comeback. Have you? What do you think is the likelihood of such a comeback? Will we one day see an American epic on the scale of Homer's?

DG: American poets have never stopped writing epics—from the *Columbiad* to the present. The problem is that most of these epics aren't very good.

A great epic poem is a very rare thing, something that happens only once or twice in the history of a language. I also suspect it is almost impossible to write in a literary culture that does not esteem narrative poetry. Masterpieces are not created *ex nihilo*. They are the peak expressions of rich and vital traditions.

KEVIN BEZNER / 2000 **73**

I would suggest that rather than look for new epics we should note the recent reemergence of powerful narrative poems. I can't think of a finer narrative poem written in the past decade than David Mason's *The Country I Remember*. It is both ambitious and powerfully focused. Sydney Lea's "The Feud" is also a perfect midlength narrative. The best narrative poet of recent times was probably James Merrill, though he is not often praised in those terms. His midlength poem, "The Book of Ephraim," was a masterpiece, but when he extended it into the trilogy *The Changing Light at Sandover*, he fell into the common traps of the American epic—grandiosity, obscurity, and egocentricism. The poem was inflated beyond its means just like *The Cantos*. I never hear anyone mention Merrill's two other half-booklength narratives, *From the Cupola* and *The Summer People*, but they are both gems. Another midlength masterwork is Anthony Hecht's *The Venetian Vespers*.

I wonder if the American genius isn't better suited for such novella-length works rather than the epic. The reality of our country may simply be too vast and unruly for the narrative mode. It requires the prophetic strain of a Walt Whitman. For expressions of our native narrative genius, give me *The Great Gatsby, The Day of the Locust, Ethan Frome*, and *A Turn of the Screw*—all of which could fit into fewer pages than the first volume of the *U.S.A. Trilogy*.

KB: What do you plan next?
DG: I'm not sure. Maybe I should write an epic. If I fail, I'll be in distinguished company.

Dana Gioia Interview

Christina Vick / 2001

From *Louisiana Review* 4 (Fall/Winter 2004–2005): 161–69. [Interview conducted 2001.]
Reprinted by permission of Christina Vick.

Christina Vick: When did you first conceive a love for literature?
Dana Gioia: I can't ever remember a time when I did not love poems and stories, but who knows how it all began? Oddly, I don't recall my parents ever reading books to me, but my mother often read or recited poems. I remember hearing hundreds of poems as a child. As soon as I learned to read, I devoured books. We had—because of political graft—an enormous library in my otherwise rundown hometown. I used to go there after school and wander the shelves. No one ever advised me on what to read, so I sampled everything. On the same visit I might bring home a book of Roman history, another of horror stories, and a third of Italian paintings. Reading was in many ways more real to me than my daily life. It opened up a world of possibilities beyond the dreary limits of working-class, urban Los Angeles.

CV: Were there any special circumstances in your childhood that made books so important to you?
DG: I spent a great deal of time alone. Both of my parents worked. My first brother wasn't born until I was six, and except for my cousins next door there were almost no children in my neighborhood, which was made up mostly of small cheap apartments. Our home, however, was full of books, records, and musical scores from my uncle, Theodore Ortiz, who had served in the Merchant Marines before dying in a plane crash in 1955. He was an old-style proletariat intellectual who spent all of his money on music and literature. His library lined nearly every room and spilled over into the garage. There were books in six languages and hundreds of classical LPs. My

parents never read the books or played the records, but they kept them for sentimental reasons. The books were not especially interesting to a child— the novels of Thomas Mann, the plays of George Bernard Shaw, Pushkin in Russian, Cervantes in Spanish—but growing up with this large library around us exercised a strong magic on me, and later on my brother Ted.

CV: At what point in your life did you know that you wanted to be a poet?
DG: I remember quite exactly when I decided to become a poet. I was a college sophomore studying in Vienna on a Stanford exchange program. I had gone to Europe as a decisive gesture to figure out if I really wanted to be a composer. Living abroad for the first time and speaking a foreign language, I brooded a great deal in my room or else wandered the labyrinthine streets of the inner city in a fever of loneliness. Soon I found myself constantly reading and writing poetry—both in English and German. By the time I returned to America, I had decided to be a poet.

CV: Who or what do you read for pleasure or inspiration?
DG: I read all the time—newspapers, magazines, journals, and books—usually several books at once. I don't read as many novels now as I did when I was younger, though I still read forty or fifty a year. Now I tend to read more biographies and history. I also read theological and philosophical books. And, of course, I read—and reread—poetry all the time. I find myself habitually rereading certain books and authors, especially Virgil, Horace, St. Augustine, Shakespeare, and the Bible. I read science fiction for fun at bedtime. I also devour classical music and opera magazines. I sometimes worry if I have spent too much of my life reading, but how much narrower my life would have been without books.

CV: Who are your favorite authors?
DG: I have too many to list, especially poets. Some of my favorite novelists include Stendhal, Balzac, James, Cather, and Nabokov. I have a special passion for the short story, which seems to me perhaps the greatest single achievement of American literature, and I adore the short work of Poe, Cheever, Hemingway, O'Connor, Faulkner, Porter, Welty, Malamud, and Carver—though I would award Chekhov top international honors in the form. Philosophers and theologians like St. Augustine, Albert Schweitzer, Dietrich Bonhoeffer, Thomas Merton, Friedrich Nietzsche, Miguel de Unamuno, Mircea Eliade, Marshall McLuhan, Jacques Maritain, and Georg Lukacs have all been important to me.

CV: Who have been your mentors? What influence have they had on your professional and personal life?

DG: I have moved around a great deal in my adult life and changed my profession three times—from academics to business to writing. No one person served as a mentor across all those changes, but at particular points in my life certain people had a crucial influence. The older writers who helped me the most—not so much in terms of external assistance but in internal clarification—were Robert Fitzgerald, Elizabeth Bishop, Donald Davie, Howard Moss, and Frederick Morgan. Each helped me in a different way, sometimes just for a short but critical period. There have also been some important relationships with older writers who were not so much mentors as dear friends—like Donald Justice, John Haines, Daniel Hoffman, X. J. Kennedy, William Jay Smith, Janet Lewis, William Maxwell, and Anne Stevenson.

CV: What influence have these mentors had on you?

DG: They provided useful models of what a writer's life might be like. Their work also kept my standards high. Each relationship was necessarily different. Elizabeth Bishop, for example, encouraged me, whereas Donald Davie discouraged me. Both interventions helped me develop as a writer. Robert Fitzgerald taught me essential things about poetic craft. He also provided me with a model of a modern Catholic man of letters. Frederick Morgan quietly encouraged me to write in my own way. I should also add that these writers were all remarkable human beings. Knowing them confirmed my sense of the importance of friendship, generosity, and integrity in literary life.

CV: Do you compose a poem in longhand or on a computer? What is the reason for your choice? Do you think the electronic age has helped or hindered creative writing?

DG: My methods are quite primitive. My poems begin as words in the air. I talk to myself—usually while pacing the room or walking outside. Any observer would assume I was mad. After I coax a line or two aloud, I jot it down. Very slowly and painstakingly I shape those lines and phrases into a poem. I pay equal attention to the way the poem sounds and how it works on the page. Only after many handwritten drafts do I type the poem up. That transition allows me to see the poem differently and revise it further. Since I believe that poetry not only originates in the body but also communicates largely through physical sound, I am skeptical of the putative advances of the electronic age. Though computers offer great convenience, they cannot substitute for direct physical embodiment of one's medium.

CV: Mark Twain, famous for his prose style, once said, "The difference between the right word and the nearly right word is the difference between lightning and a lightning bug." How do you know when you have found the "right" word for a poem?

DG: This is an excellent question because so often the expressive effect of a line or stanza depends upon a single word. In poetry no effect is too small to matter. I revise a great deal and often focus on a particular word or phrase which I instinctively feel is crucial to the poem's impact. I like to combine words in a way that initially seems slightly odd but also oddly appropriate. I hope to discover a new combination that the language was waiting to have happen.

CV: When you begin work on a poem, what is your method? Do you have the poem, or the concept of the poem, in its entirety in your mind before you set it down in words, or is writing the poem a process of discovery?

DG: My poetic method is best described as confusion, followed by madness, exhilaration, and despair. I advise others to avoid my conspicuously bad example. For me, a poem begins as a powerful physical sensation. I can feel the poem in my throat and temples—a sudden illumination that is mostly beyond words but which is also partially embodied in a few specific words. That line or phrase suddenly opens a doorway. I usually have no idea what the final poem might be beyond its opening line. Writing the poem is discovering what one meant to say. People who aren't poets have trouble understanding how mysterious the process is.

CV: Many of your poems seem so heartfelt and personal, particularly the poems in your recent collection *Interrogations at Noon*. I'm thinking especially the title poem, which discusses "the better man I might have been, / Who chronicles the life I've never led," as well as "Curriculum Vitae," "A California Requiem," and certainly "Pentecost" seem to speak to the reader about the author. To what extent do you chronicle your own experiences, and to what extent do you adopt a persona in your poems?

DG: My poems are personal but almost never entirely autobiographical. I combine my own experiences with observations from other people often adding elements of pure fantasy to create situations and stories that feel true. I deliberately try to eliminate myself in literal terms from the poem. The speaker of the poem may resemble me, but he or she is also a surrogate for the reader. Paradoxically, I find that the more I invent the more candid and truthful I become.

CV: How does the audience affect your poetry? By that I mean, when you give a reading of your poems, does that situation dictate your choice of poems to be read?

DG: When I write poetry, I don't consider the audience except in the most general terms—as fellow human beings who share the English language. But when I give a public poetry reading, I always consider my immediate audience. I don't worry much about its level of literary sophistication. If a poem is good enough, it should communicate at some essential level to most audiences. What I consider mostly is each audience's range of life experience. To understand a poem it helps to have lived at least a little of its contents. I take readings seriously. The sort of poetry I love best is meant to be spoken aloud and heard.

CV: Does the act of reading in public transform the experience of those poems for you? What do you wish your audience to receive or take away from a reading?

DG: Yes, over time the act of giving poetry readings has gradually transformed my attitude toward my own poems. Now that the finished poems exist independently of me in print I find that I am merely one of their readers, and I begin to see them very differently. They often mean things I never initially realized or intended.

CV: In the title essay of your 1992 collection, *Can Poetry Matter?*, you lamented the fact that "most poetry is published in journals that address an insular audience of literary professionals." Nine years later, do you see any reasons for optimism about the dissemination of good and accessible poetry to a large reading public?

DG: A great deal has changed since the publication of *Can Poetry Matter?*—some for the good, some for the worse. The most important development has been the astonishing growth of the poetry world outside the university. There has been an explosion of poetry readings, festivals, broadcasts, and conferences based in libraries, bookstores, galleries, and community centers. These new poetry venues range from the sublime to the ridiculous, but collectively they have had the effect of democratizing our literary culture. Most of this activity happens on a local basis, so it has hardly challenged the established reputation-making power of New York and the Northeast, but this new bohemia does allow poets to speak directly to a broader and more diverse audience than ever before.

CV: Writing has been called a lonely profession because it is performed of necessity in solitude. Do you have a support system—family, friends, colleagues—people who offer encouragement in your practice of what is generally considered, in America at least, an unorthodox profession?

DG: Writing is mostly a solitary endeavor—sometimes terribly so. For many years I wrote after work and on the weekends. I had to give up a great many things to make the time for poetry. That decision exacted its price in human terms, but I paid it gladly because I felt most truly myself, most intensely alive when writing or reading.

Now my life is even more solitary. I no longer work in a busy office but alone in a studio across the hill from my house. Many days I see no one except my family—and a great many animals. I accept that loneliness as a necessary part of who I am. I should be lost without my friends, even though I seldom see them. Solitary people feel friendship deeply. There are a few fellow poets I love quite deeply. They sustain me.

CV: In your experience, can writing poetry be a therapeutic exercise as well as an imaginative, creative endeavor? Do you sometimes turn to writing poetry as a means of coping with difficulties in life, past and present?

DG: I associate therapeutic poetry with bad writing—especially my own. I guess there is some therapeutic aspect in much poetry, but it also seems to me that it concerns the emotional impulse behind the poem rather than the poem itself. I have often sat down and poured my suffering soul onto some innocent piece of paper, but surrendering to a powerful subjective emotional state does not create an imaginative structure that will replicate the experience in the reader's mind. A poem is a mysterious verbal device, a sort of magic spell, directed not at the author but the reader. If a poem is therapeutic, then the patient must be the reader, not the writer.

CV: In your experience, how much of writing poetry is art, and how much is craft?

DG: All art depends on craft. Without proper technique a poet, however talented, can amount to very little. Despite the proliferation of graduate writing programs—perhaps because of them—our age has seen both a denigration and ignorance of poetic craft. Today any poet who wants to master verse craft must do it mostly on his or her own. Technique is the necessary beginning, but it is only a means to an expressive end. Having something genuinely compelling to express is essential. That gift can't be taught.

CV: Your considerable background in the business world might come as a surprise to readers familiar only with your poetry. Could you comment on this background?

DG: I originally went to graduate school in literature, but it seemed a bad place for me as a writer. I liked it too much. Harvard aggravated my inherent tendency to be overly intellectual and self-conscious. Working in business gave me a chance to construct a different sort of writing life—more private, independent, and contemplative. I went to Stanford Business School, and in 1977 I joined General Foods in New York. When I resigned fifteen years later, I was a Vice President. I still miss the people I worked with. They were smart, friendly, and funny. There were a few idiots, scoundrels, and egomaniacs, but no more than I've encountered in literary life.

CV: Were you engaged in creative writing at the same time that you were involved in a business career?

DG: Yes. I went into business to be a poet. For me, business was always just a job, even though I ended up doing quite well. I would work ten or twelve hours a day at the office, and then I tried to squeeze two or three hours of writing in each night at home. It wasn't easy, but I managed—mostly by giving up other things.

CV: Did you consider these pursuits antithetical or complementary to each other?

DG: I never considered business as either antithetical or complementary to my writing. Business and poetry were simply different occupations.

CV: In your essay "Business and Poetry," in which you create an intriguing exploration of such poets as T. S. Eliot, Wallace Stevens, James Dickey, and others who sustained themselves and their families in business careers, you pose the question: "How did their business careers affect the lives and works of these poets?" This issue has personal relevance to you. Would you answer the same question you posed in your essay? How has your experience in the business world affected your literary work?

DG: My years in business offered at least two advantages. First, they allowed me to develop as a poet at my own pace and in my own way. I had no pressure to publish or need to conform to any academic or intellectual fashion. I made my own mistakes and discoveries. Working in isolation, my most intense literary relationships were with the great dead, the most demanding and yet attentive colleagues. Had I stayed at Harvard I would have been too vulnerable to the many captivating influences around me. Neglect, obscurity, and loneliness are the necessary nourishment of a young poet.

Second, working in business greatly broadened my life experience. It permitted me—indeed forced me—to see the world and literature from a different angle than I had in graduate school. Working with intelligent but non-literary people for nearly twenty years made me conscious of the cultural elitism I had acquired at Stanford and Harvard. I no longer took certain assumptions for granted. Most important, I understood the importance of writing in a way that does not exclude intelligent people.

CV: Could you discuss your writing life outside the university?

DG: It is an odd enterprise to make a living as a poet outside academia. It's definitely not a career for the faint of heart. The poems—no matter how good—won't pay the bills. I work seven days a week. I travel constantly giving readings and lectures—always working on airplanes and in hotel rooms. I edit anthologies, write for BBC Radio, review books and music, and collaborate with composers. The practical challenge is to pay the bills, which I've gradually learned how to do. The deeper challenge is spiritual—how to create and sustain a passionate sense of living the right life. That is far more difficult. Loneliness, exhaustion, disappointment, and despair are always nearby.

CV: You have recently published an intriguing libretto for the opera *Nosferatu*, based on the silent German expressionist film directed by F. W. Murnau. What drew you to this particular retelling of the Dracula myth?

DG: The subject chose me. I was looking for an idea for a libretto, and by lucky coincidence I happened to read an essay on Murnau by my friend Gilberto Perez. By the time I had finished the piece I knew that this was the subject, the *only* possible subject for the opera the composer Alva Henderson and I were planning. What drew me to *Nosferatu* was the depth and complexity of the heroine, and the symbolic possibilities of the vampire myth. Opera is the last surviving form of poetic theater, and I wanted a subject that would allow my imagination a wild freedom.

CV: To what extent did your background in musical composition influence your decision?

DG: I knew I wanted to write a libretto that revived and explored traditional musical forms—arias, duets, trios, choruses, and ensembles. I also wanted the language and the dramatic structure to be inherently lyrical. I had no interest in writing a prose drama to be set to music. I tried to give every scene a dramatic shape embodied in musical and poetic structures.

CV: You have published a number of college textbooks, including *Literature: An Introduction to Fiction, Poetry, and Drama* coedited by X. J. Kennedy, an anthology I have used for a number of years. Has this been a rewarding experience for you?

DG: Editing anthologies has been enormously interesting and rewarding. It has also been exhausting. To edit them responsibly, I must constantly read and reread poems, stories, plays, and scholarship to make the right selections. I am also perpetually writing critical overviews, historical notes, author biographies, and commentaries. I sometimes feel I am living in an eternal finals week. My private goal has been to manage this task without ever letting the writing become insipid—in other words never to let the book sound like most textbooks.

CV: Why do you work so hard on textbooks?

DG: Because they are important. A great anthology can change a student's life. A dull one can turn him or her away from literature forever. I take anthologies seriously because they represent the logical extension of my concerns as a poet and critic. What better way is there to correct, improve, and expand literary taste? I also love to bring new or neglected writers to a broader audience.

CV: On what current projects are you working?

DG: I have too many projects. Graywolf Press will publish a tenth anniversary edition of *Can Poetry Matter?* in late 2002, and I am writing a special introduction about the reception and impact of the book. I am also putting together a new collection of critical essays. I am now just finishing up two large anthologies on twentieth-century American poetry and poetics. I'm coediting these ambitious and comprehensive books with David Mason and Meg Schoerke. The critical apparatus is itself several hundred pages long, and it gives me the opportunity to discuss writers and issues I have not written on before. I also plan to edit an anthology of California poetry with Chryss Yost and Jack Hicks for Heyday Books, as part of the California Legacy Project. I am also writing a second opera libretto—a phantasmagoric one-act work that mixes comedy and tragedy—for the composer Paul Salerni. And I hope to finish a few new poems. No rest for the wicked.

CV: You recently won the American Book Award for *Interrogations at Noon*. Has the prize changed your life in any way?

DG: The award made me slightly more respectable in official circles. More important, it greatly impressed my nine-year-old son, Mike, who likes the gold-foil sticker that went on the cover of my book. I was pleased to win a prize for my poetry since my criticism so often dominates my public image. I was also delighted to win an award given by a jury of writers, who were all strangers. Mostly, I consider the event sheer good luck, which should be enjoyed but not taken too seriously.

CV: What advice do you have for poets who are relatively new to their craft but who want to pursue it as a serious endeavor?

DG: Read widely and memorize the poems that move or delight you. Immerse yourself in the medium. All writers begin as readers. I also recommend spending your twenties lonely, broke, and unhappily in love. It worked for me.

An Interview with Dana Gioia

William Baer / 2001
From *The Formalist* 13.1 (2002): 18–49. Reprinted by permission of William Baer.

William Baer: Were there many books in the Gioia home?

Dana Gioia: Yes, we were a working-class family, but we had an exceptional library of books and records that had once belonged to my uncle, Theodore Ortiz, a merchant marine. He was an old-style, proletariat intellectual who unfortunately died in a plane crash at the age of twenty-eight when I was six years old. He was apparently a brilliant polymath who had been a member of the Communist Party, but who had eventually left the party and converted to Catholicism. So I grew up in a house filled with books in five or six different languages, musical scores, art books, and recordings. Even though my parents took no interest in these things, they kept them out of a sense of family duty. This extraordinary library had a marked influence on my life.

WB: Did your interest in the arts start very young?

DG: It did. I realized, at a very early age, that many of my interests were different from those of other boys my age. I was thrilled by music, poetry, and art in a way that wasn't typical. I did everything I could, within my limited environment, to involve myself with those things. I can still remember, quite vividly, the complicated steps I took to attend my first symphonic concert in the company of the nuns when I was around ten or eleven. That first concert was a great experience for me, comparable to the way other boys felt about sports games and athletic achievements.

WB: At Stanford, you became the editor of the University's literary journal, *Sequoia*, which you greatly improved. What was that experience like?

DG: *Sequoia* allowed me to immerse myself in the literary life. At the time, *Sequoia* was on the verge of bankruptcy, but we managed to turn it into the largest "little" magazine on the West Coast. In all honesty, I feel that I learned more about both literature and business by running *Sequoia* than I did in either my literary graduate studies or business school.

WB: In what ways?

DG: Well, as you know, Bill, being a literary editor forces you to develop a strong but flexible criterion for accepting poems. It also forces you to visualize a broad view of what you'd like the journal to become—and then to do whatever it takes to create that journal. When I took over at *Sequoia*, we made lots of changes. We began doing long interviews for the first time. We also began to solicit work from a wide range of writers and started doing theme issues. I'm still very proud of a special translation issue that we did, which featured interviews with Robert Fitzgerald and Mary de Rachewiltz, Ezra Pound's daughter, who had translated *The Cantos* into Italian. So the challenges of creating a small journal definitely helped develop my own aesthetic. It also deepened my knowledge about how the literary world works.

WB: You also published a lot of formalists.

DG: That's true. Back in the seventies, it was almost impossible to publish formal poetry except in a few places like the *Southern Review*. But *Sequoia* was different. We published many of the writers who later became known as New Formalists at the very beginnings of their careers, people like Timothy Steele and Robert Shaw, and many others.

WB: After finishing at Stanford, you went to graduate school at Harvard where you studied under Robert Fitzgerald in the Comparative Literature program. Could you discuss Fitzgerald's impact on your thinking and your work?

DG: Robert Fitzgerald was, without doubt, the single most influential poetry teacher I ever had. He was an extraordinarily charismatic man— and to know him was to love him. He was also someone with a profoundly spiritual understanding of the importance of literature, which was always in evidence when he discussed his favorite poems—Homer's *Odyssey*, Virgil's *Aeneid*, and Dante's *Inferno*. I learned a great deal from having a teacher who placed human, rather than merely intellectual demands, upon poetry.

I also took a class with Fitzgerald on the history of English versification. In addition to the readings and scansions, we had to write a poem every week in whatever form we were studying at the time—beginning with classical meters and continuing all the way through the history of English poetry. In the process of writing those poems, I truly learned metrics. Before taking the class, I thought I understood poetic form, but Fitzgerald's class greatly refined my understanding—he saved me five, maybe ten years, of mistakes. Finally, Robert Fitzgerald was Catholic, and it was, in personal terms, extremely valuable to study under a great literary intelligence who professed his Catholicism. He was the first and only openly Catholic teacher that I had in my eight years of study in college and graduate school.

WB: How about Elizabeth Bishop? You also studied with her.

DG: Bishop wasn't as good a teacher as Fitzgerald, but she was a delightful person. I was very fortunate to become a good friend of hers during my last year at Harvard. After most classes, in fact, we would go off for tea together. As Bishop herself admitted, she wasn't an especially good teacher, and she didn't really like to teach. Nevertheless, she did instill in me a number of very valuable lessons.

Probably the most important thing that Bishop taught me was that the surface of the poem *is* the poem—that, in other words, to understand a poem one must begin and end by paying attention to every word, image, and detail in the text. Her deliberately literal approach came as quite a shock. Initially I thought she was rather naive as a critic, but as I continued to study with her, I realized how much more I was learning about the way a poem really operates because of her relentlessly precise examination of the surface of the poem. This was quite different from my classes in the German department, for example, where we got lost in deep speculations about the philosophical implications of a poem, or the possible meanings of its subtext.

WB: So she emphasized the craft over the interpretation.

DG: Yes. Elizabeth Bishop had almost no interest in interpreting poems. What she loved was experiencing good poems. And I gradually came to realize the great wisdom in her approach. By the time I finished her class, I was, in some sense, a changed person, in the same way that, through Robert Fitzgerald, my understanding of the harmonics of verse had altered and expanded. Both these experiences proved decisive for me as a poet. I threw away every poem I had ever written before I studied with Fitzgerald and Bishop.

WB: You were very lucky. It takes most people ten or fifteen years to discover that the craft is as important as the meaning, assuming that they ever learn it.

DG: We tend to intellectualize too much, out of the fear of seeming naive. So it takes us time to appreciate the basic lessons of the art form. Poetry is not a conceptual kind of language. It is a uniquely different way of knowing and speaking, which is experiential and holistic. Conceptual intelligence only gets you so far in poetry.

WB: After your MA at Harvard, you returned to Stanford for an MBA. Naturally, this seems a bit incongruous. What was your thinking at the time?
DG: I went to Stanford Business School to become a poet. People find that hard to comprehend, but to me the choice was fairly clear. Harvard was the best intellectual experience of my life, and I was, in many ways, sad to leave it. But Harvard was also training me to become a literary theorist. When I first entered the discipline of comparative literature, I really didn't understand what it was all about. I thought I'd be reading great literature in the original language to develop my taste and understanding. But academia was, even back then, beginning to change into what we have today with a primarily theoretical—and therefore ideological—approach to literature.

One of my teachers at Harvard, for example, was Edward Said who was then in the vanguard of the theory school. He made us read Michel Foucault in French, and, at the time, all I could think was that I had learned French to read Flaubert and Baudelaire, not Foucault. Harvard was trying to turn me into an academic trained to speak in an elaborate and complex Mandarin code. But the more efficient I became at mastering that code, the weaker my poems became. I was also aware that I had a natural propensity for theoretical discourse. After all, I had gone to Catholic schools for twelve years, and I was trained in theology. But literary theory wasn't what I wanted. It wasn't useful for my poetry, and I decided that I had to get out of it. So my challenge, at the time, was to find a way of making a decent living while also creating some time in which to continue my writing.

WB: Why did you choose business rather than other possible professions?
DG: The most respectable choice for literature students leaving graduate school was, of course, law school. But I noticed that all my literary friends who'd gone off to law school had all pretty much stopped reading. For some reason, the law seemed to occupy that portion of the brain previously inhabited by poetry and literature. On the other hand, I had never noticed any MBAs whose minds were particularly cluttered with conceptual thoughts. As a matter of fact, whenever I walked by the Stanford Business School, most of the students were sitting outside on the steps drinking beer. So I

said to myself, "I can do that." In retrospect, I think it was a good choice. In business school, most of the skills I learned were mathematical, logistical, and practical, and they didn't, for the most part, invade the same part of my mind inhabited by the poetry.

WB: How did you find the time?
DG: I made the time. When I decided to go to business school, I made a promise to myself that I would spend three hours every day either reading or writing before I did any of my business studies. While I was in business school, I published about forty essays and reviews on writers including Nabokov, Bellow, Cavafy, Pound, Montale, Burgess, and many others. I also published poems and translations.

WB: Your earliest collections of poetry were, interestingly enough, various fine press editions by well-known printers like Kim Merker, Harry Duncan, and eventually Michael Peich. For a number of years, you actually turned down publication offers from larger publishing houses. What was your thinking back then? Most young writers would have jumped at the chance.
DG: I was always very aware that a writer has only one "first" book, and I felt certain that I shouldn't rush into it. The process of discovering one's self as a poet is not an easy one, especially in recent times when there are so many influences, styles, and aesthetics. So I made up my mind to have a good sense of who I was as a poet before I brought out my first book.

It's true that I did turn down several unsolicited offers from various presses, but I felt I wasn't ready yet. I waited until 1986 when Graywolf brought out *Daily Horoscope*. In the meantime, I felt that the smaller fine press books of my work allowed me to establish some sort of literary identity without going all the way to a full first book. They struck me as a very valuable intermediate step towards full publication.

WB: You also had a serious commitment to fine press publishing.
DG: Yes, and I still do. I've always loved beautiful books, and it remains a great privilege and pleasure to have someone actually design a book specifically for your own poems. I was very fortunate to have some of the most distinguished literary letter-press printers in American history—people like Harry Duncan, Kim Merker, Gabriel Rummonds, and Michael Peich—do books of my work.

WB: After Stanford, you worked for the General Foods Corporation in White Plains, New York for fifteen years, eventually becoming a vice-president.

How did you have the energy to write poetry after your long days in the business world?
DG: I forced myself. I would come back from working ten- or twelve-hour days, and I'd make myself something to eat, and then I'd sit down and write for about two hours every night before I went to bed. Even when I was utterly exhausted, I discovered that if I could just get started, I could get a second wind and get something done. If I were writing prose, I would simply recopy by hand the last paragraph I'd written the night before, and in the process of copying it, I'd begin to revise it and gradually re-enter the argument of the piece. Usually by the end of the paragraph, I was full of ideas again. Generally, I'd set myself very small but attainable goals—like one useable paragraph if I were writing prose, or a single good line or stanza if I were writing verse. For me, the most important thing was to just keep writing every night, to keep the continuity of the imaginative effort flowing.

WB: You once told a class of my students that it was like a runner's second wind.
DG: That's right. When I was in college I took a curious one-credit-PE class, called "Conditioning." It was the class that the athletes took in the off-season, so one quarter I'd be with the football players, and then the next quarter with the basketball players, and so on. In that class, we would do various exercises, but we always ended up running four miles. Now, even though I'd been running since high school, after about 2 miles, I'd start feeling sick and exhausted. Everything would ache, and I wanted to quit, but I knew that if I could get around the track one more time, do another quarter mile, then suddenly I'd get a second wind. Then I could run forever. Later, I found that the same thing was true with the writing. No matter how exhausted I was when I'd come home from work, if I could just get through that first paragraph, then I'd get that second wind. This trick, however, led to another problem a few hours later. I would often have trouble getting to sleep because my mind was so jazzed up.

WB: Given your later success as a poet, people tend to forget that most of your early literary work was as an editor. You continued your association with *Sequoia* even after you graduated from Stanford, and you were also the editor or coeditor of your first two books: a collection of Weldon Kees's short stories and an anthology of Italian poetry with William Jay Smith. How did these experiences prove valuable?

DG: During my early years in business, I was always working on poetry, but I stopped sending it out. I wanted to figure out who I was without the external pressure of publication, so for nearly seven years I wrote privately. My public literary identity was as an editor, critic, and translator. Working in the corporate world, I was hungry for literary life. Editing had the practical advantage of allowing me to meet many writers, translators, and publishers I would not otherwise have encountered. Editing has always seemed to me one of the essential literary tasks. So much of the health and vitality of literary culture depends on the people who edit the journals, anthologies, and presses.

WB: While you were working at General Foods, you kept your "other" life as a poet secret. Why did you do that?

DG: I felt that it wouldn't do me any good in the business world to be known as a poet. It might turn out to be a distraction, or a curiosity, or worse. At the same time, I really didn't feel the need for some kind of outer affirmation of my vocation as a poet. In fact, I feel that this need for external approval is a mistake that I often see in younger poets. Some of them seem to need institutional validation in order for them to write. But, of course, if you're a real writer, you'll write anyway, regardless of what anyone else thinks.

I've always admired Flannery O'Connor's rejoinder when someone asked her what should be done to "encourage" young writers, and she replied, "I don't think we discourage them enough." Obscurity, suffering, loneliness, and difficulty are all nourishments for a poet. They may not be pleasant, but they are the fire in which we refine our sense of mission.

WB: In 1984, your "cover" was blown by *Esquire* magazine when you were chosen for their first registry of "Men and Women Under 40 Who Are Changing the Nation." Included in that group were Steven Spielberg, Julius "Dr. J" Irving, Whoopi Goldberg, and Bill Clinton. How did this affect your working situation at General Foods? Was it as bad as you expected?

DG: When *Esquire* called to say that they were planning to write an article about me, I tried to discourage them. But they made it clear that my own wishes had nothing to do with it since they intended to run the article anyway. Most people at General Foods were pretty shocked, especially my boss who was an Annapolis graduate who'd been an all-American in two sports and a commanding officer in combat. He was a big, athletic, dark-haired Irishman who chomped on cigars and looked quite a bit like the old comic book hero Sgt. Fury. So when he heard the rumor that I wrote poetry, he called me into his office, and he asked me if it was true. When I reluctantly conceded that it was, his only response was "Shit."

WB: How did it turn out?
DG: By that time, I was already recognized as a valuable senior executive at General Foods, but I have to admit that being known as a poet didn't make my life any easier.

WB: In 1986, Graywolf published your first book-length collection, *Daily Horoscope*, to a wide range of diverse commentary. You've pointed out in the past that your evolving poetic aesthetic was very much influenced, in a negative way, by the Beats and the Confessionals. Could you discuss that more specifically?
DG: When people talk about literary influences, they inevitably list the writers they love and admire. The familiar argument is that one imitates the writers that one most admires, or, at least, learns from them. That is certainly true, but it's only half the story. There is also a natural impulse to be consciously different from the writers you dislike.

Growing up in the sixties and seventies, I didn't care for most of the contemporary poetry I read. I thought it was dull and self-indulgent. I also felt that it lacked music. So, to a considerable degree, my gradual process of self-definition as a poet consisted of consciously rejecting the contemporary fashions in poetry and trying to discover who my own true ancestors really were. That required a lot of reading and much trial and error.

WB: Could you be more specific?
DG: Well, I've come to believe that poetry casts a kind of auditory spell over the reader. It creates a kind of mild hypnotic trance, which invites the listener to pay heightened attention to the poem, and which also helps the listener access his or her own deepest memories and unconscious impulses. But most of the poems that I read or heard back in the seventies lacked any kind of verbal music. They were, in general, flat and unmemorable. I also felt that the confessional poetry of that era was long-winded and self-pitying to the extreme, and that the so-called Deep Image poetry of the time was mostly pretentious, being either simplistically symbolic or intentionally incoherent. So it seemed that on every side—be it the New York School, Deep Image, the Confessionals, Black Mountain, or Beat—I was being offered models for various kinds of poetry that were unable to move me in any significant way.

Perhaps I'm wrong, or maybe I have a blind spot for those kinds of writing, but the fact remains that I couldn't build on sources which didn't move, fascinate, or delight me. I believe that the greatest mistake a young writer can make is to fake responses. Any work that is built on inauthentic responses will create a void in the reader. My own early work was very much a reaction to what I felt were the various failures of the contemporary poetry of those times.

WB: Who were your most important positive influences and models?
DG: In high school, I discovered Eliot and Auden, and they have remained among my favorite poets. In college, I became besotted with Ezra Pound. For years I tried to educate myself according to his suggestions, and I'm still very grateful for that apprenticeship because he encouraged me to learn foreign languages and to immerse myself in the history of European poetry. But by the time I was writing the poems that were included in *Daily Horoscope*, my models had definitely shifted a bit to certain writers whom I'd read in the past but whom I now came to appreciate much more, especially Robert Frost and Wallace Stevens. Also, Weldon Kees. From the first moment I read Kees, he dazzled me. He was doing brilliantly the sort of things that I was, independently, trying to do. So Kees was, to use Baudelaire's term, *mon frère*, right from the beginning. Other poets who were especially important to me were Theodore Roethke, E. E. Cummings, Elizabeth Bishop, and Philip Larkin.

WB: The "big" one missing there is Yeats, especially since some of the delicacy and lyricism in your own work seems reflective of his poetry.
DG: I have always had a complicated relationship with Yeats. I adore his music, and I've definitely been influenced by it. Under Robert Fitzgerald, I studied Yeats's extraordinary use of tetrameter, but I've always resisted Yeats in other ways. He had a lamentable capacity for talking himself into dubious philosophical assumptions which hurt his later poetry. By contrast, Auden remained a great poet without sacrificing his intelligence. The same could be said, in different ways, for Stevens, Larkin, and Bishop.

WB: In writing your own poetry, you always took a stand against the standard "workshop poem" of the time, once dubbed the "McPoem" by Donald Hall. Could you delineate that type of poem and its failings?
DG: The typical workshop poem of the 1970s and 1980s was a one-page, free verse, autobiographical poem usually about childhood or young adulthood.

Those were *exactly* the kinds of poems I didn't want to write. I was always deeply suspicious of confessional poetry. Once we start to speak of ourselves in openly autobiographical terms, we lose critical distance and objectivity about both our subject matter and our tone. These are very serious problems. As a result, I have written almost no directly autobiographical poems.

WB: I'd like to turn now to a few themes in your work that begin in *Daily Horoscope* and then continue through your subsequent collections, *The Gods of Winter* and *Interrogations at Noon.* One of the most consistent motifs in your work is the persistence of loneliness—often related to lost love or a nostalgia for the past—as in such poems as "Cruising with the Beach Boys," "The Memory," "Speaking of Love," "Summer Storm," and many others. "Corner Table," for example, ends:

>   What matters most
> Most often can't be said. Better to trust
> The forms that hold our grief. We understand
> This last mute touch that lingers is farewell.

How conscious have you been of that recurring motif?
DG: I'm not sure a poet always has the ability to recognize such things in his or her own work. I discover my own thematics just as my readers do. I'm often quite surprised as my books are taking shape, by how thematically unified they are, which was certainly not conscious or intentional on my part.

As for the specific theme of loneliness, I suppose a lot of my poetry does deal with solitude. My life, even in childhood, was often solitary. Both of my parents worked, and I had a happy, lonely childhood. It was even true in the business days because I wrote in isolation. So solitude has been my natural element from childhood. I don't think that's necessarily a bad thing. I believe that most people have a profound sense of solitude in their lives. What usually breaks that up for most people is marriage and parenthood, when we bring other lives into our own, but up until that time in my life, I think solitude was very much my medium. Even today I spend most of my days working alone. I don't think it's a negative thing, so I'd prefer the word "solitude" rather than "loneliness." Many poets whose work I love—like Stevens, Frost, Cavafy, and Kees—are poets of solitude.

WB: A number of your poems, like "Insomnia," for example, go beyond either loneliness or solitude, and fall into a kind of self-recrimination for the narrative "I." For example, in your poem "Interrogations at Noon," an uncompromising voice accuses the narrator, saying "you cultivate confusion": "And play the minor figures in the pageant, / Extravagant and empty, that is you." So, in some of your work, the poetry is being used to remind us, in no uncertain terms, of our potential failings.

DG: That's true. I like to make poems out of unresolvable arguments, and I try to avoid going for more than eight lines in a poem without some kind of dialectical shift. As I write my poems, I think of them as a statement, countered with an argument contesting that statement, and then followed by more debate. I think that's the way we experience life. We have a thought, an experience, or an emotion, and we begin, almost immediately, to qualify or challenge it. So it seems to me that poetry should mimic that particular process of the mind and heart by which we clarify our perceptions, rather than just stating a static emotion. One problem I find with a lot of the poems is that they don't go anywhere. They offer an emotion, an intellectual state, or whatever, but they never challenge or clarify it. But as Yeats pointed out, "We make out of the quarrel with others, rhetoric, but of the quarrel with ourselves, poetry." And I absolutely agree.

I also think, in response to your question, that the kind of self-recrimination you mention has something to do with being Catholic. A Catholic is trained from an early age to undertake spiritual self-examination. We not only examine our actions, but we also question our motives for those actions. For many years, I wasn't aware just how deeply Catholic my process of thinking is, but it was formed by not just twelve years of Catholic education, but by my lifelong existence within the church.

WB: That's exactly what I was thinking of—the examination of conscience that prepares the sinner for the sacrament of penance.

DG: Once again, let me go back to the poetry of the sixties and the seventies. It seemed to me that a great many male poets of that era were writing what I would call "confessional" poems that were, in some sense, sexual self-advertisements of themselves as sensitive, caring lovers. I always found that distasteful and dishonest. I strongly dislike any kind of self-congratulatory, moralizing poetry in which the author advertises his or her own moral perfection. Yet that type of poetry is *still* quite common. It's a kind of new didacticism with a narcissistic bent. Do I sound too grumpy?

WB: Not at all, I couldn't agree more. Now let's talk about your narrative poetry, specifically the dramatic monologues. I'd like to ask you about

your exceptional tercet poem, "Counting the Children," where the narrator, a Chinese American accountant, sees a roomful of abandoned and/
or dismembered dolls, and then later, in his sleeping daughter's bedroom,
observes her dolls staring at him with "contempt." But he's still moved by
their future abandonment:

> I felt like holding them tight in my arms,
> Promising I would never let them go,
> But they would trust no promises of mine.
> I feared that if I touched one, it would scream.

What was the genesis of this poem? Where did the dolls come from?
DG: I remember the genesis of that particular poem very well, although
it was quite complicated. The poem began after I'd visited a madwoman's
museum in rural Alabama. The poet Chase Twichell took me there after I'd
given a reading at the University of Alabama at Tuscaloosa. The museum
consisted of a series of chicken shacks full of bizarre objects, the last one
being a tiny barn full of dolls, not unlike the collection I describe in the
poem. I first attempted the poem as a short lyric, but I didn't feel that it
communicated the extraordinarily powerful emotions that I'd experienced
in that unbelievably disturbing room full of discarded dolls.

So I rewrote the poem, adding two characters who witnessed the dolls
together, thinking that this would allow me to project the appropriate emotion through their experiences. But as soon as I'd done that, I realized that
in order to *really* show the impact of the dolls, I needed to give one of the
characters a past and a present life. So I gradually created Mr. Choi as the
protagonist, who is in some ways very much like me, but in other ways,
quite different. The Chinese, for example, are very much like Sicilians in
their family devotion.

I did an early version of the poem which I thought was almost finished. I
thought I was just a few lines from the end when I wrote the passage that is
now in part three:

> I felt so helpless standing by her crib,
> Watching the quiet motions of her breath
> In the half-darkness of the faint night-light.
> How delicate this vessel in our care,
> This gentle soul we summoned to the world,
> A life we treasured but could not protect.

Within a few days of writing those lines, my first son died unexpectedly at four months of sudden infant death syndrome. The almost-completed version of the poem was very much about the experience of fatherhood, but now that experience had taken a terrible turn. I didn't write anything for many months, but eventually I tried to finish the narrative. Almost immediately, however, I realized that what I'd previously thought was the ending of the poem was actually only a mid-point, so I drastically revised it, creating a much more complicated narrative. The poem now consists of four parts: an experience, a nightmare, a memory, and a vision. It also has a covert three-part structure based on Dante's *Commedia*. It goes from hell through purgatory to a vision of paradise. Most of the Dantean elements emerged only after the death of my son.

WB: Was it changed to tercets with Dante in mind?
DG: No, the poem was always conceived in tercets, right from the beginning, but it's about twice as long now as it would have been. The poem began before my son was born; it was seemingly finished while he was still with us; and then it was completely revised and expanded after his death.

WB: The original "dolls" aspect of that poem leads me to my next topic regarding a selection of your poetry that I'm especially fond of: your eerie, creepy poems, like "Beware of Things in Duplicate . . . ," "Thanks for Remembering Us," "Guide to the Other Gallery," and "Time Travel." These and many others have a definite *Twilight Zone* ambiance, as in "The Letter," where people are characterized as waiting rather desperately for a possibly misplaced letter that would set "Everything straight between us and the world," and for which we eagerly wait: "Checking the postbox with impatient faith / Even on days when mail is never brought."
DG: My favorite television show as a child was *Twilight Zone*, and I grew up reading science fiction and supernatural novels. H. P. Lovecraft was an early enthusiasm of mine, and I wrote my senior essay at Stanford on Edgar Allan Poe's short stories after having researched the whole *doppelgänger* motif through German and English language literature. I've always felt that the eerie and the supernatural are a natural subject matter for poetry, and I'm surprised that there isn't more of it.

WB: The critical commentary on your poetry tends to avoid those poems.
DG: You're right. I think critics are much more comfortable talking about those poems that come out of the more mainstream literary traditions.

But one of the things that I'm proudest about is the variety of my poetry, even though, for many critics, that kind of diversity raises the suspicion of inauthenticity. I believe that such thinking is yet another one of the more unfortunate legacies of Confessional poetry: the notion that a writer's work is simply an extension of his or her personality and should never be allowed to wander into the realm of the imagination.

WB: Which is very limiting.
DG: It definitely is. In both fiction and poetry, there are two great traditions. One is the realistic tradition, and the other is the romantic tradition, which includes supernatural literature, horror literature, and science fiction. Both realms—it seems to me—are viable products of the human imagination. I wouldn't want to participate in a literary tradition that didn't offer both.

WB: You once said that "the task of a serious poet is to master the craft without ever losing sight of the spiritual purpose." A number of your poems, like "Prayer" and "The End of the World," clearly relate to the spiritual dimension of human existence, but, in general, how do you try to approach spiritual concerns in your poetry?
DG: I believe that the writer's most important spiritual obligation is to be truthful. Sometimes the truth can be difficult to determine, so the writer needs to begin by refusing to lie, since we generally know when we're not saying what we truly believe. As a result, I've always been wary of what Auden called the "resonant lie."

Another aspect of the spiritual consciousness is the understanding that much of the world that the poet describes is invisible. Certainly our emotions, our thoughts, and our dreams are quite intangible, but I also have the conviction that there is another world which coexists with ours, which is invisible, but no less real—and that there's something very significant beneath the fabric of reality. Even though I don't consider myself a devotional poet, much of my work is religious.

WB: In 1991, your essay "Can Poetry Matter?" appeared in the *Atlantic Monthly*, and it created much discussion, both positive and negative—as did your subsequent collection of essays, *Can Poetry Matter?: Essays on Poetry and American Culture*, published by Graywolf the following year. At the time, you became, as April Lindner has pointed out, "something of a lightning rod for criticism against Expansive poetics," meaning a poetics more open to traditional forms and poetic narratives. How did it feel to be so controversial?

DG: I have never had much desire to be famous. In fact, I prefer privacy. My ambitions have been to write as well as I possibly could and to be well-known enough to have the freedom to pursue the things that interest me. So I feel very lucky right now. As a writer I'm well enough known that, even though I have to earn a living as a writer, I can still choose the projects which sincerely fascinate me. Years ago, after *Esquire* wrote that article about me, I suddenly became "famous" as the "businessman poet." An endless stream of articles appeared about me in newspapers, magazines, and other media, saying I was the new Wallace Stevens. And no matter how much I discouraged those articles, they continued to appear.

So when "Can Poetry Matter?" appeared in 1991 and created what proved to be a literary event, I was not unprepared for dealing with the media, but it still quickly took on a life of its own. I was on the *Charlie Rose Show*, the BBC, Canadian Broadcasting, and many other places, and I must confess I didn't enjoy it very much. On the other hand, I felt an intellectual obligation to appear on those shows and talk to reporters about literary ideas that I thought were important, but it soon became an extraordinary drain on my time. The truth is, if you're picked up by the media in our society, one article generates another, and another, and another, and soon you can get lost in the "fame" game. So, one of the primary reasons I moved back to California six years ago was to get away from New York where I'd become a public figure in the arts. I felt that while, in some ways, my minor celebrity was fun and useful, it was very bad for me as a writer.

WB: Because of the time?

DG: Yes, because of all the time it takes, but also because once you start talking and thinking in news bites, you begin to suffer intellectual damage. About a year and a half ago, BBC wanted to do a TV show about me and I turned them down. They were completely dumbfounded, but I told them I was already famous enough. It is unusual for a poet to become well-known in our society, and when it happens, it is usually for extra-literary reasons. Then the media fosters some sort of stereotype, which is always a reduced version of your real personality. I guess I'm now famous as the "bad boy" of American poetry, the maverick who challenges the establishment. Well, some of that is true, I suppose, but I don't really think that it summarizes my true identity as a writer. But fame always requires a reduction of identity.

WB: You're always identified with the formal revival of the late eighties and early nineties, often called the New Formalism, and I'd like to ask you about that. The term, unfortunately, seems to imply that the younger poets choosing to write in forms were somehow doing something different from Donald Justice, Howard Nemerov, Anthony Hecht, Richard Wilbur, Mona Van Duyn, and the other distinguished voices of the senior generation. Now I realize that the term came from some critics as a way to lump you and Tim Steele and others together, but I've never liked the "New" business, and I'm just curious how you feel about it.

DG: I've always disliked the term "New Formalism," but it's the term that's been adopted by the culture, so we're stuck with it for the foreseeable future. It was coined by Ariel Dawson in an attack on young writers working in forms in the AWP newsletter in 1986. She was attacking what she called "yuppie" poets, some of whom were named, and some of whom were not. I believe she specifically had in mind Brad Leithauser, Vikram Seth, and me.

But I disagree with you in one sense. I think there is something, if not entirely new, at least meaningfully different in the use of form by the American poets of my generation. Unlike Wilbur, Justice, or Hecht, we were raised in a literary culture which had openly and conclusively rejected rhyme and meter in poetry. While it's true that the older poets were still able to get published, one forgets now how often they were attacked back then. *American Poetry Review* regularly mocked Richard Wilbur in its early issues. We grew up in a culture where rhyme and meter were forbidden techniques, and we were met from the very beginning with bitter hostility. That was not a bad thing in some ways. While it destroyed a number of young poets, it toughened up the rest of us. It made us understand that what we were doing would come at a cost to our careers, and the situation bred a certain amount of necessary courage and passion.

In such a hostile environment we found few useful models for our own work. Consequently, we looked back two generations to several poets who were then very much out of fashion—Robert Frost, E. A. Robinson, and Robinson Jeffers. They suggested enormous imaginative possibilities not offered by the current literary scene—most notably narrative poetry. This commitment to the narrative mode, to telling stories about imagined lives rather than autobiography, is one of the things that separate our generation most clearly from both the Confessional poets and the midcentury formalists. Another significant difference between us and the generation of Wilbur, Justice, Hecht, and Hollander is our comfort with a more emotionally direct and less ironic style. That also comes from Frost and Jeffers as well as, I think, from popular culture.

So what we did, in a sense, as all new generations of poets do, was invent our ancestors. Since there was almost no one to help us within the generation of our "parents"—because those were the very people that were teaching the creative writing classes and editing the magazines—we went back to rediscover who our "grandparents" were, and we began reconnecting with poets like Robert Frost, E. A. Robinson, and for the narrative, Robinson Jeffers.

One of the great curiosities of American literary history was why Robert Frost, who is arguably the greatest American poet ever, had so little influence on posterity. But Frost's broad influence became apparent for the very first time in our generation. This didn't happen by some kind of group consensus. Each of us, working independently, searched through our history and saw in Frost the unrealized potentials that we could pursue. We did what all new generations do—we reinvented the tradition.

I also think that the New Formalists are postmodernist in a way that Richard Wilbur, for example, was not. By the time the New Formalists began writing, it was clear to all of us that Modernism, whatever its literary achievements, was now a dead tradition. We began to try and find a way to balance the useful elements of Modernism with the things that had been lost, especially form and narrative. That sense of Modernism being dead doesn't exist in Justice, Wilbur, or Hecht.

WB: I wouldn't disagree with most of that, although I feel that Frost had a much greater influence than you recognize—early Lowell, Wilbur, Kumin, Hall, even Walcott, for example. But I still don't think that your points indicate that there's anything really "new" about the formalism itself. Certainly those younger poets faced a different environment than the previous generation, but that's always the case. Coleridge's environment was different from Dryden's.

DG: Well, I don't like the term either, but it's there, and it's interesting to speculate why it caught on. One of the crucial things that distinguished those younger formalist writers was that they were deeply nourished by the great, dead poets, and not by the contemporary workshops of the time. They came to their various practices by returning to the great tradition, rather than by conforming to the current official culture.

WB: One more question about the New Formalism. One of the supposedly "new" aspects of the movement was a closer relationship with the popular culture—despite the fact that the senior generation of formalists had done so in the past. Richard Wilbur, for example, wrote a very clever poem about the film version of *The Prisoner of Zenda* (1937) and even mentioned the film's star, Ronald Colman, in the poem. How do you feel about that?

DG: I think the New Formalists' debt to popular culture is often misunderstood. People tend to think that it means writing poems about subjects drawn from the popular culture. There was certainly a bit of that. I've written a poem that refers to the Beach Boys, and others have written poems about pop songs and movies.

But years ago, when I was trying to introduce this concept into the critical discourse, I had something very different in mind. I felt that we should learn from the forms and modes of popular culture—the power of narrative, the pleasures of form and genre, and the intrinsic relationship between song and lyric poetry. It seemed to me, for example, that there are ways of telling stories that the cinema has developed that are also natural to poetry. I also thought we could learn from the various ways that rock music effectively projects emotions. There is a kind of direct emotionalism exhibited throughout the popular arts that the midcentury generation of poets was deeply suspicious of, but which my generation felt was very useful in creating an expressive sort of lyric poetry. It was really the methods of popular culture that we found most useful.

WB: Isn't it true that those popular culture methods were learned from earlier literary and artistic sources? And that, for example, the western film, which learned its narrative from Homer and Shakespeare, made us long for those older methodologies once again, especially since they weren't being used in contemporary poetry?

DG: Yes, our generation's deep familiarity and affection for popular culture always reminded us of the viability of traditional modes of storytelling and song-making that had existed since the origins of literature, whereas late-Modernist and contemporary poetry seemed to hold itself aloof from those things. In the end, I think that we learned as much from the movies as we did from the Modernists.

WB: One more question about pop culture. I must admit that I'm always wary of the pop culture since, by definition, most of it will end up forgotten and its references footnoted. On the other hand, useful references to aspects of the popular culture can be made clear in the poem, even if the reader doesn't understand the specific reference. For example, a hundred years from now the Beach Boys may be totally forgotten, but in your poem which refers to the band, it's perfectly clear that they're a singing group who once sang a song in the narrator's youth that now incites a powerful nostalgia. On the other hand, the reference to the filmmaker Cecil B. DeMille in the same poem is not clarified, and will, most likely, need an explanatory footnote in the future. In other words, it seems to me that there are two ways to use the pop culture. One is to drop it in the poem without clarification, and the other is to use it in such a way that the reader will understand the allusion even without knowing the specificity of the reference.

DG: I absolutely agree. I've consciously crafted the poems in my last two books to exclude almost any reference that might create difficulties fifty or a hundred years from now, unless they're clarified in the context of the poem. Poems that are laden with contemporary references will be fatally damaged in the future. Even Cecil B. DeMille, that great Hollywood director, is already becoming a footnote. There is a wonderful epigraph in a poem by Edgar Bowers that is a quote from one of his students: "Who's Apollo?" When I wrote "Cruising with the Beach Boys," I did so with the conscious intention that the reader could insert any song by any group that he or she has had a similar relationship with. Over the last ten years, I've come to the conclusion that part of the way poetry communicates is by leaving out essential details and by inviting the reader to project appropriate ones from his or her own life into the poem. Those projections, in fact, are a crucial part of the experience of reading a poem.

WB: One of the ambitious goals of Expansive poetry—and the related New Formalism—was the difficult task of attempting to reclaim poetry's "lost" audience—to try and appeal beyond the universities to a more general readership. Do you feel much progress has been made?

DG: I do, and I would like to emphasize the positive aspects of the situation. Although we faced an open hostility by the official literary culture and were excluded from many venues, the resurgence of form has, nevertheless, not only survived, but actually thrived. Our books get published, and many sell quite well. Form is back in many of the journals again. And most importantly, from my point of view, audiences respond positively and deeply to our work.

If we're not too famous, that might be a good thing. Being well-known enough to have the freedom to continue our work is all that we should really expect. Most important, over the past twenty years some extremely fine poets have emerged who have written work that will eventually become part of the canon of American poetry.

WB: Those were all important successes, but what about the appeal to a wider audience?

DG: I think that over the last ten years there has been a noticeable resurgence of interest in poetry by the general public. There are now poetry readings at bookstores, libraries, museums, everywhere. There are community-based poetry festivals all around the United States. Poems are regularly quoted in movies and on television, in a way that you didn't see twenty years ago. There are many poetry radio shows. Newspapers are providing more coverage of poetry than they used to. I'm not saying that all these things qualify as a renaissance, but it's certainly a resurgence. The populist instincts of New Formalism are one of the important reasons for the revival.

WB: Let's return to your own poetry and talk about your excellent third book, *Interrogations at Noon*. In what ways do you see it as different from *Daily Horoscope* and *The Gods of Winter*?

DG: I think that *Interrogations at Noon* is meaningfully different from my earlier books. My life has become so busy with other activities—criticism, editing, and my role as a public commentator—that it took me quite a long time to bring the new book out. The poems grew very slowly, one by one, over the last decade, and when I finally began to put them together, I noticed certain changes in my work.

Firstly, the poems have gotten shorter. I've developed a passion for cutting things out. A poem, almost by definition, should leave quite a bit to the imagination of the reader. Secondly, I'm now using rhymed stanzas more than I did in the past. I want to make the poems more overtly musical and song-like. Thirdly, I've begun working in non-iambic meter much more than before. Aside from the iambs the book has anapests, trochees, dactyls, and various kinds of stress meters. I much prefer that kind of metrical diversity. I've often felt that the New Formalism could have been called the "New Iambicism" because most of the poems were written in either iambic tetrameter or iambic pentameter. Lastly, I think my newer poems are more emotionally direct. They are, I believe, much closer to Hardy than to Stevens.

WB: Do you set aside specific time for writing your poetry?

DG: I have to. I now make my living as a writer, and I publish something every week—an article, a review, editorial work, or narratives for BBC broadcasts. So, I have to set aside time to write my poems; otherwise they would never get done. Since I work seven days a week, it's hard to find the time during a given week so I try to isolate a few weeks for nothing but poetry writing. Also, when I travel, I often bring along drafts of my poems, and I work on them in the airplane and in my hotel room—where the phone isn't ringing all the time. Ironically, it's been harder for me to write poems leading a "literary" life than it was during my "business" life. In my corporate days, my two lives were entirely separate. Now they're entirely intermingled.

WB: How do you go about crafting your poems?
DG: Well, let me start by saying that I'm a slave to inspiration. Poems are "given" to writers. I actually experience inspiration as a physical sensation that I feel in particular parts of my body. I get a strange feeling in my throat and a burning across my temples. Then I know I have a poem emerging.

WB: Will this happen anywhere? As you're walking down the street?
DG: Yes, and if I'm walking down the street, and I don't get to some quiet place where I can write down some notes, I'll lose it. Over the years, I've lost many poems because something has interfered. The man from Porlock follows me everywhere!

WB: Do you carry paper in your wallet?
DG: Whenever I travel, I always have a pen with me and usually something to write on. Often, it's just the back of an envelope or the margins of a magazine or concert program. As I'm writing, I usually go into a kind of trance for about thirty or forty-five minutes, sometimes an hour. When I emerge, I find that I've written down some notes that wouldn't make much sense to anyone else. Sometimes, it's just some lines written in a particular rhythm. I usually don't know what my poems are *really* about until they're done.

WB: So, is the original idea usually a concept or a rhythm?
DG: Often, it's the first line or an image—or something that I'm certain will appear within the poem, even if I'm not sure why. Most of the poems that begin in this first flush of inspiration never go beyond that sketchy set of notes. In order for me to continue with a poem, I have to determine what its form is. If it's metered verse, I need to know what the line length is, and the stanza shape, and whether it's rhymed. Sometimes it takes a long time to determine those things. It took me about seven years to figure out the form for "The Litany" which was included in *Interrogations at Noon*. I kept going back to my notes, and I'd play with the lines again, over and over, but I couldn't find the right shape. Eventually, when I finally get the form, I can proceed with the poem.

WB: Where do the forms come from?
DG: A poet has to listen closely to the language and then determine what shape the language suggests. Form is never imposed from outside the poem. It grows naturally out of the language that is there. Only after you've recognized the shape that the language itself suggests, can you finish the poem. This is something that opponents of form have never fully understood. They think that form is a conceptual template that is imposed on the poem. But I see form as the language itself revealing the secrets of its being.

WB: Then what happens?
DG: Then I try to get what I call a "first finished" draft. I always write in longhand with a fountain pen on lined paper in a tablet, but most of the composition is done while I'm walking around mumbling to myself. I like to compose aloud. If anybody ever saw me doing this, they'd probably think I was psychotic.

WB: Wordsworth did that, and Yeats sometimes.
DG: For me, at least, the physical movement is very conducive to composition. Back when we still lived in New York, there was a long country path I'd often take, mumbling things to myself and jotting them down as I went. I might say a hundred versions of a line before writing one down. For me, it is the most natural way to write.

WB: Are you actually composing the poem as you walk along?
DG: Yes, I'll often do a stanza at a time, especially when I'm working in rhyme. I feel oral composition is absolutely essential when I'm going after sound. I need to recite the lines aloud. Much of the pleasure of poetry, of course, comes from hearing it and saying it. Poetry should always consist of a language that's pleasurable to recite—to wrap your tongue and larynx around. Eventually, after a few long walks, I get back to my desk and complete the "first finished" draft—which might take twenty or thirty intermediate drafts. By this point, I have a very good sense of what the finished poem is going to be like. Only at that point do I type the poem up to see what it looks like in cold print.

WB: Then the revising begins?
DG: Yes, the poem might go through another twenty or thirty drafts, cutting lines or adding new stuff as I go, but now it's easy because I've got a real sense of what the poem is all about. Finally, when I think it's done, I put it on

the computer and print it out so I can, once again, look at it freshly. By that point, I'm usually just making a few tiny corrections, but it's helpful to see it "new." I do wonder if many contemporary poets aren't shortchanging themselves by working directly on the computer. They miss the new perspectives one gets by going from handwriting to typewriting to laser printing.

WB: You have quite an involved writing process.
DG: Yes, isn't it appalling? I wish I could just sit down and write a poem. That has happened a few times in my life, but usually I work in the slow, neurotic fashion I have just described.

WB: I'd like to shift now to the very successful Exploring Form and Narrative Poetry Conference that you and Mike Peich created in 1995. How did it come about?
DG: Mike and I are old, dear friends, and one night at my parents' house in Sebastopol, when we were having dinner, we noted the fact that although there were, at that time, over two thousand writers' conferences in the United States—several of which I was involved with—there was not a single place where a young writer could go to learn the traditional craft of poetry in any systematic way. Having just finished a bottle of pinot noir, it occurred to us it would be a wonderful thing to start such a conference. So we did, even though we had no budget, no staff, and no other visible means of support.

We drew up what we thought would be a model curriculum—classes in meter, the sonnet, the French forms, narrative poetry, etc.—and next to each subject, we put the name of the person who we thought would be the best younger poet in the country to teach that course. We felt that it was important that these techniques be taught as living traditions by younger writers who were actively using them. We also wanted to honor our elders, and so we decided to recognize, as a keynote speaker, some writer whose work we felt confident had an enduring place in the canon of American letters. We invited Richard Wilbur to be our first keynote speaker. We had no money to pay our faculty, so I called each of them up to explain why it was important that we all do this, and everyone said "yes."

Initially, we thought that the conference would probably be a onetime event, but when it was over, nobody went home. People stuck around because they'd enjoyed themselves so much, and we realized that we should do it again. Since 1995, the conference has grown and developed. Last year, for example, we had fourteen classes ranging from blank verse to dramatic monologue. We've also started critical seminars as part of a scholarly conference that runs simultaneously with the writing conference. A few years ago, we also initiated the world's first and only prosody prize, the Robert Fitzgerald Award for a lifetime contribution to the study of versification and prosody. Next year the award will be given to Paul Fussell who will attend the conference.

WB: For those interested in attending the conference, what are the various opportunities for poets at West Chester?

DG: We created the conference to provide three things for the individual poet. The first is focused, informed, and practical instruction in verse craft. The second is an intellectual forum where critics and poets can talk about subjects of mutual interest. And third, and perhaps most important, we try to create a community of poets and scholars who share certain values. Probably the most important contribution that West Chester is making to American letters is the creation and fostering of a new generation of writers committed to the importance of technique, who now realize that they have both colleagues and an audience.

WB: I can attest to the sense of community at West Chester, and it's always beneficial to meet like-minded people.

DG: That's right. Very few people leave West Chester without having made new friends.

WB: Back in 1992, when you resigned your position at General Foods, you decided to earn your living entirely as a writer. Much of your time has been spent editing textbooks for universities, especially a number of widely-used texts originally established by X. J. Kennedy. Are things going well? Or is it too absorbing?

DG: To be honest, if I'd wanted to be just a poet, I would have stayed in business, but I wanted to be a man of letters in the old-fashioned sense of the term. I wanted to continue writing poems, but I also wanted to write criticism, edit books, write for the stage, and engage in the public conversation about literature and culture. Fortunately, I've been able to do all those things. It's not easy to make a living as a literary writer in our society without institutional connections. I work seven days a week and also travel constantly on the lecture and reading circuit. I've had some good financial years and some bad ones. But I've managed to maintain my independence. I have never applied for a grant or taken a full-time university job. Over the years, I've been offered a number of academic positions, some quite distinguished and lucrative, but I feel that it's important for me to stay independent from institutional life.

WB: One of your more interesting recent projects has been the writing of *Nosferatu*, an opera libretto which was set to music by Alva Henderson. This has allowed you to combine your interests in musical composition, poetry, and performance.

DG: Over the last ten years, I've written quite a bit for the stage and concert hall. I translated a Latin tragedy by Seneca that was produced in SoHo, and I've collaborated with about a dozen composers on all kinds of projects, from choral pieces to song cycles. But my most fascinating endeavor was the creation of *Nosferatu* with Alva Henderson. I wanted to write a libretto that could work both as a poetic tragedy on the page and as a musical drama on stage. I believe that the libretto is one of the great unrealized poetic genres in the English language.

If you go back a few hundred years, it was taken for granted that poets could work in a wide range of genres, from hymns to epics, from ballads to verse tragedies, from satires to lyric poetry. But when I started writing poetry in the seventies, the possibilities of contemporary verse had been pretty much limited to the lyric poem and the occasional modernist epic. While they're both fine and fascinating forms, they didn't begin to exhaust the many possibilities of poetry. As for me personally, I'd always been drawn to verse drama. I loved the plays of W. H. Auden, T. S. Eliot, W. B. Yeats, and Christopher Fry, but, unfortunately, there is no longer a living tradition of spoken verse drama in English. The only aspect of the verse drama that's still active and open to contemporary poets is opera.

WB: Do you plan to do more?

DG: Absolutely. I'm already working on a second libretto—for the composer Paul Salerni. It's a long phantasmagoric, one-act opera titled *Tony Caruso's Final Broadcast*. It contains four levels of language—prose, doggerel, Latin and Italian, and poetry—each of which is associated with a slightly different musical world. I also expect to write another opera for Alva. He and I are currently discussing the possibility of a contemporary requiem, which is an idea that I've wanted to try for many years. I would like to write a sequence of lyric poems that replicate the spiritual and liturgical journey of the Latin requiem mass. The idea of creating a large liturgical work that would be genuinely poetic excites me. I'm not sure if I can successfully bring it off, but I plan to try.

WB: What other projects are you working on right now? Isn't your second collection of essays, *Barrier of a Common Language*, coming out soon?
DG: Hopefully. The book's been finished for quite a while and the University of Michigan Press is ready to publish it as soon as I write the preface. It deals with contemporary British poetry. I also have several other books coming out.

WB: Any new poems?
DG: I've got quite a few new poems in the draft stage, but I have to admit I don't finish most of the poems I start. I also don't publish many of the poems I finish, and I don't collect all of the poems I publish. But I'm reconciled to my paltry level of production. My ambition is simply to write as well as I can, and I intend to keep writing poetry for as long as the muse is willing.

WB: I hope so, Dana. As we finish up today, I'd like to read the lovely ending of your poem "Do Not Expect . . ." from *Daily Horoscope*:

> One
more summer gone,
and one way or another you survive,
dull or regretful, never learning that
nothing is hidden in the obvious
changes of the world, that even the dim
reflection of the sun on tall, dry grass
is more than you will ever understand.

> And only briefly then
you touch, you see, you press against
the surface of impenetrable things.

Thanks, Dana.

Dana Gioia and the Role of the Poet-Critic: An Interview

Garrick Davis / 2003

From *Contemporary Poetry Review*. Reprinted by permission of Garrick Davis.

Garrick Davis: When did you begin writing criticism?

Dana Gioia: I began writing criticism for my high school paper—reviewing music, books, and films. In college I wrote for the *Stanford Daily*, mostly about music, and I edited *Sequoia*, the campus literary magazine. Ironically, I only began publishing literary criticism regularly when I was in business school. For two years I wrote a piece on poetry or fiction every two weeks in the *Stanford Daily*. The editor gave me complete freedom, so I was able to review what interested me most—an invaluable circumstance for a critic. Consequently, I wrote on serious writers like Vladimir Nabokov, Eugenio Montale, Ezra Pound, Constantine Cavafy, Anthony Burgess, and Seamus Heaney. Like many young writers, I educated myself in public.

GD: Did you see criticism as an inevitable task—an obligation—of your poetry?

DG: For me, it was inevitable. Criticism seemed the most natural activity imaginable. I loved books and enjoyed talking about them. Why not open up the conversation by bringing it into print? Criticism is not only a fascinating enterprise in its own terms. It also helps a young writer understand and refine his or her own sense of the art.

GD: What do you think the role of the poet-critic should be?

DG: The poet-critic plays a crucial role in modern literary life, especially during times of artistic innovation or cultural stagnation. The critic creates the perspectives and standards by which new work can be understood and judged. "Poets are the antennae of the race," Pound asserted—meaning that poets notice cultural change earlier than their fellow citizens. That ability explains the importance of poets writing criticism. They observe changes in the art, the audience, and the culture before non-artists do. They also write about their art with the passion of personal commitment.

GD: What modern critics or poet-critics do you consider exemplary in this regard?

DG: I have always been drawn to poets who were active and versatile men of letters. My exemplary poet-critics would include T. S. Eliot, Ezra Pound, W. H. Auden, and Paul Valéry—each a great poet as well as a great critic. They are my intellectual patron saints. Other important poet-critics for me are Jorge Luis Borges, Randall Jarrell, Yvor Winters, Kathleen Raine, Donald Davie, and William Everson. There are also some poets like Robert Frost and Robinson Jeffers who wrote very little criticism but nonetheless left a few extraordinary essays.

I must also mention the special case of Thomas Merton, a minor poet who became the most significant Catholic religious writer that America has produced. His books and essays on the contemplative life are also very much about the poetic imagination. Finally, I would add that several novelists are central to my canon of exemplary critics. George Orwell is the greatest of these. He has been an indispensable guide. I also owe debts to D. H. Lawrence and Anthony Burgess.

GD: Do you see your own criticism as that of a poet's, partial and dogmatic, or an ideal reader's? Is there a vital link between your own poetry and prose?

DG: I try never to be dogmatic or partisan in my criticism, though I cannot help being personal. If a critic tries to ignore his or her own personal reactions, all that is left is ideology. Emotion, imagination, and intuition can be useful tools in criticism as long as they don't overwhelm intelligent observation and analysis. Art is about specifics, not abstract categories. Good critics respond to their subjects with the fullness of their humanity.

I divide my critical prose into two categories—literary journalism and serious essays. The journalism I try to make intelligent, interesting, and accurate. It is usually written to a set length—say 1000 or 1500 words—for a particular journal like the *Washington Post* or *San Francisco Magazine*. Journalism usually assumes a particular audience. I am writing in such cases according to someone else's rules.

My essays, however, are written according to the dictates of my own imagination—in my own way and to my own length. Here I try to use all of my resources as a writer. Nabokov asserted that there was no essential difference between poetry and "artistic prose." I tend to agree. There is little meaningful difference between my best discursive prose and poetry. In my essays I worry about sound, tone, mood, imagery, and rhythm just as I do in my poetry.

GD: What do you think of the present situation of poetry? Of its current health as an art?

DG: The art of poetry is reasonably healthy at present. Unfortunately, most of the machinery of literary culture—criticism, scholarship, anthologies, journals, prize committees, and the like—has broken down. As a result, the best new poetry no longer necessarily gets identified and brought to a wider audience. It gets lost in the clutter of Po-Biz. Art is an affair of individual genius and a passionate dedication to the highest standards. It is not an affair of institutions and ideologies.

GD: What do you think of the present situation of poetry criticism?

DG: Poetry criticism is currently in dreadful shape. Most of it is dull, timid, and unoriginal—badly argued and indifferently written. No wonder few journals publish it, and so few readers pay it any attention. The situation makes it difficult for critics, especially young critics. There are now very few places where someone can write seriously about poetry for the general intellectual public.

GD: If one compares the poetry criticism written in the first half of the twentieth century to that written in the second half, there has been a marked deterioration. What caused this decline?

DG: There has been an indisputable decline in the quality and importance of American poetry criticism over the past century. There are probably several reasons. First, the clustering of poets in the academy created a narrow professionalism. Too many critics feel it is proper to write only for one another. That may be an adequate aim for scholarship but not criticism. Second, the general press has largely abandoned the coverage of poetry. This retrenchment meant that it was no longer easy for nonacademic critics to play an active role in the art. It also hampered the necessary conversation—and debate—between academic and public criticism. Third, I suspect that there is also an obvious practical reason no one wants to admit—the lack of major talent. Why would any first-rate literary talent continue writing poetry criticism? The audience is tiny, divided, and unappreciative. The venues are few and unremunerative. When someone first-rate comes along like Clive James, Paul Fussell, or John Simon, they often gravitate toward popular culture—areas that will provide a living and some notoriety.

GD: Is there some way to account for the fact that the majority of American poet-critics have been, and continue to be, politically conservative? From the New Critics to the New Formalists many of the important poet-critics have been denounced for their political allegiances as much as their aesthetic ideas.

DG: Critical excellence has less to do with political ideology than intellectual independence. The best criticism tends to come from dissenters—poets who reject the prevailing opinions. Since the intellectual mainstream of the twentieth century was progressive, indeed often revolutionary in its worldview, it is not surprising that the most provocative critical writing would challenge those assumptions. Archibald MacLeish, for example, perfectly reflected the progressive liberal establishment of his day, and his criticism is invincibly dull and intellectually complacent. By contrast, T. S. Eliot, Wallace Stevens, Allen Tate, and Marianne Moore (not to mention the extreme example of Ezra Pound) were political reactionaries, and their criticism remains profoundly vital—even to readers who do not share their politics.

Not all of intellectual dissent, however, came from the right. The anarchistic left produced some important poet-critics like Kenneth Rexroth and William Everson. Delmore Schwartz was an independent-minded Trotskyite. (Free inquiry and disinterested literary judgment didn't thrive among Stalinists.) It is also important to remember that some culturally conservative critics like Yvor Winters were political leftists. What matters is not political allegiance but a stubborn determination to get at the truth rather than merely acquiesce to the currently popular platitudes.

GD: What do you think of the yoking of politics to poetry, which is such a fixture of recent American poetry?

DG: To judge poetry as political speech is to misunderstand the art on the most basic level. Poetry is not primarily conceptual or ideological communication. It is a different way of knowing—experiential, holistic, and physical—that is largely intuitive and irrational. To treat poetry as political statement reduces a complex and dynamic art to a few predetermined categories. No wonder the urge to politicize art proves irresistible to the ignorant, the lazy, and the small-minded of all persuasions.

GD: Much has been made in recent years of the proliferation of creative writing programs in the United States. Do you think this academicization has had a beneficial or baleful effect on poetry?

DG: In principle, there is no reason that writing programs should be bad for American poetry. The proliferation of music programs in the US has helped raise the standard of orchestral playing and broadened the access to classical music. But, for a variety of reasons, the growth of graduate writing programs has had some unfortunate effects on both American poetry and poetry criticism.

GD: What do you think of the vast subsidized system of grants, prizes, and awards that poets currently compete for?

DG: I worry that many poets care too much about external validation—prizes, grants, fellowships, competitions, and other forms of institutional recognition. However pleasant to receive, official honors have nothing to do with the real work of an artist. Once poets start thinking about their activities in terms of institutional approval, their art suffers.

A poet needs enough faith in his or her own vocation to work endlessly at perfecting it—despite indifference or even hostility. Think of Osip Mandelstam or Anna Akhmatova. Or, in a less dramatic way, consider Wallace Stevens or Lorine Niedecker, who toiled for decades without grants, prizes, readings, or much public recognition. Stevens was fifty-seven when he published his second book. By today's Po-Biz standards, he was a complete failure.

GD: Which contemporary poets do you read with pleasure?

DG: The older generation of American poets has some dazzling writers, especially Richard Wilbur, Donald Justice, Anthony Hecht, Louis Simpson, Anne Stevenson, and Adrienne Rich. I also love comic poets and children's poets like X. J. Kennedy, William Jay Smith, Nancy Willard, and Tom Disch. (To me, it says everything about academic critics and anthologists that they usually exclude comic poetry from their canons.) There are also some lesser-known writers like Ted Kooser and Kay Ryan whom I consider important.

There are also some superb British poets who are little read in the US—Charles Causley, James Fenton, Tony Harrison, Dick Davis, and Wendy Cope, just for starters.

GD: Which contemporary critics?

DG: I read many critics with profit and enjoyment. I particularly admire how the British still manage to practice serious criticism in a public idiom.

I was a great fan of Ian Hamilton and was heartbroken to hear of his death. He was a brave, smart, lively critic with a wicked sense of humor. I still miss Anthony Burgess—as a critic, novelist, and poet. His 1995 novel-in-verse, *Byrne*, is enormously enjoyable. The generosity, range, and energy of Burgess's criticism were astonishing. I wish Clive James would return to poetry criticism. Why does he waste his time becoming rich and famous on TV when he could be reviewing slim books of modern verse for tiny magazines? Among the other Brit-crits I also like James Fenton, William Oxley, and Kathleen Raine.

GD: What about American critics?

DG: Among living Americans I especially admire Donald Hall, Anne Stevenson, Louis Simpson, John Haines, and Daniel Hoffman—a rather elderly crew, I'm afraid. I wish Richard Wilbur and Donald Justice had written more criticism. The work they have published is astute and original. I enjoy Richard Kostelanetz on the avant-garde. He writes well, thinks clearly, and is enormously well informed. Jack Foley's theoretical essays on speech and writing have influenced me deeply.

Among non-poets I would single out Leslie Fiedler, William Pritchard, Hugh Kenner, Susan Sontag, Paul Fussell, Joseph Epstein, and Guy Davenport. These critics are skilled and inventive writers. I admire excellent writing. I find it hard to trust the critical judgments of people who can't compose a memorable sentence.

Not many poets of my generation have taken criticism seriously as a medium. If they have written criticism at all, they have rarely put their full artistic intelligence and energy—not to mention moral courage—into the enterprise. The deep dedication to the art itself that one saw so frequently in Pound and Eliot's generation or Jarrell and Berryman's seems to have largely vanished. Recently, I have been heartened to see the emergence of a few strong young critics like Christian Wiman and Adam Kirsch.

GD: Are there any books of poetry published in the last few years that you would particularly recommend to readers?

DG: I read a great many new books of poetry, but there are so many published that I have no confidence that I or anyone else really knows the best new work. If we had better critics, we might *collectively* clarify the situation. But we have very little informed and demanding evaluation of new work—mostly just bland patter that is hardly distinguishable from the blurbs.

Some of the old masters of American poetry are still writing well—Richard Wilbur, Anthony Hecht, Donald Justice, Anne Stevenson, and X. J. Kennedy. Their recent volumes are among their finest work. Such creative longevity is actually quite rare. In American letters it is quite common for writers to decline precipitously in the second half of their careers. Just look at the later work of James Dickey and Anne Sexton—or more recently Adrienne Rich and Robert Bly. Some poets, like Allen Ginsberg, had only a few good years before they fell into pretentious banality.

But you are probably more interested in less-established poets. In this regard among the best new books I've seen in the past decade are Kay Ryan's *Say Uncle*, David Mason's *The Country I Remember*, and H. L. Hix's *Perfect Hell*. Each of them is radically different from the other, but each seems destined to last. It interests me how little critical attention these writers have received. I was the first person ever to write an essay on Ryan, who had by then published four books. She seems to me as good as anyone in her generation. Mason and Hix have also been shamefully neglected.

GD: Can poets regain the common readers they once had? Will poetry ever exert itself again in American culture as it did a century ago? Does criticism have a role to play in this?

DG: I doubt that poetry can ever regain the role it once had in American society. There are now too many competing forms of art and entertainment. But surely poetry could and should play a much larger role in our culture than it has in the past half century. To win back the intelligent common reader is the obvious task for the poet, the critic, and the teacher. Criticism's role in this revival is self-evident. It must create the public conversation about poetry that will renew the reader's curiosity and interest in the art.

GD: Do you think your criticism has hurt the reception of your poetry?

DG: I have been the victim of my own success as a critic. I maintained a balanced reputation between my criticism and poetry until the publication of "Can Poetry Matter?" The international controversy caused by that essay—and later the book—quickly changed my public image. I went from being known as a poet who wrote criticism to a public intellectual. That situation was reinforced by my slowness in finishing my third book of poems. *Interrogations at Noon* (2001) did not appear until ten years after *The Gods of Winter* (1991). I risked a great deal by refusing to publish a new book of poems until I was sure of the work. Luckily, the book won the American Book Award, but I am still in the process of reasserting my identity as a poet.

GD: Have your reviews cost you anything?

DG: The candor of my criticism has cost me a great deal. A number of influential poets have made no secret of their anger at particular reviews, and they have been assiduous in their attempts at revenge. No poet in my generation has been attacked in print as often or so ferociously as I have. I reconciled myself to this situation years ago. I knew that unless I gave up reviewing, I would win no major prizes, no fellowships, no residencies, no swank invitations from the establishment. So I stopped worrying about such things. I took myself out of the running for external rewards. I apply for nothing and expect nothing. I make my living as a writer and seek no institutional support. It is a small price to pay for the freedom to write honestly.

GD: The title essay of *Can Poetry Matter?* received the most attention, but there are other pieces in the book which have had a lasting influence, since they significantly altered the critical opinion on their subjects. Your essays on Weldon Kees and Robinson Jeffers have helped to revive interest in these underappreciated poets, while your retrospective on Robert Bly seems to have initiated the decline in his reputation.

DG: I have tried to write essays that have something new to say—pieces that might make a difference. So much literary criticism merely repeats the current consensus. I'm particularly proud of having written the first full-length essay on Weldon Kees as well as the first essay ever on Kay Ryan. I have probably helped change critical—though not yet academic—opinion on Kees and Jeffers. I've also helped build the reputations of Ted Kooser and Kay Ryan. At the very least I have helped increase their readership, or so people tell me.

I fear my essay on Bly did help turn literary opinion against him. It articulated criticisms and reservations that many other readers seem to have shared but had not yet voiced. Ever since my piece appeared, his poetic reputation has been in steady decline. Bly may be a sanctimonious goof—half shaman and half Shriner—but his heart is in the right place. He knows that literature has an essential connection to spirituality and emotional development. At the height of deconstructionism and postmodernism, he championed the ancient human purposes of myth and poetry. He also wrote one brilliant and original book of poems, *The Light Around the Body.* These are not small accomplishments—despite his other failings.

GD: The Preface to the Tenth Anniversary Edition of *Can Poetry Matter?* sounds an optimistic note on the vitality of the art, which seems at variance with the pessimism you expressed in the original introduction. How would you explain that shift in your opinion?

DG: I don't consider "Can Poetry Matter?" pessimistic. I may have described a bad situation, but I wrote without bitterness or despair. I even outlined some measures that might correct the situation. I had an unswerving faith in poetry itself. Ten years later, it is reassuring to see that substantial progress has been made in broadening the audience of American poetry. There are still plenty of problems, but surely we can all gloat a bit at present about poetry's renewed popularity. Isn't it nice to have something to celebrate?

Bringing Art to All Americans: A Conversation with Dana Gioia

Michael J. Bandler / 2003

From *US Society & Values* 8.1 (April 2003): 5–8.

Michael J. Bandler: Let's begin by viewing the arts in America through your unique prism—the NEA itself.

Dana Gioia: I come to the NEA with a very simple vision. A great nation deserves great art. America is the wealthiest and most powerful nation in the history of the world. But the measure of a nation's greatness isn't wealth or power. It is the civilization it creates, fosters, and promotes. What I hope to accomplish here, in the broad sense, is to help foster the public culture that America deserves.

Although we are the largest arts funder in the United States, the NEA's budget represents less than 1 percent of American philanthropic spending on the arts. So the federal government could never "buy" a certain kind of culture. Our role at the NEA is leadership. We are in the unique position of being the only institution that can see all of the arts from a national perspective. Enlightened leadership from us could accomplish goals in American culture more quickly and more pervasively than efforts by any other institution might. What excites me about my position is the possibility of using the arts to make America a better place in which to live.

MB: Contrast, in general terms, American philanthropy with the European model with which the world is quite familiar.

DG: The European model grew out of a tradition of royal and aristocratic patronage that in modern times has been assumed by the state. Over there, the majority of an arts institution's budget comes from federal or local subsidies. The American model rests on private philanthropy. And it works. We have an enormous range and depth of museums, symphonies, theaters, opera houses, and ballet companies.

Historically, particularly during the 1970s and 1980s, the NEA used federal funds across the country to seed the development of regional dance, theater, and opera, as well as, to a lesser degree, museums and symphonies. The enormous number of these institutions that now exist in middle-sized American cities is evidence of the power of the NEA to lead.

MB: How do we explain the emergence of significant private funding for the arts, over the decades, even the centuries?
DG: The arts in America grow out of American culture. The reason that America has had this diversely distinguished history of art, this unprecedented breadth of achievement—ranging from movies to Abstract Expressionism to jazz to modern literature—is because America was and is a society that recognizes the individual freedom of its citizens. American philanthropy follows the same model. America is perhaps the only nation in the world in which there have been hundreds of people who created enormous fortunes and gave them away within a single lifetime to philanthropic enterprises.

MB: Is there a corner of culture that might have escaped wide notice?
DG: The original mission of the NEA was to foster excellence and bring the arts to the American people. We would now probably qualify that as bringing art to *all* Americans—recognizing the multitude of special communities in the United States, some cultural, some geographic, some related to language, and some related even to age and physical capabilities. All of those groups are our constituencies. We've also come to realize that to support our goals, we must have a role in education. And so providing leadership in arts education is now another goal of the NEA.

MB: What excites you the most about American culture these days?
DG: There are several huge, overarching trends in the arts today. The first I would characterize as a kind of aesthetic crisis. As America enters the twenty-first century, there is a growing conviction that the enormous explosion of energy that came out of the Modernism movement that began after World War I has reached its end. We still appreciate the rich legacy of Modernism and the avant-garde, but it no longer seems to have the generative power it once possessed. There is a growing consensus on the need for

synthesis between the intensity and power of Modernism and experimental art, with the kind of democratic accessibility and availability that traditional and popular arts have. In every art form in which I have an active participation, I see this trend of artists trying to reconnect themselves to the public. What is emerging—whether one likes it or not—is a kind of new populism.

MB: How does this play out, for instance, in music?
DG: Look at classical music—which leads me to the second major trend, the notion of fusion—disparate traditions coming together. For example, there is a very powerful movement in American music called world music, spanning everything from classical to pop—an attempt to combine and harmonize Eastern and Western traditions. You also see a kind of technological fusion—taking traditional performing arts and applying the potential of new technology. Twenty years ago, the emerging trend was postmodernism. But I think postmodernism in some ways was just an attempt to add to the life span of Modernism. Today, the movements are not so much characterized by manifestos and methods as by intuition and outreach.

MB: And outreach is how you make the arts accessible?
DG: Yes. The history of the arts in America, to a certain degree, reflects the excellence and depth that comes from elitist traditions tempered by the human possibilities of art in a democratic culture. That is a dialectic that will probably never be exhausted, but will take a different form with each era. No art can cut itself off from its history. Even Futurism and the avant-garde have deep and complicated traditional backgrounds. What often happens in the arts is that you reject your parents while embracing your grandparents.

MB: You mentioned world music as an example of technological fusion. Talk about music in terms of the first trend you cited—the new populism.
DG: The major tendencies in American classical music at the moment all have traditional roots. There is the new romanticism, which is the most overtly traditional. There is the world music movement, which uses non-Western traditions. And there is minimalism, which basically combines classical and pop traditions. All of these styles aim at accessibility.

MB: How do the megatrends play out in some of the other art forms?
DG: In painting, interestingly, one of the major trends has simply been the reaffirmation of paint as a medium—as opposed to construction or collage and various other forms of expression. There has also been a

revival of figurative and landscape painting as viable alternatives to conceptual art and abstraction.

In poetry, there has been a revival of form and narrative. One of the major literary trends in America has been the re-creation, entirely outside of official intellectual culture, of popular poetry—rap, cowboy poetry, poetry slams (oral competitions in which the audience selects the winner). Almost always, the new popular poetry employs meter and rhyme, even if it's a syncopated jazz rhythm as in rap, or, in cowboy poetry, a revitalization of the kind of stress meter of the border ballads. What you see is an attempt to reestablish a relationship between the past and present, to mix the modernist and traditional modes to create something contemporary.

In theater, the most highly regarded American playwright in midcareer is August Wilson. Wilson, essentially, has revived the Naturalist tradition that you see in Eugene O'Neill and Tennessee Williams.

MB: Take a play of Wilson's, like *The Piano Lesson*—tradition, family history?
DG: Exactly. It focuses on social issues. Yet more interesting, perhaps, in American theater is what a European would call *Gesamtkunstwerk*, or "together artwork"—the Wagnerian notion of a theatrical piece that involves multiple media. New operas and opera productions are more overtly literal because the subtitles make their dramatic and poetic elements accessible to the audience. Meanwhile, in theater, you have someone like Julie Taymor, who brings together elements of *commedia dell'arte*, music, and spectacle that one usually considered the province of opera or ballet. You have the notion of trying to fuse media—dance, opera, musical theater, spoken theater, even puppetry—into a total theatrical experience.

MB: Your own work is a mirror on this kind of fusion, isn't it?
DG: Yes. I'm a poet, and before I took office here, I was collaborating with dance and opera companies. There are dance companies in the United States that employ resident poets and use texts with music and dance.

MB: I'd like you to place your personal history—someone who worked in corporate America while nurturing a career as poet and critic and essayist—against the backdrop of the responsibilities in which you'll be engaged for the next phase of your working life. What does that renaissance duality—the worlds of business and culture—mean for the Endowment?
DG: If I am a renaissance man, it is only because it was the only way I could survive as a working artist. I wanted to be a poet, and I didn't want to have

a career at a university—which meant I had to find some other way of making a living. I'm a working-class kid from Los Angeles who spent fifteen years in corporate America working ten to twelve hours a day while writing nights and weekends. I did that to survive as a writer, but I also discovered that I was good at business. I learned things in the business world that I don't think writers necessarily learn in their art form, like teamwork—the fact that you can accomplish so much more if you can create a situation in which, by working together against common goals, everyone can succeed. Business also taught me the importance of understanding what you want to do in the long term, and working toward it. Ironically, when I left business, I promised myself that I would never work for a large corporation again.

MB: What spurs your cultural sensibility these days?
DG: I've long felt that one of the missing pieces in American culture is a new generation of public intellectuals—serious intellectuals, that is, who are not affiliated with universities. America needs more artist-intellectuals who can speak without condescension in a public idiom. We have had a distinguished tradition in this regard that goes back at least as far as Emerson and Poe, up through the extraordinary explosion of New York Jewish intellectuals in the 1930s and 1940s—which may have been the high point in the American tradition.

MB: When did the system change?
DG: In the decades after World War II, the university system in the United States grew so large in the midst of a prosperous society that academia employed most of the intellectuals. Increasingly, these men and women began to speak within a narrow discipline rather than to a diverse audience of intelligent readers. At the same time, the various media that once employed these public intellectuals grew smaller. One of the issues that most interests me is how to reinvent the media for public intellectual life. How can we create opportunities for artists and thinkers to address a general audience?

MB: How is American intellectual life currently changing?
DG: I believe America is currently seeing the creation of a new bohemia. The old bohemia, in American terms, was an urban neighborhood characterized by a concentration of artist-intellectuals who crossed disciplines and were organized without regard to social class. The poet E. E. Cummings, for example, also painted, wrote fiction, and did theater. Ezra Pound wrote music, criticism, and poetry. Wyndham Lewis was a superb painter as well

as a novelist. A lesser-known American writer I greatly admire, Weldon Kees, was a poet, a writer of fiction, an Abstract Expressionist, an art critic, and also an experimental filmmaker. Bohemia is based on the notions that the different arts reinforce and nourish one another, and that creativity happens best in a classless situation where talent and energy are the currencies.

Today, a new sort of bohemia is emerging—not as neighborhoods in big cities, but as a virtual community through technology. It moves through the Internet, inexpensive phone calls, the fax, overnight delivery, electronic publishing—and also through the creation of such temporary bohemias as writers' conferences, artists' colonies, and artists' schools, where people come together for a week or more. These communities are not defined by local geography but by cultural affinity.

In the broadest sense then, the question is, how do you create artistic and intellectual life outside the institutional support of the university? Not that the university is bad, but rather that a culture is richer when art is created in many places in a society and when academic and bohemian cultural life create a healthy dialectic.

Money Talks: A Conversation with Dana Gioia

Johanna Keller / 2003

From *Chamber Music* (October 2003): 27–30. Reprinted by permission of Johanna Keller.

Johanna Keller: Let's start *in medias res* with the question everyone asks—can the NEA survive? During the 1990s culture wars over Robert Mapplethorpe and other controversial artists, the NEA came close to extinction. Since then, funding has inched upward to $115.7 million currently (down from its peak of $150 million two decades ago). In your opening statement to the appropriations committee, you mentioned your goal to restore the public stature of the NEA. How will you go about this?

Dana Gioia: I want to change the public conversation about the NEA and the role of government funding in the arts. It's important to put those bad years in perspective—the NEA gave 120,000 grants of which eleven were controversial. Unfortunately, the NEA allowed itself to become reactive rather than proactive and became notorious for the missteps rather than the many successes. It has an impressive legacy. Over the past four decades, thanks in part to the NEA's funding, museums and orchestras expanded, and a national network of regional ballet, theater, and opera companies has been established. Think of the successes of the Spoleto Festival USA, the Sundance Film Festival, and the design for the Vietnam Memorial in Washington, DC, just to name three NEA-supported initiatives.

My aspiration is to be the second-best chairman after Nancy Hanks. I'd like to restore the NEA to the premiere position it enjoyed under her as one of the leading cultural institutions. I'm completely confident that things are going to work. In the past few months, we've already changed the perception of the NEA from being embattled to being confident and active.

JK: Arts education has suffered a lot in the past few years, going from bad to worse. Many nonprofit arts organizations have stepped in to help fill the gap. But their resources are limited.

DG: There is a crisis in education. The choir, the band, and all music instruction are being cut. Unless there is strong national leadership, we'll have a generation of Americans raised without elementary or secondary music education.

My feeling is that the NEA is the agency best suited to understand and address this issue. However, the solution is not just to throw money at the problem. No one wants a monolithic federal program, a onesize-fits-all. So what I'm working on is this. There are thousands of education programs in the field, some great and some not so good. We need to identify the superb model education programs and validate them. It would be like offering a Chinese menu: here are sixty programs with materials, everything ready to go, and here is substantial seed money to bring this into your schools. Music education has to be at the center of this: instrumental and choral training are communal arts.

JK: Your early musical training was your primary exposure to art, as I recall.

DG: Yes, I studied piano in the second grade, alto clarinet in the eighth grade (because I could rent it for practically nothing and I had no money). In high school, I played alto and bass clarinet, tenor sax, and piano in a jazz band.

JK: When you codirected the poetry conference at West Chester University (from which you resigned this year because of your new position), you and your codirector Mike Peich programmed a musical event each year. It has been an inspired combination of music and poetry.

DG: The arts are all related. We need to break down the disciplinary boundaries. It surprised me to find out that so many poets had never been to an art song recital. We presented some serious music each year—opera or art song. If you expose people to excellence, it's going to catch on.

JK: You have also played the role of music critic in the past few years, writing for *San Francisco Magazine*.

DG: In fact I was so pleased someone just gave me a bronze award for my criticism in the category of city magazines.

JK: How did the music criticism come about?

DG: The editor asked if I would write on literature, but I didn't want another literary gig. They didn't have a classical music critic, and I offered to write a column. I think the extra exposure helped the classical music world in the Bay Area, which is very distinguished. And it allowed me to write about a variety of things, from Philip Glass and Michael Tilson Thomas to Lou Harrison and Giuseppe Verdi. It kept me going to opera and concerts, and often I brought along my two sons. Now my son Teddy loves opera, and my younger son, Mike, was recently assigned a school project and came up with the idea all on his own of reporting on the San Francisco opera.

JK: You are a devoted opera buff—and we've had an ongoing argument for years about Donizetti and Bellini! But what about chamber music? Where is its place in the American arts landscape?

DG: In a very personal sense, chamber music is the heart of abstract art music. I've squandered a lot of money on CDs and if you ask me what I listen to in my personal time, it's opera and chamber music. For a lot of people, chamber music doesn't have the razzmatazz, but I have a deep affection for and familiarity with the standard chamber music repertory.

JK: Chamber Music America has always defined the art form broadly as "one on a part with no conductor." This ecumenical attitude welcomes in the standard classical configurations of all shapes as well as jazz ensembles and folk groups.

DG: And I agree with this definition. There are basically two great traditions: the one that plays written music and one that is improvisational. At the NEA, we don't differentiate. We fund symphonic, jazz, and chamber music in the same program.

What I like about chamber music particularly is its portability. You can bring a world-class string quartet or jazz ensemble to remote places at minimal expense. Some of the NEA programs have reflected that. For instance this year, we gave $250,000 to Chamber Music America for a four-year initiative to bring innovative chamber ensembles to underserved communities, which would not otherwise hear this music.

JK: As a poet and critic, you never shrank from controversy. But at the NEA, you are representing more than yourself and your own aesthetic. What is your strategy for navigating the rough shoals of the aesthetic politics of art?

DG: My goal as the NEA chair is to create a broad mainstream public consensus for funding arts and arts education. We are not going to accomplish this by creating a divisive or polarized message. My vision for the endowment is that artistic excellence and democratic reach are not incompatible. We need to be inclusive and democratic but also relentlessly committed to artistic excellence.

The danger in the arts world is that you trade excellence and outreach against each other. More art is not better art. Better art is better art. My conviction is that we must never condescend to the American citizen. We must bring the best art of each kind and make it widely available.

Do I sound too idealistic? Perhaps. But if one can deal with the politics of the poetry world, one can deal with anything.

"If Any Fire Endures Beyond Its Flame": An Interview with Dana Gioia

Robert Lance Snyder / 2006

From *Christianity and Literature* 56.1 (Fall 2006): 87–111. Reprinted by permission
of Robert Lance Snyder.

Robert Lance Snyder: In *God and the Imagination: On Poets, Poetry, and
the Ineffable* (2002), Paul Mariani quotes the concluding lines of Wallace
Stevens's "Final Soliloquy of the Interior Paramour":
[reads lines 10–15 of "Final Soliloquy of the Interior Paramour]
Mariani states that the passage indicates this poet's "self-humbling before
the Sublime," but he also points out how shiftily evasive is the modernist
qualifier "We say" in the line: "We say God and the imagination are one."
How do you construe Stevens here? Are God and the imagination one?
Dana Gioia: Stevens's splendid "Final Soliloquy of the Interior Paramour"
is one of his last poems, written after a lifetime of meditation on the problematic meaning of existence in a world without God. Stevens tried to posit
the human imagination as an adequate substitute for divinity. He developed
a complex and subtle worldview in which all values were created by the
human imagination.

On his deathbed, however, Stevens reportedly asked the hospital chap-
lain to baptize him into the Catholic Church. Once you start to ponder that
spiritual decision in the face of death—which is at once both extraordinary and commonplace—you notice that Stevens's late poetry is saturated
with his longing for faith in some transcendent reality. I would, therefore,
interpret Stevens's famous line in light of his own spiritual journey. It is
not the ironic utterance of an atheistic aesthete. It is an existential gesture of hope by a profoundly reflective man standing on the threshold of

death—a philosophical poet looking from the outermost border of reason across great vistas of mystery.

What did Stevens mean when he wrote, "God and the imagination are one"? As the Modernist most deeply engaged in the romantic tradition, Stevens saw the imagination as both a creative and cognitive force, but he must have suspected that the human mind was not an adequate substitute for God. At the end of his life, did he recognize the imagination as a pathway to divinity? I don't think that is too Wordsworthian a view of Stevens—if one is to take the account of his baptism seriously.

RLS: Elsewhere in his book Mariani cites Stevens's observation, "One of the visible movements of the modern imagination is the movement away from God." He then proposes that the statement "suggests its corollary—as the subtle master well knew—that one of the *invisible* movements of the modern imagination may therefore be *toward* that same God." What evidence do you see in contemporary poetry, and more broadly in the arts, that might corroborate this hypothesis?

DG: I find Mariani too hopeful here. Most of what modernity has accomplished has been the secularization of culture and society. Contemporary consumer culture not only makes the individual the center of values; it also caters to the lowest elements of human nature—greed, vanity, gluttony, lust, and sloth. Conformity, complacency, and creature comfort hardly represent the ideals of a great culture. They may be economically powerful motives, but they inhibit any genuine spiritual development. In a healthier culture the arts would stand in opposition to these forces of vulgarity, triviality, and excess, but in contemporary culture the arts increasingly reflect them. Our culture has largely lost its sense of the sacred.

RLS: Which poets writing today do you think of as being religious or, more specifically, Christian?

DG: Most poets consider themselves "spiritual" in some sense, but there are few poets today in America who write from a specifically religious perspective, and fewer poets still who write especially well from such conviction. The best religious poet now active in the US is surely Richard Wilbur, who may also be the best poet now writing in English. His work is deeply Christian, permeated by a spiritual joy unusual for modern religious poetry. He has no peers among American religious poets of his generation.

Equally distinguished is the poetry of Charles Causley, a Cornish writer who died in 2003. Idiosyncratic, visionary, and unabashedly musical, his verse combines mystery and immediacy in ways hard to describe. He somehow married the forms of traditional ballad and popular song with the sensibility of surrealism—half Bob Dylan, half William Blake. Then there is the dense, dour, and magnificent Geoffrey Hill. He is not to everyone's liking. He is a poet's poet. But Hill rewards study. Other interesting contemporary Christian poets include Marilyn Nelson, Jody Bottum, Kathleen Norris, and Robert B. Shaw. Then there is an interesting Christian poetry of doubt in writers such as X. J. Kennedy, Andrew Hudgins, and Mark Jarman.

RLS: Have these contemporaries influenced your own work or sense of poetic vocation?
DG: Not significantly. I adore Wilbur's poetry, but his sense of language and religious experience seems curiously distant from my own. He writes English of enormous originality, with an ear greatly influenced by French. His most direct impression on me has been a reminder that lyric perfection is still possible today. Causley has had a little more influence on me—mostly in his gift of mixing the mundane and the magical. Hill's work is remote from my own practice, though I admire the density of his language and the authenticity of his spiritual struggle. The Christian poets who influence me most deeply came from an earlier generation—T. S. Eliot and W. H. Auden. I read them both in early adolescence, and they have exerted a constant influence on both my poetry and criticism. In recent years they have also shaped my sense of verse theater and operatic drama. Auden is my favorite modern poet. Eliot is surely the greatest modern critic, though Auden's criticism is nearly as fine and much more compassionate.

RLS: What about the presence of Christianity in other arts?
DG: There has been a great revival of sacred music in the last twenty years. Two composers of genius I would recommend are Arvo Pärt and Morten Lauridsen. Pärt, an Estonian, is now a figure of international stature. He has fundamentally reinvented sacred music for our time, incorporating elements of Medieval, Renaissance, and Eastern Orthodox vocal writing in a minimalist but deeply expressive manner. His importance at the moment is hard to overstate. Lauridsen is less prolific, but his *Lux Aeterna* is one of the few true masterpieces of recent American music. Other significant sacred composers include Henri Gorecki, Osvaldo Golijov, Dave Brubeck, James MacMillan, Gavin Bryars, and John Tavener.

RLS: Let me ask you about two different notions of poetic language. Certain poets seem to discover through language a power of disclosure, unveiling, or unconcealment, whereas others appear to take that dimension of *aletheia* for granted. If this distinction makes sense, how do you conceive of explicitly Christian faith as functioning in the writing of poetry?

DG: This is an important distinction, but both attitudes toward language have poetic potential. The first poem in my third collection, *Interrogations at Noon*, is called "Words." The final poem is "Unsaid." Both poems discuss the limits of language—what can be said about the world and what cannot be expressed. Both are very Catholic poems, although there is nothing overtly religious in either work. The relationship between language and reality is a fundamental question for any serious poet. That relationship differs profoundly for a Christian and a postmodernist skeptic. My basic view of lyric poetry is both sacramental and metaphysical. It is not enough to show the surface of the world or the exterior of existence. It is also necessary to reveal, or at least suggest, what lies beyond the physical senses. The relation between the visible and the invisible is an inevitable theme for the poet.

RLS: In all your collections to date one detects a pervasively elegiac undertone related to what April Lindner, commenting specifically on *Daily Horoscope* (1986), describes as "themes of loss and displacement," a "sense of exile from essential things." Would you kindly reflect on whence that "sense of exile" arises?

DG: The notion of exile has always been present in my life. I was raised in an immigrant family in an immigrant neighborhood. There were Italians, Mexicans, Cubans, Filipinos, Vietnamese, Japanese, and Chinese around me every day. Almost everyone's family had been forced to leave its homeland by poverty or persecution. Even the native-born Americans had mostly fled the Dust Bowl. Everyone had come seeking a new life—at the cost of an old one. Exile was never an abstraction. It was our common background.

My adult life has been a series of exiles—from the place, family, language, and social class of my childhood. They were voluntary but nonetheless exacted a great personal cost. The first move was the shortest in physical distance but the biggest in impact. I left working-class Latin Los Angeles for the privileged environs of Stanford University. Since then I have lived in Vienna, Boston, New York, Rome, Minneapolis, San Francisco, and Washington, DC. My family and relatives have usually been far away. How could that not affect my poetry?

RLS: In *Daily Horoscope* motifs of loss have both personal and cultural dimensions. Poems such as "California Hills in August," "In Chandler Country," "Eastern Standard Time," and "In Cheever Country" chronicle your own transcontinental migration and memory-forged impression of "feeling out of place." Other poems in *Daily Horoscope*, however, seem to universalize the experience. I am thinking especially of "Waiting in the Airport," a poem that incisively dramatizes the anonymity of what Marc Augé has referred to as the "non-places" so predominant in "supermodernity." Do you consider such displacement as merely symptomatic of our age or as endemic to human existence?

DG: The themes of loss and displacement are central to lyric poetry. They arise naturally from the human condition—from the recognition of our mortality and the irresistible ravages of time. As Stevens observed, "Death is the mother of beauty." If we were all immortal, there would be no need for poetry. No need for any sort of art or philosophy. Look at how petty, vain, and self-indulgent the gods in Homer are—worse than a Hollywood brat pack.

I am a Latin Catholic—a mixture of Italian and Mexican. I was raised by working people who had been born in poverty and suffered enormous losses in their lives. My mother's childhood was a nightmare of deprivation. My family had a stoical view of existence. You bore your sorrows quietly. When I read Seneca and Marcus Aurelius in college, I felt an immediate sense of recognition. Their voices sounded like my Sicilian uncles and grandfather. Stoicism is the Mediterranean and Mexican worldview.

RLS: Is displacement, then, merely part of the human condition?

DG: Displacement has always been a factor in human existence, but historically it has mostly been an exceptional condition that arose out of dire circumstances like war, plague, famine, or natural disaster. Most people wanted lives of human continuity, deeply rooted in a particular place, clan, faith, and culture. Modernity and America have created situations where displacement is necessary for success and upward mobility. The average American moves every seven years—often thousands of miles. Children are raised hardly knowing their grandparents or extended family. Neighborhoods are torn down and rebuilt. Families split up. Old people retire in places where they have never lived. The mobility of our society has greatly contributed to our material prosperity, but it has enormous human cost.

RLS: I am curious about the voice deployed in the title sequence of *Daily Horoscope*. On the one hand, the omniscient speaker asserts that "nothing is hidden in the obvious / changes of the world," but shortly thereafter we are urged to "look toward earth" rather than the zodiac for evidence of "another world":

Look for smaller signs instead, the fine
disturbances of ordered things when suddenly
the rhythms of your expectation break
and in a moment's pause another world
reveals itself behind the ordinary.

How are we to reconcile these two divergent views?

DG: I try never to interpret my own poems for two reasons. First, if the poem is any good, it should convey its own meanings. If the poem isn't any good, then who cares what it means? Second, I feel that I have no monopoly on saying what a poem of mine means or doesn't mean. Having published a poem, I become only one of its readers. I may remember things about its origins, but I am also likely to be blind to other aspects of the final work. I may know what I intended but not what I actually created.

RLS: But will you nonetheless say something about the seemingly divergent views expressed in this poem?

DG: I don't want my poems to provide answers. I want them to pose questions worth pondering. I am glad that you have noticed that my poetic sequence "Daily Horoscope" presents contradictory points of view. The poem is a conversation—an argument in soliloquy. Virtually all of my poems proceed this way. I can't write more than a few lines without shifting the mood or arguing with myself. The structure of lyric poetry is dialectical. Isn't that how thoughts or emotions unfold—up and down, back and forth? Consciousness never moves in a straight line.

RLS: What appears to be at stake in "Daily Horoscope" is the idea of immanence, as well as the concept of *aletheia*. Would you agree?

DG: Yes, immanence and *aletheia* are motives in "Daily Horoscope," though I might have described these themes using different terms. Those are among the issues that the poem argues about.

RLS: I would like to invoke Robert McPhillips's canny judgment that your work is "marked by a distinctive poetic style of visionary realism in which memory imbues details of the ordinary world with a sensuous luminosity, making them at once seemingly tangible yet tantalizingly elusive, as if existing in a border region between time and eternity." Does the creative act itself effect for you an epiphanic passage through what McPhillips terms "a border region between time and eternity," or what in "Song from a Courtyard

Window" you refer to as "that strange place / that's always changing, constantly drifting / between the visible and invisible"?

DG: For me, most poems begin as a small epiphany. Some ordinary object or event makes a small rip in the fabric of time and place, and I sense something lying beyond. The passage you quoted earlier from "Daily Horoscope" could describe the beginning of my own creative process. For me, inspiration has always been involuntary—sudden, surprising, and often disturbing. The finished poem attempts to recreate that experience of awe and wonder.

RLS: *The Gods of Winter* (1991) is dedicated to the memory of your first son, Michael Jasper Gioia, who died in December 1987 at four months of age. In a 1992 interview you admitted that after this grievous loss you "saw poetry differently": "Writing took on a spiritual urgency I had never experienced before." Would you please elaborate?

DG: After my first son's death I fell into a terrible period of grief, which was prolonged and intensified by several other family deaths. I kept reaching for poetry but found that very little poetry, especially contemporary poetry, could reach me. It seemed mostly trivial, self-absorbed, and pointlessly clever. I needed poetry strong enough to bear the weight of my emotions. I stopped writing for nearly a year. When I started writing again, I put different demands on my work. I wanted my poems to concern things of consequence. I also wanted them to be true—not platitudinously true like so much political or devotional poetry but to work assiduously toward grasping difficult fundamental truths of human existence.

RLS: Did this experience change your sense of an audience?

DG: It broadened my sense of audience. I knew that I had to resist the constant pressure nowadays to write for a coterie audience of poets and critics. My poetry is deeply literary—carefully written, informed by tradition, deeply allusive—but I do not write for the literati. I try to engage any alert and intelligent reader or listener. I attempt to make the surface of the poem, whether of sound or story, as arresting as possible so that the other elements do their work on a subconscious or semi-conscious level.

RLS: In the opening section of *The Gods of Winter*, "All Souls,'" "Veterans' Cemetery," and "The Gods of Winter" explore the blank sense of nullity that overtakes one upon great personal tragedy, but the section closes with "Planting a Sequoia" and a poignant rite:

But today we kneel in the cold planting you, our native giant,
Defying the practical custom of our fathers,
Wrapping in your roots a lock of hair, a piece of an infant's birth cord,
All that remains above earth of a first-born son,
A few stray atoms brought back to the elements.

Is the writing of such an autobiographical poem, which memorializes the act of memorializing, part of what you understand Robert Hayden to mean by "love's austere and lonely offices," which you quote as an epigraph to your book's second section?

DG: "Planting a Sequoia" is one of the few entirely autobiographical poems I have ever published. Most of my poems are fictional to a greater or lesser degree. The events in "Planting a Sequoia" actually happened as they are described in the poem. I shaped the narrative only by dropping a few unnecessary details. I wanted the poem to commemorate my son as a living presence and not merely grieve over his death. What is an elegy except a poem that tries to "memorialize the act of memorializing"?

RLS: "Counting the Children," the first of two long narrative poems in *The Gods of Winter*, develops further your meditation on mortality. The poem presents Mr. Choi, an "accountant sent out by the State / To take an inventory of the house" in which a wealthy woman died intestate. Arriving at the dead woman's home, he is ushered into a bedroom containing shelf after shelf of discarded dolls that have been sorted by kind. Witnessing this silent horde, Mr. Choi wonders: "Was this where all lost childhoods go?" He then is terrified by a dream that bodes his daughter's death unless he can prevent ledger numbers from "slipping down the page, / Suddenly breaking up like Scrabble letters / Brushed into a box to end a game," and "find the sum." This nightmare section soon modulates toward a visionary conclusion. What was the source of this poem?

DG: "Counting the Children" is based on a real incident—a madwoman's private museum I happened to visit years ago in rural Alabama. ("Guide to the Other Gallery," another poem in *The Gods of Winter*, also describes this eerie museum.) At first I drafted a short lyric poem, but it didn't convey the overwhelming weirdness of the place. I decided to recast the experience in a narrative. I gradually created a story and a narrator in which to relocate the image of this woman's macabre, terrifying doll collection. The story took on a life of its own and expanded beyond my original idea. I was working on this poem when my son died. When I resumed writing many months later, I radically revised the poem and added the final section. I looked to Dante for both the form and the narrative structure. I had initially written about hell. I decided to continue the narrator's journey through purgatory and at least give a glimpse into paradise. I don't mention Dante anywhere in the poem, and the reader needn't catch the allusion to understand the story. But if you notice the Dantean correspondences, other layers of meaning become apparent.

RLS: Let me ask another question about "Counting the Children." Years later, having "learned the loneliness that we call love," Mr. Choi no longer worries—his daughter is now seven—but has a vision concerning which he asks:

> What if completion comes only in beginnings?
> The naked tree exploding into flower?
> And all our prim assumptions about time
> Prove wrong? What if we cannot read the future
> Because our destiny moves back in time,
> And only memory speaks prophetically?

I am intrigued by the conditional clause in the final lines. How is it that "our destiny moves back in time, / And only memory speaks prophetically?"
DG: We can understand human destiny as easily moving back in time as by moving forward. Isn't this a central truth for Christians? We look back toward the Redemption, which wouldn't have been possible without the Incarnation. And to answer why the Incarnation was necessary, we must go all the way back to the Garden of Eden. The future is the past unfolding into the present. The same thing is true of us biologically. We are the sum total of our genetic inheritance.

RLS: Your poetry is rarely overtly religious, yet there is a constant sense of spiritual struggle in your work. Why is it that religion becomes an explicit subject in only a few instances?
DG: With the exception of a few short poems like "The Burning Ladder," "The Litany," or "The Archbishop," my poems seldom have religion as their overt subject. My poems, however, are deeply theological. The most specifically Christian works I have written tend to be my long ones—the narrative poems in *The Gods of Winter* and *Daily Horoscope* as well as my two libretti, *Nosferatu* and *Tony Caruso's Final Broadcast.* If you read "The Room Upstairs," "Counting the Children," and "The Homecoming," you will see what I mean. The poems are not in any sense devotional, but they dramatize

aspects of the Christian mythos, especially the journey from despair to grace, from confusion to redemption. Or in the case of "The Homecoming" they portray evil—the choice of sin and the refusal of grace. "The Homecoming" is essentially a theological poem about the nature of evil and free will. As for my two libretti, they contain overtly religious elements and even incorporate portions of Catholic liturgy.

RLS: Why is it that the narrative rather than lyric form proves more conducive for you in composing poems that deal with such Christian mysteries as grace and our response to it?

DG: Lyric poetry need only convey the feelings and insights of an instant. It may hint at broader meaning, but there is no obligation to provide a fuller account of human existence. The poet needs only to create "a moment's monument." A single small insight expressed in memorably beautiful language is enough to sustain a lyric. A narrative poem, however, needs to depict something far more extensive—a significant action along with its motives and consequences. There is no way to convey the significance of an action, neither its motives nor consequences, without being alert to its morality.

As I began working on narrative poems thirty years ago, I faced a series of problems. The tradition of verse narrative was officially dead. Writers were supposed to use prose for telling stories. There were almost no viable contemporary models for poetic narrative. Modernism had mostly rejected narrative poetry in favor of the lyric mode. A few poets had attempted cumbersome book-length epic works—usually cluttered with cultural content and almost totally lacking in narrative momentum. Those poems didn't offer much help. I needed to find a style at once flexible enough to tell a story but still capable of poetic force and lyric resonance.

RLS: What solution did you bring to this dilemma?

DG: The essential thing was to tell a story of moral consequence. Something of life-or-death importance had to be at the heart of the poem. Otherwise it was hard to build a work of sufficient intensity that transformed narrative verse into real poetry. I gradually came to realize that the most compelling stories had some mythic resonance. As Geoffrey Hill wrote, "No bloodless myth will hold." Reaching that deep resonance inevitably brings out a writer's core beliefs. In my case that meant the mythos, signs, and symbols of Catholicism. None of this was conscious on my part. It just happened as the poems developed. The mythic elements inherently and unconsciously arose out of the subjects. You can't write about what is important without revealing your own values and beliefs.

RLS: Your work, especially the narrative poems, seems fascinated by the idea of evil. Needless to say, this is not a common theme in our relativistic age. Why does evil play such a significant role in your work?
DG: I believe in evil. I believe some people choose evil because it frees them from moral restraints and gives them power over others. In most cases, choosing evil is not a matter of ignorance. These people usually know that they are doing wrong, no matter how they later try to justify or excuse their actions. Neither Hitler nor Stalin would have become a just and liberal ruler had he taken a seminar on ethics. Their corruption was a matter of will. They chose cruelty and evil as a road to power. I am archaic enough to believe in sin. Why else do we need redemption? I deal with these questions most explicitly in "The Homecoming" and *Nosferatu*, but they haunt many of my poems.

RLS: Am I correct in seeing the devil, or at least demonic figures, present in your poems?
DG: With Marlowe, Milton, and Goethe among my favorite writers, how can I resist introducing the devil? Sometimes he is present quite explicitly as in *Nosferatu*. Sometimes he is there implicitly, as in the poem "Guide to the Other Gallery," which is narrated by a demon in hell. I think Flannery O'Connor showed me the compelling possibilities of introducing the demonic into the mundane, just as T. S. Eliot and Baudelaire demonstrate ways to bring hell into the modern city.

RLS: You seem to make the demonic figures in your work articulate and persuasive characters. Does this risk glorifying evil?
DG: It is an interesting poetic challenge to give voice to evil. Milton and Marlowe understood that you have to give the devil the best lines. How else can you make his unpleasant notions seductive? If you want to create the dramatic and narrative power to sustain a work that examines these moral issues seriously, you must create a real struggle between good and evil. Too many contemporary writers can't create plausible villains. Perhaps they are unwilling to recognize their own potential for evil, which is probably necessary to create some sense of authenticity. A poet must give the devil his due.

RLS: Between "Counting the Children" and "The Homecoming" in *The Gods of Winter* are ten very diverse poems. At least four ("News from Nineteen Eighty-Four," "The Silence of the Poets," "My Confessional Sestina," "Money") demonstrate a more public voice emerging in the collection. Your books seem consciously arranged in contrasting suites of poems. When so

many contemporary poets strive for books with a unitary style and thematics, why do you prefer such diversity?

DG: I consider variety an important poetic virtue. I generally find it dull to
read a book in which all of the poems are alike in mood, form, and style—
unless the book is an integrated sequence like Meredith's *Modern Love* or
Rilke's *Sonnets to Orpheus*. I especially prize formal and musical variety.
Since poets cannot choose their own imaginative obsessions—those tend
to be involuntary—they can at least strive for different forms of expression. One reason I so greatly admire W. H. Auden, Weldon Kees, Elizabeth
Bishop, and Philip Larkin is their enormous versatility. Despite the powerful
sense of individual personality in their work, their poems are so often surprising in shape, length, or mood.

I strive for diversity of expressive means. In *Interrogations at Noon* I
wrote poems in almost every English measure except syllabics. I even used
triple meters and strong-stress verse. No critic noticed, at least in print, but
I like to think many readers felt and enjoyed the variety unconsciously.

RLS: I want to ask about a shorter poem in *The Gods of Winter* that attests
to something far deeper than ordinary rapprochement with the immediacy
of grief. "On Approaching Forty" describes, in the first person, a midlife
transformation motivated by suffering and sorrow. The poem concludes:

> The years rise like a swarm around my shoulders.
> Nothing has been in vain. This is the work
> which all complete together and alone,
> the living and the dead, to penetrate
> the impenetrable world, down open roads,
> down mineshafts of discovery and loss,
> and learned from many loves or only one,
> from father down to son—till all is clear.
> And having said this, I can start out now,
> easy in the eternal company
> of all things living, of all things dead,
> to disappear in either dust or fire
> if any fire endures beyond its flame.

In these magnificent lines is registered, obviously, a new stage of spiritual
insight and acceptance, one whose expression reverberates with all kinds of

scriptural as well as literary echoes. Might I invite you to comment on this passage in light of my observation?

DG: "On Approaching Forty" is a translation from the Modernist Italian poet, Mario Luzi, so I did not invent the situation or imagery, though I freely recreated it in English. What drew me to Luzi's poem are exactly the qualities you mention. Luzi shares my admiration for T. S. Eliot, especially his use of liturgical language and sacramental symbolism. My translation is also alert to something deeply embedded in Luzi's poem—the Augustinian notion of the communion of saints that unites the living and the dead. "On Approaching Forty" is a deeply Catholic poem. I should have mentioned Luzi earlier in this interview when you asked about contemporary Christian poets. Luzi died at ninety in 2005. He was one of the great Christian poets of the past century—an Italian equivalent to T. S. Eliot.

RLS: Much of what I see as your poetic integrity in *The Gods of Winter* derives from its fifth and final section. Rather than extrapolating the recognition that "Nothing has been in vain" into a homiletic valediction, you instead trace the difficulty of endurance after an irreversible loss.

"Becoming a Redwood" harks back to "Planting a Sequoia" and posits that healing "change is possible," while "Maze without a Minotaur" speaks of the impulse to "raze each suffocating room" of remembrance. In this context "Speaking of Love" conveys powerfully the parental survivors' struggle to surmount the impasse of denial and silence, which "can become its own cliché," in the wake of "How little there seemed left to us." The work's final lines, however, are suffused with ambivalence, if not something darker:

> And so at last we speak again of love,
> Now that there is nothing left unsaid,
> Surrendering our voices to the past,
> Which has betrayed us. Each of us alone,
> With no words left to summon back our love.

Because this passage anticipates the coda of *Interrogations at Noon* (2001), would you address what it describes? Certainly more is involved here than what Emily Dickinson communicates in writing that "After great pain, a formal feeling comes."

DG: Once again I hesitate to offer interpretations of my own poems, especially when you so capably demonstrate your own understanding of them. Let me say only that "Speaking of Love" portrays the fragility of language—how easily it can be exhausted, cheapened, or misused. When language is debased, then all the essential things we need it for—love, learning, communication, ritual—are threatened and weakened. The poem also reflects the sad truth that we often despoil or destroy things without intending to.

As for my resisting the homiletic and valedictory impulses, I hope you are right. I want my poems to express ideas but not in any neat or modular way. I admire poetry that conveys hard wisdom won from and still inseparable from experience. The impulse of my poetry originates mostly in mystery, anxiety, and uncertainty. If something can be said unequivocally and unambiguously, I see no purpose or pleasure in saying it in poetry.

RLS: To what extent do you regard the trauma of loss and the experience of despair as essential to the life of faith?

DG: Some people may be lucky enough to lead lives untouched by pain, loss, struggle, and despair. I am not one of them. My life has been difficult—full of physical, emotional, and spiritual pain. Some people may also be able to learn life's lessons effortlessly. Not me. I have done many stupid and destructive things. I may be a quick study for intellectual things, but whatever real wisdom I possess came slowly and painfully. I would not have learned much about humility, compassion, patience, and generosity if suffering had not so often instructed me.

RLS: Do you consider suffering, then, a necessary element for spiritual growth?

DG: Isn't suffering central to Christianity? Certainly the Mediterranean Latin Catholicism I was raised in was based on the unavoidable but redemptive nature of suffering. The Stations of the Cross, the Rosary, and the Lives of the Saints were all meditations on the centrality of suffering to spiritual development. I was taught to bear pain quietly. If you accept suffering, it teaches you courage, patience, and compassion. If you refuse to bear life's inevitable pain, you become bitter, resentful, and self-pitying. Properly accepted, suffering is a gift.

RLS: Having already alluded to "Unsaid," with which *Interrogations at Noon* ends, I would like to pose a question about the book's opening poem, "Words," which begins by admitting:

The world does not need words. It articulates itself
in sunlight, leaves, and shadows. The stones on the path
are no less real for lying uncatalogued and uncounted.
The fluent leaves speak only the dialect of pure being.
The kiss is still fully itself though no words were spoken.

However, if language is superfluous to nature, which speaks "only the dialect of pure being," words clearly transform our experience of the world:

Yet the stones remain less real to those who cannot
name them, or read the mute syllables graven in silica.
To see a red stone is less than seeing it as jasper—
metamorphic quartz, cousin to the flint the Kiowa
carved as arrowheads. To name is to know and remember.

In a vein reminiscent of Gerard Manley Hopkins, you then close the poem by writing,

The daylight needs no praise, and so we praise it always—
greater than ourselves and all the airy words we summon.

How for you is poetry a vehicle of praise?

DG: Rilke once asserted that the role of the poet was to praise. When I first read his poem "Praise" as an undergraduate, I thought it was merely a literary pose. I have come to accept that I was wrong. The central purpose of poetry is to praise existence—without, of course, denying the harsher realities. Rilke understood that difficult spiritual truth, ultimately the same lesson that Job learned at the end of his suffering. Wisdom comes from seeing and accepting reality—from understanding the vast beauty of creation and our own humble place in it. If poetry is to be a vehicle of truth and discovery, and not merely a pleasing fiction, then it must see, love, and praise the world, not as we imagine it but as it truly is.

I am not saying that poetry must be optimistic or upbeat. Absolutely not! Nothing depresses me more in poetry than "uplift." Poetry must deal with suffering, loss, despair, and death, but it needs to see them in the broadest context as the necessary preconditions of enlightenment, grace, and redemption. How can we understand the good without experiencing evil or appreciate joy without first knowing pain? I have sat by the deathbeds of both my parents and watched them die. I have held the dead body of my little son in my arms. That is how I learned to appreciate the unimaginably great gift of being alive.

RLS: The concept of praise also emerges in "The Litany." If I am correct in regarding the collection overall as examining, from a Dantean midpoint or figurative "noon" in life, the specious illusions we weave about our lives, then "The Litany" strikes me as profoundly central to the work as a whole.

DG: "The Litany" is one of the central poems in *Interrogations at Noon*. It is also probably the most difficult poem in the book. It is easy to misunderstand if you focus on any one part out of context. The poem needs to be read as a progressive journey or argument in which each part rejects or qualifies what came before.

RLS: What I wish to ask concerning this poem requires an explanatory prologue. "The Litany" begins by announcing that it will be an inventory:

> This is a litany of lost things,
> a canon of possessions dispossessed,
> a photograph, an old address, a key.
> It is a list of words to memorize
> or to forget—of *amo, amas, amat,*
> the conjugations of a dead tongue
> in which the final sentence has been spoken.

By the third stanza these tropes of our attachment to "lost things" belonging to a memorialized past give way to the persona's barren offering of "a prayer to unbelief," his resistance to spiritual divestiture making even the Crucifixion appear a blasphemous parody of the sacrifice necessary for atonement:

> It is the smile of a stone Madonna
> and the silent fury of the consecrated wine,
> a benediction on the death of a young god,
> brave and beautiful, rotting on a tree.

A turn occurs, however, in the ensuing *memento mori*. With its mandate to savor "the bitterness of earth and ashes" the poem takes us beyond captivity by "time's / illusions" toward a vision of "pure paradox"—the apprehension of "our life" as a "shattered river rising as it falls." Reading this incantatory poem, I cannot help but think of Eliot's *Four Quartets*, the second movement of which ("East Coker") proclaims "the way of dispossession," associated with the apophatic tradition within Christianity, as the path to a redemptive understanding of human existence. Would you grant this suggestion of a parallel? My question stems in part from your fourth stanza's declaration that "This is a prayer to praise what we become, / 'Dust thou art, to dust thou shalt return.'"

DG: "The Litany" may parallel Eliot's "East Coker" in some respects, but I did not have *Four Quartets* in mind when I wrote the poem. What you are sensing is our common roots in Catholic ritual and Christian mysticism. As for the apophatic tradition, one of the most effective means of lyric poetry is apophasis. This is especially true of religious poetry, which cannot literally show the very subjects it purports to present. Likewise all lyric poetry is in some sense a *memento mori* since its intensity depends on a sense of our mortality and the irreversible flow of time.

I began sketching out "The Litany" at the same time I wrote "Planting a Sequoia," but I had trouble getting beyond the opening—and a few scattered lines. I couldn't figure out the shape the poem needed to take. I knew that to succeed the poem had to create a powerful musical spell, but the melody kept eluding me. I couldn't even decide whether the poem should be in meter or free verse. I kept jotting down lines and playing with stanza patterns for several years before I figured out the right rhythm for the lines and images. Once I finally hammered out the opening stanza, the rest of the poem came quickly. Something that "The Litany" does borrow from Eliot is a technical element from his early work in *vers libre*—the intricate maneuvers of a poem moving around "the ghost of a meter," slipping in and out of form.

RLS: Another poem in *Interrogations at Noon*, "A California Requiem," seems closely linked to "The Litany." "A California Requiem" begins with the speaker's surveying a contemporary West Coast cemetery:

I walked among the equidistant graves
New planted in the irrigated lawn.
The square, trim headstones quietly declared
The impotence of grief against the sun.
There were no outward signs of human loss.
No granite angel wept beside the lane.
No bending willow broke the once-rough ground
Now graded to a geometric plane.

My blessed California, you are so wise.
You render death abstract, efficient, clean.
Your afterlife is only real estate,
And in his kingdom Death must stay unseen.

The speaker then hears the whispered confession of those interred there. What the chorus of ghostly voices intones is a shared failure. Those who "claimed the earth but did not hear her claim" while alive seek now to earn "Forgiveness from the lives we dispossessed." Disinherited by what they have despoiled and cannot even name, these self-portrayed "shadows" that "the bright noon erases" can only shrink back into the void they created by shunning the fact of mortality. Could you say something about this striking poem?

DG: There was a tradition in Medieval and Renaissance literature of the vision poem, often an allegorical sort of narrative in which the protagonist is given a supernatural vision. The vision could be of the past, the future, the afterlife, or something else not normally open to human scrutiny. *The Vision Concerning Piers Plowman* and Dante's *Commedia* are two famous examples of this religious literary genre. "A California Requiem" seeks to rehabilitate this venerable but neglected genre in a contemporary setting.

Obviously the vision presented in "A California Requiem" is rooted in the ecological disaster of my native state, but it also borrows a moral premise from Dante. Early in *Inferno* Dante depicts vacillating crowds of souls in Limbo—the lost souls—who were neither good nor bad. Even hell won't let them enter. I borrowed this curious theological notion for my poem. These souls had never been truly alive, and so they can't truly die. It's pure heresy, I know, but it opens up certain poetic possibilities. I was disappointed that the Vatican recently dismissed the concept of Limbo. I don't dispute their theology, but I felt Limbo was a place I actually had seen.

RLS: In contrast to the stark outlook of "A California Requiem," "The Lost Garden" limns an alternative reaction to "The Litany." If "the old estate" of prelapsarian innocence has been forfeited, a compensatory principle is still operative:

The trick is making memory a blessing,
To learn by loss subtraction of desire,
Of wanting nothing more than what has been,
To know the past forever lost, yet seeing
Behind the wall a garden still in blossom.

How is this "trick" of "making memory a blessing" actually wrought in the living of one's life? Extending the query further, is it also something that for you occurs during, or perhaps accrues from, the process of writing poetry? **DG:** The trick of making memory a blessing is twofold. First, one needs to recognize that everything that happens in life, even the hardest things, when seen from the proper perspective is a gift. Every loss bestows its blessing, if one is humble or patient enough to receive it. Second, memory and imagination constitute our human means of conquering time and mortality. Memory allows one to revisit lost places and lost people. If one can resist the powerful urge to regret and mourn—and there is a period of grief after any deep loss when such resistance is impossible—then one can recapture an enormous amount of the past. "What thou lovest well remains," as Ezra Pound said, and "the rest is dross." I often converse with the dead.

RLS: Many of your poems in *Interrogations at Noon* are adaptations, variations, or imitations of other writers, among them Rainer Maria Rilke ("Entrance"), Constantine Cavafy ("After a Line by Cavafy"), Seneca ("Descent to the Underworld" and "Juno Plots Her Revenge"), and Valerio Magrelli ("Homage to Valerio Magrelli"). With the sole exception of Weldon Kees ("Lives of the Great Composers") in *Daily Horoscope*, however, the same is not true for your earlier two collections. Is this simply a reflection of the fact that throughout the 1990s you were committed to various other projects, including translations of Seneca's *The Madness of Hercules* and Eugenio Montale's *Mottetti* and composition of the libretto for Alva Henderson's opera *Nosferatu*? Or might this interest in translation and adaptation suggest that you increasingly have come to recognize that your creative voice has been inflected by that of others? **DG:** Although my third volume contained more translations than the earlier books, it wasn't as radical a change as you suggest. *The Gods of Winter* contained versions of Rilke, Mario Luzi, and Nina Cassian. I included these particular translations because I felt that each of the three poems—from German, Italian, and Romanian—had been successfully transformed into an English-language poem with a theme and style almost indistinguishable from my own. There were no translations in *Daily Horoscope*, but the book did include poems that directly drew from other literary texts. "In Chandler Country" borrows the voice of the detective Philip Marlowe from Raymond Chandler. "In Cheever Country" is an homage to the landscape and milieu of John Cheever. "My Secret Life" is a commentary on the Victorian memoir of that title. These poems all appropriated or argued with literary works, though their sources were all prose works. I simply used translation and allusion more overtly in *Interrogations at Noon* than in earlier books. In writing this way, I am not merely acknowledging literary sources but calling attention to the nature of poetry.

RLS: How do these translations and adaptations call attention to the nature of poetry?

DG: All poetry achieves its particular resonance by playing off the reader's experience with tradition. By "tradition" I don't mean any monolithic literary canon but rather the reader's total previous engagement with all sorts of literary texts—from nursery rhymes and popular songs to classic poems and novels. Those works set up a network of expectations and associations that provide contrasts and comparisons. Whether in its form or genre, subject or rhetoric, image or diction, the new poem engages and exploits the reader's experience. A strong poem compels the reader to readjust his or her interior sense of things to make room for this new account. Poems exist as conversations that simultaneously engage the reader, the language, and the literary past. Literary theorists call this type of communication "intertextuality." I find that a useful and commonsensical notion. All literature works this way, but poems do it with special intensity and compression. There is a special effect when an author openly acknowledges another text. It also lets the reader into your confidence as in "After a Line by Cavafy" or "In Cheever Country." Allusion is a powerful effect, though it can easily be misused. Eliot reveled in the possibilities of allusion. Look at "Marina" or, better yet, *The Waste Land*, which even includes prose notes. The poetic possibilities opened up by allusion are simply too enticing to ignore.

RLS: Having just finished Norman Sherry's three-volume biography of Graham Greene, I was moved by his account of how this prominent Catholic novelist, in the final decades of his long life from 1904 to 1991, found that he had lost his capacity for belief, all the while doubting his unbelief, yet retained an unwavering faith. If we assume that "belief" in Greene's case refers to theological propositions, whereas "faith" denotes an underlying expectancy of assurance, would you say that his spiritual journey may be paradigmatic of other "religious" writers in the last century?

DG: I am glad that you mentioned Greene. Not only is he a writer whom I admire enormously, but he also is part of a literary tradition that has been essential to my own poetic development. Greene belonged to the great tradition of modern British and Northern Irish Catholic novelists, which includes Evelyn Waugh, Muriel Spark, Anthony Burgess, and Brian Moore. I would like to list James Joyce, who is another personal favorite, but as an Irishman he is a slightly different case. I have been reading and rereading these extraordinary novelists since I was a teenager. What gives their writing such spiritual power—one might even say ferocity, especially among the comic novelists—is that they were Roman Catholic in a nation in which Catholics were a downscale and marginal minority. These writers took for granted they were addressing an audience that would treat their beliefs with condescension at best and at worst scorn. That isn't bad training for an American Catholic writer today.

RLS: What religious characteristics in their work impressed you?
DG: Their novels are not often religious in any conventional sense, but their books usually play out deep theological issues—often in violent and disturbing ways. (Among American Catholic writers only Flannery O'Connor matches their ferocity of vision.) It may seem odd for a poet to acknowledge prose writers as central models, but for a Catholic writer they are the best modern guides, except Eliot and Auden. Novels such as *The Power and the Glory, The End of the Affair, A Clockwork Orange, Nothing Like the Sun, Memento Mori, The Prime of Miss Jean Brodie, Black Robe, A Cold Heaven, Decline and Fall,* and *A Handful of Dust* shaped my imagination as much as anything in contemporary American poetry. One of the many things these books taught me was to present the terrible human struggle of sin, despair, grace, and redemption—not to preach about the fruits of faith and salvation.

RLS: What role has belief *or* faith played in your career as a poet? Has doubt also been essential to sustaining either one or the other?
DG: I was raised by Italian and Mexican Catholics and attended Catholic schools for twelve years. I attended daily Mass and studied religion, church history, and theology. I learned Church Latin before Classical Latin and can still read the Latin Bible with ease. Catholicism is in my DNA—my ethnicity and my upbringing. I refuse to join the ranks of ex-Catholics, who so slavishly follow intellectual fashion as a part of upward mobility. My sympathies are with the poor and the faithful—the people who raised me. No genteel Ivy League agnostic is going to shame me into renouncing my working-class Latin identity and heritage.

All of this is only to say that every poem I have ever written reflects my Catholic worldview, especially my sense of struggle in living with my own imperfections in a fallen world. Besieged by failure and despair, tempered by humility and suffering, I hope to remain alert to God's presence in the world.

RLS: Thank you for your candid responses throughout this interview, and all best wishes in your future endeavors.

A Public Catholic: An Interview with 2010 Laetare Medalist Dana Gioia

Cynthia L. Haven / 2010

From *Commonwealmagazine.org* (May 13, 2010). © Commonweal Foundation, reprinted with permission. For more information, visit www.commonwealmagazine.org.

Cynthia Haven: In commending you for this year's Laetare Medal, Fr. John Jenkins, president of the University of Notre Dame, said you have "given vivid witness to the mutual flourishing of faith and culture." You have spoken in the past about the need for a Catholic culture—what exactly do you have in mind?

Dana Gioia: What I envision is quite simple. In the diverse social mix of the United States, there would be a recognizable Catholic element in the arts and culture. It wouldn't be a unified dogmatic block, but a vibrant and varied range of recognizable Catholic activity—rather like Jewish cultural life. This culture would not be the product of the church but of the laity.

CH: You have said that anti-Catholicism remains the only acceptable prejudice among intellectuals in America today. Has the situation improved in recent years?

DG: No, it has grown worse. Much worse. There has been a revival of militant atheism, which views all religion as a hindrance to social progress. This movement hates Catholicism in particular because of its size, authority, and continuity. In many circles now, anti-Catholicism isn't considered bigotry, but a virtue.

CH: You have commented that today's Catholic writers see their religion "as a private concern rather than a public identity."

DG: Catholic writers and artists have lost any sense of a meaningful cultural community. There is, of course, a meaningful spiritual community, but how do they connect it to their artistic vocations? They rightly feel as if they struggle in isolation without either the support or attention that a vital subculture should afford. Even unfavorable attention would indicate that what they are doing is important enough to argue about.

For most artists and intellectuals, their only havens are the institutions of secular culture, which have grown increasingly anti-Catholic in recent years. This situation compels most Catholic artists and intellectuals either to shed or disguise their core religious identities.

CH: In light of this prejudice, what do writers, artists, and humanists stand to gain from what you have called a "Catholic identity"?

DG: They would gain authenticity, integrity, continuity, and community. Catholicism is not only a religious identity, it is also a rich range of cultural and ethnic identities—Italian, Polish, Mexican, Irish, Haitian, Vietnamese, Austrian, and so on. Catholicism is universal without being uniform. I have regularly attended services in Mexican, Polish, and Italian parishes over the years, and each had a different sort of vibrancy.

American Catholicism needs to resist the suburbanization of consumer culture. Keeping in touch with one's ethnic and cultural roots is an essential form of resistance to social homogenization.

CH: Such a culture used to exist—at least much more than it does today. What happened?

DG: Affluence, assimilation, and social ambition—all aided and abetted by the church's general indifference to the arts and the secular culture's distaste for Christianity. The situation is not entirely new. The American Catholic Church has always been an immigrant church populated by the working poor. Consequently, it has never had much social cachet for the upwardly mobile. Meanwhile, the church has never had much use for artistic culture, which is a serious mistake since great art, especially sacred art, speaks across cultures and classes.

CH: How can individuals foster this culture?

DG: Catholics need to be better stewards of their cultural and intellectual traditions. Too often, they seem either ignorant or apologetic about their own legacy. Catholics also feel they need to cultivate humility and charity at the expense of culture, which is seen as a dispensable luxury. I think many

Catholics feel especially virtuous for excluding the arts—as if having better music at services might be a luxurious indulgence that would morally undermine their commitments to homeless shelters and food kitchens. The poor do not live by bread alone.

CH: Speaking of your own resonance with this culture: A recent article by Janet McCann, "Dana Gioia: A Contemporary Metaphysics," described you as having a "sacramental imagination," where heaven and earth are "closely bound to this world."

DG: Being raised Catholic makes you deeply aware of symbols. That isn't bad training for a poet. Catholicism also trains you to ponder the mysterious relationship between the visible and the invisible aspects of the world.

CH: Your poems sometimes presuppose the Christian, if not Catholic, conviction that history has a point, and is not merely a random succession of moments in some Zen-like eternal now—I think of "Song for the End of Time," "The End," "The Stars Now Rearrange Themselves," "Pentecost," "The Litany," "California Requiem," the list goes on.

DG: I am reluctant to gloss the meanings of my poems. If they don't speak for themselves, no amount of commentary will redeem them. But let me make one general comment: Art craves teleology. It's not necessarily a theological point. Hegel and Marx say it as clearly as Augustine and Aquinas. Unless one wants to write only impressionistic miniatures, poems need to go somewhere. Human nature also looks for patterns and meaning. If poetry is language charged with meaning to the utmost possible degree, then you need to charge it with real meanings large and small. I like to connect small and large things in my poetry, especially to link the mundane and the mysterious.

CH: One of the themes of *Interrogations at Noon* is the limits of words to reach reality. I tend to agree with your conclusion in "Words": "To name is to know and remember." But the same volume ends with "Unsaid": "the tongue-tied aches / Of unacknowledged love are no less real / For having passed unsaid." Is the jury still out for you on the relationship of words to reality, and our perception of it?

DG: Words are an imperfect medium through which to understand and express the world. But they are also the best medium we possess as long as we don't expect them to express everything. Language is probably the greatest achievement of humanity—how can a poet think otherwise?—but reality is greater. Language is vastly expressive, but we should also not forget the eloquence and mysteries of silence—be it human or nonhuman.

CH: In a number of poems—*Nosferatu* and "My Secret Life," for example—you write not only about the risk of losing love, but of the risks of love distorted. In "California Requiem," a powerful voice-from-the-dead laments environmental plunder: "What we possessed we always chose to kill." You wrote of Breton in "Elegy with Surrealist Proverbs as Refrain": "'Better to die of love / than love without regret.' And those who loved him / soon learned regret." Love lost, love distorted—is this Dantesque theme the essence of the darkness that hovers on the edge of your poems?

DG: I don't think I can briefly answer that large and interesting question, but let me go to the heart of it: Our vices and our virtues are related. Both arise from the same core human energies and impulses. Love, in particular, is such a powerful and dynamic emotion that it can lead us to heaven or hell.

The object of love is crucial. Love and desire the wrong thing, and it can corrupt you. The challenges, responsibilities, dangers, and failures of love are probably the things I've written about the most, though they aren't themes that today's critics find interesting. But that's okay. Readers understand.

CH: When did you begin writing poetry?

DG: The first poem I ever wrote was in fourth grade. We had a class contest to write a poem about our guardian angel. Manny Di Benedetto won first place, but I could tell his mother had helped him. A little later, like everyone else, I wrote a few self-pitying poems in high school. At that point music was my chief passion, and I intended to be a composer. By the age of twenty, I discovered that poetry was what most excited me. It's really not as if I chose poetry. Poetry chose me. I simply recognized my vocation. It took years of study and practice to write anything good, but the hard labor of mastering the craft gave me a great pleasure.

CH: How has your Washington post as National Endowment for the Arts chairman affected your poetry—besides obviously limiting your time to write it?

DG: Not writing was the essential thing. It's not an altogether bad thing for a poet to stop writing for a while when the rest of life becomes engrossing. The unconscious works all the time. The poems will come eventually and probably be better for the wait. There is a silly pressure on American poets to publish constantly. So much new poetry seems dilute and underpowered.

Running the Arts Endowment for six years also reminded me of the larger purposes of art—both for individuals and communities—I never thought deeply about art's communal role before coming to Washington. At the Arts Endowment, I had a very simple goal—to bring the best art and arts education to the broadest audience possible. I tried, in other words, to be true to both art and democracy.

CH: Any indication of what your new poems will look like, how they have changed?

DG: Poetic inspiration is an involuntary process. I never know what a new poem will look like till it arrives, and I'm often astonished by what appears.

I just finished a long narrative poem—a sort of short story in verse. I would never have predicted writing a psychological ghost story dealing with themes of wealth, ambition, and destructive sexual attraction. But one day the first three lines popped into my head, and suddenly the story and the characters were almost fully visible.

What will my future poems look like? Who knows! I just hope that poems keep coming. Poetry is a more mysterious art than writing workshops would lead us to believe.

CH: Given last year's events at Notre Dame, with President Barack Obama being awarded an honorary degree and Mary Ann Glendon declining the Laetare Medal, do you feel under more pressure or scrutiny this year?

DG: I always feel under scrutiny. It's a sort of psychological disability. And no occasion brings out more anxiety than speaking at a large college commencement. But these worries have nothing to do with Barack Obama and Mary Ann Glendon.

The problem is practical: How does one avoid being pompous and boring and manage to say something of value while addressing a large, restless audience which has other things on its mind?

The only harder gig is talking about poetry to sixth graders.

An Interview with Dana Gioia

Andrew McFadyen-Ketchum / 2010

From *Poem of the Week.org* (August 23, 2010). Reprinted by permission
of Andrew McFadyen-Ketchum.

PRAYER

Echo of the clocktower, footstep
in the alleyway, sweep
of the wind sifting the leaves.

Jeweller of the spiderweb, connoisseur
of autumn's opulence, blade of lightning
harvesting the sky.

Keeper of the small gate, choreographer
of entrances and exits, midnight
whisper traveling the wires.

Seducer, healer, deity or thief,
I will see you soon enough—
in the shadow of the rainfall,

in the brief violet darkening a sunset—
but until then I pray watch over him
as a mountain guards its covert ore

and the harsh falcon its flightless young.

Andrew McFadyen-Ketchum: The first three stanzas of "Prayer" are a fragmentary list of metaphors for God, or so I assume, disguised as sentences. It seems that sentence fragments and lists are used quite often in lyric poems, which this poem most certainly is. Why do you think this is a device often used by lyric poems and why, in this instance, did you feel compelled to open "Prayer" in this way?

Dana Gioia: I consider "Prayer" an unusual poem in tone, shape, and texture. It was certainly different from my own earlier work. I rather like the way I suspended both the sense and syntax for several stanzas. But, of course, poets admire their own work. Vanity is our occupational vice.

As for lists, they have always been a major poetic technique from Homer's catalogue of ships to Whitman and Borges. Why? Surely because there are so many things in the world that poets want to put into poems.

Sentence fragments are also natural for poetry. People tend to speak in sentence fragments and phrases rather than complete sentences. Poetry imitates and heightens aspects of speech. Only a grammarian should be troubled by what is granted by poetic license.

AMK: At first these metaphors seem built on imagination but, after a second look, it's clear that sound is what drives them. There's the "Echo of the clocktower" with its repeating *O*-sounds, the "Jeweler of the spiderweb, connoisseur" with its *R*s, *W*s and *I*s, and "Seducer, healer, deity or thief" with the opening short-*E* turned long. I think that without this use of sound, we might get tired of this opening and our attention would wane. Is all this music-making something that came via revision or did it come more naturally?

DG: The poem began as words and phrases that felt fraught with both sound and sense. Revising sharpened it a bit, but the auditory sense was always inseparable from the emotional sense. In poetry music makes meaning. Otherwise it's just perfunctory prose.

AMK: Can you talk about music more generally? Why is it important for a poem and what are you willing to sacrifice in your work for the sake of it?

DG: If a poet is doing a good job, he or she never sacrifices anything for music. Verbal music is what gives force and cadence to a poem. A poem casts a spell or it isn't much of a poem. The poems that first moved me did so by their sound. I was enchanted by their music, not by their paraphrasable meaning. Sometimes I didn't even understand the sense of the poem, but I experienced something deep and genuine almost entirely from the sound and images. Poetic meaning is not primarily analytical and abstract; it is physical, sensory, and emotive.

For me, poems begin as resonant first lines or phrases, not as ideas. If I have a tune, then I can finish the poem. Otherwise the words just sit mutely on the page.

AMK: You utilize the em dash in the fourth and fifth stanzas, which is typically used to set apart a "violent disruption" in the sentence, but this isn't a terribly violent disruption at all. I'm not sure the poem changes much if you replace them with commas, and I can see ways in which you could use fragments as in the stanzas before to get these lines into the poem with equal attention. Then again, there's a part of me that takes those em dashes as a signal to change my tone when I read and, with the repetition of "in the," a little more quickly. Is the em dash used here as a sort of stage direction to the reader? Am I overanalyzing?

DG: I do love dashes. They provide a small rhythmic pause and clear out a small semantic space without chopping up the poem. Maybe that's why Emily Dickinson loved them so much. I've never thought of the double dash as violently disruptive. It seems a mark of many moods.

AMK: There's a mysterious "him" that enters in the third to last line, whom, it seems, the speaker's prayer is for. I have no problem with this because prayers typically are for either the self or someone else, but I can also imagine a workshop of poets all clamoring over the unidentified "he" showing up so close to the end of the poem. Is this a risk you're taking or is such criticism simply misplaced?

DG: I'm sure you are right about how a poetry workshop might react to the end of "Prayer." But who cares what a workshop would think? Poems are not written for committees. Our lives are full of mystery. A poem should not be afraid to embrace a little of it. Mystery is not the same as obscurity or muddle. A mystery is a truth we feel but don't fully understand—exactly the sort of meaning poetry expresses best.

In isolation, the *him* in "Prayer" may seem mysterious, which I don't mind since it lets the reader project his or her own life into the poem. But in its original context, as the first poem in *The Gods of Winter*, a book dedicated to the memory of my first son, the identity of the *him* should be less puzzling.

AMK: I'm aware of the dangers of applying a writer's biography to that of the speaker in her/his poetry. What's your take on this issue of speaker/author in contemporary poetry?

DG: A poet necessarily creates out of his or her own life experience. Being rooted in that way isn't bad. It gives a writer authority through authenticity. The problem is when the poet can't move beyond autobiography. I believe that the best poetry is usually personal without being strictly autobiographical. There is a sense of a real human being writing, but the poet isn't simply talking about himself or herself, but finds a way to address and engage the reader. Usually the engagement is implicit rather than explicit, but the poem is about *us*, not about *me*.

AMK: Almost every poem in *The Gods of Winter* starts with a certain number of lines per stanza and maintains that number throughout. Why does this matter to you?
DG: I write best when there is some resistance. That is especially true with free verse. If I work in five-line stanzas, I find myself compressing eight or nine lines into five in ways that make the final lines richer and more evocative. There is also aesthetic pleasure in symmetry, as long as it also contains elements of variety and surprise.

AMK: Why, with that in mind, does "Prayer," the first poem in the book, end with that dangling one-line stanza?
DG: Why not end with a single line? It seems conclusive. And it adds an element of disruptive energy and surprise. I appreciate your minute attention to the formal and stylistic elements of my poems. I take these matters seriously. I ponder formal elements in my poems. I rarely use traditional fixed forms. I tend to experiment in some way and like to think I have a reason for everything I do. But it feels too self-regarding to talk about at such length. I don't want to spend time justifying the style of my poems. Either the poems speak compellingly for themselves or no amount of justification on my part will redeem them.

AMK: "Planting a Sequoia" is a similarly lyric poem to "Prayer," but the line breaks and the resulting shape of the poem is completely different, "Prayer" being made up of short tercets (save for the last line) and "Planting a Sequoia" of quintets of varying length. What's the guiding principle behind these line breaks?

Planting a Sequoia

All afternoon my brothers and I have worked in the orchard,
Digging this hole, laying you into it, carefully packing the soil.

Rain blackened the horizon, but cold winds kept it over the Pacific,
And the sky above us stayed the dull gray
Of an old year coming to an end.

In Sicily a father plants a tree to celebrate his first son's birth—
An olive or a fig tree—a sign that the earth has one more life to bear.
I would have done the same, proudly laying new stock into my father's orchard,
A green sapling rising among the twisted apple boughs,
A promise of new fruit in other autumns.

But today we kneel in the cold planting you, our native giant,
Defying the practical custom of our fathers,
Wrapping in your roots a lock of hair, a piece of an infant's birth cord,
All that remains above earth of a first-born son,
A few stray atoms brought back to the elements.

We will give you what we can—our labor and our soil,
Water drawn from the earth when the skies fail,
Nights scented with the ocean fog, days softened by the circuit of bees.
We plant you in the corner of the grove, bathed in western light,
A slender shoot against the sunset.

And when our family is no more, all of his unborn brothers dead,
Every niece and nephew scattered, the house torn down,
His mother's beauty ashes in the air,
I want you to stand among strangers, all young and ephemeral to you,
Silently keeping the secret of your birth.

DG: The only guiding principles for line breaks are music and meaning. Not all tunes fall into the same rhythm. I hate to write in the same form or meter too often. I like variety. It allows one to go after different moods, effects, ideas. I am puzzled that so many poets fall habitually into one form or rhythm and never experiment. I usually find a book dull if all the poems are written in the same shape and style. I prefer variety and surprise.

AMK: I love how you personify the earth in the line "a sign the earth has one more life to bear." It creates this notion that the earth is, in fact, bearing a life when we plant something in it and, perhaps more importantly, that it does have a limit to what it can nourish. Is this poem an environmental poem in a way?

DG: I come from peasant stock. We look to the earth to feed us. The redwood described in that poem is a real tree planted in my parents' orchard with a small working farm around it. All of my poems about nature reflect deeply held environmental concerns. This isn't politics. It's common sense. We depend on the earth to live. We need to keep it livable. Nowhere are these issues more urgent than in California, a great despoiled paradise.

AMK: Teach us a little bit about personification as an element of imagination. When is it well placed; when is it not?
DG: There are no set rules for such things. Personification works when we feel it works. A poet can do everything perfectly well, and the poem remains stillborn. Another writer does something odd and seemingly incorrect, and it succeeds. This is the mystery of art.

Read Thomas Hardy. He is often awkward and heavy-handed, and yet he so often breaks your heart. Sometimes the very imperfections endow his poems with a sincerity and spontaneity that adds to their power. So I guess the best advice is to be a genius. That seems to work.

AMK: What about metaphor? "Planting a Sequoia" is largely void of metaphor until that wonderful "circuit of bees" in the middle of the penultimate stanza. "Prayer," on the other hand, is chock full of them.
DG: I love metaphors, but I like to use them sparingly. It's also nice to have a few hiding just under the surface of the poem so that the reader feels them without exactly knowing why. But, of course, sometimes it's just fun to go hog wild. Just like changing the meter or stanza, changing the texture of the poem is a pleasure. I think a lot about creating the right texture for each poem.

Mastering poetic craft does not consist of learning a few techniques one uses habitually. Mastery comes from learning how (and when) to use all the ways in which language conveys meaning.

AMK: I think it's easy to forget that this poem is an apostrophe, a poem addressed to a person who is absent or imaginary or to an object or abstract idea. Why compose this poem in this form?
DG: Why not compose a poem as an address? In daily speech we are almost always addressing someone. It is something both speakers and listeners understand intuitively, even if it puzzles some critics. I've been rereading John Donne. Most of his poems address someone—God, a lover, a friend.

AMK: I really like that strange moment around which the poem revolves in the third stanza. It adds a ceremonial aspect of the planting of the sequoia and also reveals quite a bit about the people in the poem with few words. Is this an aspect of the economy of language or of a disinterest on your end to go any further into what the poem is largely about?

DG: Now you have found me out. I like to have turns in my poems—moments when the poem changes direction or tone. This is a fundamental element of my style. That is also how our minds work. No sooner do we focus on some idea, thing, or emotion than a contradictory notion suddenly emerges.

AMK: If you could only have five books on your bookshelf, what would they be?

DG: Dante, Shakespeare, the King James Bible, Webster's Collegiate Dictionary, and a bookdealer's catalog to order more books. I own at least ten thousand books, and that seems a bare minimum. I like having my favorite volumes within easy reach. Reading is one of life's great pleasures.

AMK: What are you working on right now?

DG: I am trying to complete my next volume of poems. I only need to finish three or four more poems before I sent it to Graywolf Press. The trouble is that some of these poems are ones I've been struggling with for years, in one case almost fifteen years. This summer I sent off poems to editors for the first time in eight years. I refrained from publishing while I was the Chairman of the National Endowment for the Arts. I thought it best for the agency if I removed any possible conflict of interest. (Not that I had much time to write since I often worked seven days a week with constant travel.) Now I am trying to rediscover who I am as a poet. That's not so easy as it might seem.

AMK: Would you be willing to share any of your new work with us?

DG: Since we have spent much time discussing two interrelated poems from *The Gods of Winter*, which was published nearly twenty years ago, may I offer a recent poem on the same subject?

MAJORITY

Now you'd be three,
I said to myself,
seeing a child born
the same summer as you.

Now you'd be six,
or seven, or ten.
I watched you grow
in foreign bodies.

Leaping into a pool, all laughter,
or frowning over a keyboard,
but mostly just standing,
taller each time.

How splendid your most
mundane action seemed
in these joyful proxies.
I often held back tears.

Now you are twenty-one.
Finally, it makes sense
that you have moved away
into your own afterlife.

An Interview with Dana Gioia

Laura Lindsley / 2010

From *Irish Rover* 8.2 (September 3, 2010). Reprinted by permission of *Irish Rover.*

Laura Lindsley: Was there a specific moment when you discovered that poetry was your passion?

Dana Gioia: There were two periods in my life that brought me deeply into poetry. The first was in childhood. I often heard my mother recite poetry, and certain poems gave me a physical thrill. The excitement had nothing to do with the subject of a poem. I was responding to the rhythms and the music. This sort of exhilaration still strikes me as the single most important aspect of poetry. True poetry displays an element of magic. The language enchants the listener. Not everything my mother recited had this effect, but I still remember the dizzy excitement of hearing poems by Poe, Kipling, Longfellow, and Tennyson. That was when I first fell in love with poetry. By comparison, my later experience with poetry in school was mostly deadening.

I loved poetry, but it never occurred to me that I might someday become a poet. The second decisive period came years later when I was studying music and German in Vienna. Speaking mostly German and living for the first time in a foreign country, I found myself reading poems constantly and also writing them seriously for the first time. Slowly I realized that I didn't want to be a composer or critic, which was what I had mostly imagined till then. I wanted to be a poet. I was nineteen years old. I've never changed my mind since that moment, though I have had to make a living in many other ways.

LL: Where did your formational experience as a writer take place?

DG: It may seem odd to you, but although I attended Stanford and Harvard, I am mostly self-taught as a poet. I had some excellent courses in literature, and I remain devoted to many of my teachers, but very little of what they did in literature courses proved useful to me as a poet. In fact, I suspect that all the fascinating and serious critical study initially hampered my writing since it made it too self-conscious and academic. Literary criticism tries to bring everything to the surface of a discussion whereas a poet learns that much of what is most important in a poem must remain unsaid. Criticism analyzes, articulates, and organizes meaning. Poetry evokes it. It took me years to shed those habits in my work.

The one notable exception was my course in the History of English Versification at Harvard with Robert Fitzgerald. Although it was a historical survey of English language prosody, we had to write exercises in each meter we studied—not poems, just verse exercises. That course probably saved me five years as a writer.

LL: You are talking mostly about literature courses. What about your creative writing courses?
DG: The only real creative writing course I took was—oddly enough—during my time at Stanford Business School. The program allowed me to take an occasional course outside Biz School, and I enrolled in Donald Davie's graduate poetry writing seminar. The class proved to be a fascinating exercise in practical criticism, but it did nothing to help my poetry. In fact, I think it mostly hurt it in the short term. But Donald and I did become good friends, and that greatly enriched my life.

LL: How would you describe your poetry?
DG: Brilliant, deathless, heartbreaking. At least that's how I'd like to hear someone else describe it.

LL: Do you belong to any recognizable literary movement?
DG: Literary critics categorize me as a leader of New Formalism. I have never liked that term, but I have reluctantly come to accept it, though I consider the name misleading. I write in both free and formal verse. If one looks at my published poetry over the past thirty years, it falls almost evenly into thirds—one-third free verse, one-third rhymed verse, and one-third unrhymed metrical verse.

My feeling has always been that the poet must be free to write in whatever shape the poem itself suggests. Thirty years ago it was considered controversial to write in meter or rhyme. I thought that was dopey, and I helped lead some of the critical battles—often called the "Poetry Wars"—to insist on the poet's freedom to write in form. I was much attacked and vilified, though that may seem incredible to you today. Critics nicknamed us—and it wasn't supposed to be a compliment—"The New Formalists." The term stuck. But we were successful in making the poetry world open to form, and one now sees formal poems in most journals. We helped make American poetry more stylistically diverse and inclusive.

But let me repeat that I have never advocated writing exclusively in form, though some people—both supporters and detractors—seem to think so. I believe that a poet needs to have all the possibilities of the art available to him or her.

LL: Do you need to be in a certain location to write your best poetry?
DG: I need peace and quiet. That has been a rare condition in my adult life since I have mostly had demanding jobs and a busy family. At present I find it almost impossible to write in Washington. I need to go off and hide in Northern California.

LL: Do you plan to write a poem or do you write when you feel moved to do so?
DG: Poetic inspiration is involuntary. It arrives when it wants to, not when you ask it. My poems come when I'm stuck in traffic, sitting in the middle of a concert, or taking a shower. They rarely come when I have a pen and paper handy. I often lose the impulse of inspiration as a result. I have a great many fantastic ideas for poems. But ideas don't turn into poems. They simply sit there lifelessly. One needs a first line—real words full of tangible imaginative energy.

LL: Although wary of putting yourself under any one category of poetry, you pointedly have avoided the modernist approach to poetry. Why? What early influences directed you away from that approach?
DG: I am so glad you asked this question because it gives me the chance to say you are quite mistaken. My poetry reeks of Modernism. Eliot, Pound, Stevens, Montale, Rilke, and Valéry are my household gods. But they are now a century in the past, and it would be a silly thing to try to copy them. Modernism died—along with most of its great practitioners—by the time I finished high school.

The real issue for me has always been what to do now? How does one combine the intensity, invention, and suggestive lyricality of Modernism with the emotional directness, narrative power, and musicality of both pre-Modernism poetry and the popular arts? Academic postmodernism gave one rather unconvincing answer. I've been looking for another. Or rather multiple answers. It is tedious to write in the same way poem after poem. That's why I like putting an experimental poem such as "Elegy with Surrealist Proverbs as Refrain" in the same book as a narrative ballad such as "Summer Storm." I prize creative range and variety. Every new poem provides an opportunity to reinvent one's medium.

LL: What influences kept you from writing the "English Department poetry" that is so common now?
DG: Guilt and shame mostly. That's the sort of poetry I began writing, and it's fun to write. The trouble is that it isn't much fun to read. I spent years trying to find a way to write poetry that interests me and the reader together. A good poem creates a secret collaboration between the author and the listener. It isn't a lecture. It is a mysterious sort of conversation in which the listener's responses are silent but essential.

LL: What does it mean to write for the reader?
DG: It means to cultivate what Keats called "negative capability." It requires a certain suppression of the ego. I found my own solution in Frost's work, which is never autobiographical but always personal. Then I noticed the same quality in Auden, Rilke, Stevens, Eliot, and others. It was one of the great lessons of Modernism—correcting the excesses of Romantic egotism. The poem isn't about me. It is about us. Doing that well is much harder than it seems. At least I find it hard.

LL: Being a poet entails more than just writing down inspired words. As you have said, it's also carrying out a conversation between the living and dead. In teaching yourself to write, how did you cultivate and maintain this conversation?
DG: I was first trained as a musician, and I have always thought of poetry as a similar art. In music, the student throws him- or herself into the art. You listen to all the music you can. You learn to play instruments. You study theory while also gaining the practical experience of performance. You memorize things you love.

Love is the key word. Your art isn't work. It's a lifelong love affair—full of romance, rapture, heartbreak, reconciliation, and constant discovery. You always want to be in the presence of your beloved.

Every musician understands the mystery of conversing with the dead. Bach, Mozart, Beethoven, Schubert talk to you. So do Louis Armstrong, Duke Ellington, John Coltrane, and Art Pepper.

Every poet has hard hours and dark nights of the soul. After my first son died, I had them every night for years. If I had not been able to talk to Dante and Shakespeare, Rilke and Frost, Borges and Cavafy about their own sorrows and losses, I might have given up.

LL: Do you really talk to the dead?

DG: All the time. Remember I'm a Latin—Sicilian and Mexican. We don't share the Anglo-Saxon embarrassment about death. In Mexican neighborhoods the Day of the Dead is a festival. Dante wrote a pretty good poem about all the dead folks he visited.

I suggest we end our campaign of discrimination against the departed. They are a pretty interesting crowd—at least if we choose our dead friends carefully. Don't forget that we are all future members of this marginalized group.

How A Poem Happens: Dana Gioia

Brian Brodeur / 2011

From *How A Poem Happens: Contemporary Poets Discuss the Making of Poems* (May 11, 2011).
Reprinted by permission of Brian Brodeur.

Brian Brodeur: When was "The Angel with the Broken Wing" composed? How did it start?

Dana Gioia: This poem started, like most of my poems, with a first line and some sense of the character speaking. It came to me in an airport. I jotted down the opening line with a few notes. A busy airport was not a place where I could do much more than that.

THE ANGEL WITH THE BROKEN WING

I am the Angel with the Broken Wing,
The one large statue in this quiet room.
The staff finds me too fierce, and so they shut
Faith's ardor in this air-conditioned tomb.

The docents praise my elegant design
Above the chatter of the gallery.
Perhaps I am a masterpiece of sorts—
The perfect emblem of futility.

Mendoza carved me for a country church.
(His name's forgotten now except by me.)
I stood beside a gilded altar where
The hopeless offered God their misery.

I heard their women whispering at my feet—
Prayers for the lost, the dying, and the dead.
Their candles stretched my shadow up the wall,
And I became the hunger that they fed.

I broke my left wing in the Revolution
(Even a saint can savor irony)
When troops were sent to vandalize the chapel.
They hit me once—almost apologetically.

For even the godless feel something in a church
A twinge of hope, fear? Who knows what it is?
A trembling unaccounted by their laws,
An ancient memory they can't dismiss.

There are so many things I must tell God!
The howling of the dammed can't reach so high.
But I stand like a dead thing nailed to a perch,
A crippled saint against a painted sky.

BB: How many revisions did this poem undergo? How much time elapsed between the first and final drafts?

DG: I don't have the drafts here in Washington, but I'd guess it went through about fifty or sixty drafts—not necessarily drafts of the whole poem but of various lines and stanzas. Probably a year passed between jotting down the first line and actually having the time to work on the poem seriously.

I finished the poem in one extended period of work, which is unusual for me. My daily life tends to be full of obligations and interruptions, and at this point I was Chairman of the NEA working six or seven days a week. I started drafting the poem on Waldron Island and finished it after two weeks of work. I had sequestered myself alone on this beautiful but remote place in the San Juan Islands of Washington, which had neither electricity nor phone service, to escape my public life. I needed real silence and solitude to write in a life that was otherwise quite destructive for a poet.

BB: Do you believe in inspiration? How much of this poem was "received" and how much was the result of sweat and tears?

DG: Of course, I believe in inspiration. That's what makes poetry so difficult.

You can't will a good poem into existence. The basic idea either comes or not. But then a different sort of work begins in trying to realize the idea in words. Inspiration is powerful, but it is also vague and elusive. A great inspiration can turn into a lousy poem. Mediocre poets have inspiration, too, but they lack the skill and fortitude to embody it compellingly in language. It is interesting to see Yeats's first drafts. They mostly aren't very impressive. But the final versions are, of course, amazing. Part of his genius was in shaping the initial impulse into something unforgettable.

BB: How did this poem arrive at its final form? Did you consciously employ any principles of technique?
DG: I wanted the poem to sing, so I knew almost at once it would rhyme. Everything else came later as I started working on it. Yes, I "consciously employed principles of technique." If you use a major form like rhymed pentameter quatrains, you'd better know what you're doing. But I didn't impose the form on the poem. I listened to the poem as it emerged and gave it the form it wanted. That's what critics don't understand about form. It has to be inherent in the material. The poet only does what the poem itself suggests.

BB: Was there anything unusual about the way in which you wrote this poem?
DG: Actually, there was. Much of the poem was composed aloud without being written down. On Waldron I could walk for miles without meeting anyone. I would work on lines and stanzas by reciting them to myself. I might go through two or three dozen different versions of a line or stanza before I jotted anything down. As I did this over a period of days, the poem gradually emerged in its present shape. Then I began reworking the draft on paper. That is one reason why the poem's sound has such physicality. I could feel in my tongue and mouth when I finally had a line exactly right.

BB: How long after you finished this poem did it first appear in print?
DG: Five years. When I wrote it, I was Chairman of the National Endowment for the Arts, and I decided it was inappropriate for me to publish. I didn't want to complicate the agency's already problematic position, so I put aside my personal career for the duration of my public service.

BB: How long do you let a poem "sit" before you send it off into the world? Do you have any rules about this or does your practice vary with every poem?

DG: I have no set rules, but it's always wise to let a poem sit. I usually let them sit for a couple of years. Sometimes I will make small changes in the interim. If a poem is any good, it can wait to be published.

BB: Could you talk about fact and fiction and how this poem negotiates the two?
DG: I almost never write strictly autobiographical poems. I usually create a fictional voice or character to speak the poem, even if this is not obvious to the casual reader. My poems are personal but not autobiographical, and that gives me a certain imaginative freedom and objectivity I would lack if I were writing confessional verse. It's hard to be entirely truthful about yourself. It's easier to be truthful in fiction. And poems should be truthful.

BB: Is this a narrative poem?
DG: It is a lyric poem with a loosely narrative structure. It is a lyric poem because it mostly explores a single escalating mood. But even in a lyric poem, there needs to be some narrative arrangement of the material. The order of the images is almost as important as the images themselves.

BB: Do you remember who you were reading when you wrote this poem? Any influences you'd care to disclose?
DG: I had probably just read the newspaper. After all, I was waiting in an airport lounge. So there was no literary source for the poem. But I had just been in Santa Fe where I had attended Spanish Market where the *santeros* ("saint-makers," as these traditional Southwestern woodcarvers and artists are called) were selling their wooden statues of religious figures. I had been haunted by these statues since I first saw them in New Mexico, and I had just bought one, a statue of the archangel Raphael by a young *santero* named Jacob Martinez.

BB: Do you have any particular audience in mind when you write, an ideal reader?
DG: Yes, the alert, the curious, and the creative. Most of these folks no longer read poetry, but that doesn't matter. The poems will be there if they need them. And oddly enough, over the years, they often find them.

BB: Did you let anyone see drafts of this poem before you finished it? Is there an individual or a group of individuals with whom you regularly share work?

DG: Since I wrote "Angel" when I was on Waldron Island, which is really very isolated, no one saw it until it was done. I could have shown it to the composer Morten Lauridsen, whom I saw each evening, but I didn't know him well enough at that point, so I felt a bit shy about reading a poem in progress to him. He and I were usually busy talking about other things. Generally, I don't show a poem to anyone until it seems pretty much done. Then I can benefit from their comments without losing the poem's individuality.

Curiously, when the proofs arrived from *Poetry*, I worried about one word. In line fifteen should "shadow" be singular or plural? I happened to be at the Aspen Ideas Festival, and Tobias Wolff sat down at the picnic table where I was working. I read the poem to him, and we decided it should stay singular. A silly story to tell, but I share it to say that in a poem every word matters.

BB: How does this poem differ from other poems of yours?
DG: It took me into a subject—both in general and specific terms—that I had never explored before. It also achieved a certain tough, formal music that was a little different from any previous poem I'd written. Most interesting for me was that it went into my own Mexican roots. My mother was Mexican American, and I was raised in a Mexican neighborhood. I had mostly written about that indirectly in the past. This allowed me to explore that part of my background more overtly as well as the deeply Latin Catholic milieu in which I had been raised.

BB: What is American about this poem?
DG: The subject, the author, and the treatment are all American. Perhaps what makes it most American is that the statue itself is a Mexican immigrant of sorts—an artifact brought from his native village to be displayed in an American museum. It is also a religious poem. That's very American, at least in a contrarian sort of way. No one in England or Europe writes religious poetry nowadays.

BB: Was this poem finished or abandoned?
DG: When I had finished the poem, I thought that it still needed another stanza, though I wasn't sure what it would say. But once I read the poem to a friend, I realized that it ended exactly where it should. It had finished itself without telling me. I had been so preoccupied with the details that I didn't notice until I heard it with someone else in the room.

Poetic Collaborations: A Conversation with Dana Gioia

Michelle Johnson / 2011

From *World Literature Today* 85.5 (September-October 2011): 27–35.
Reprinted by permission of Michelle Johnson.

Michelle Johnson: You are often identified with New Formalism, a literary movement now thirty years old, which revived meter, rhyme, and narrative. Much of your own work, though not all, employs form. What is New Formalism's status at the beginning of the twenty-first century?

Dana Gioia: The revival of form and narrative was one of the central events in late-twentieth-century American poetry, and the controversy that still simmers over this unexpected shift of sensibility only proves how significant it was. The movement connected literary poetry to the energy of the popular culture—which had remained rooted in auditory forms like song and storytelling. In this sense the revival was populist and democratic. It also helped reconcile modernist poetic practice with the vast possibilities of traditional techniques. It moved poetry forward while also reconnecting it to its primal roots in orality and performance. (It's no coincidence that revival of form and narrative among young literary poets exactly coincided with the creation of hip-hop and slam poetry.) This movement meaningfully enlarged the possibilities of contemporary poetry.

It's easy to forget how odd things were back in the 1970s. Form and narrative were almost universally denounced as dead literary modes. They were considered retrograde, repressive, elitist, antidemocratic, phallocentric, and even (I'm not making this up), un-American. It was impossible to publish a formal or narrative poem in most magazines. One journal even stated its editorial policy as, "No rhyme or pornography." Poems were supposed to be free verse lyric utterances in a confessional or imagistic style. I'm happy to say that journals and presses are now open to formal or narrative poetry. This is a direct result of the so-called "Poetry Wars," the long and loud debates over these issues that lasted from the early 1980s through the 1990s.

MJ: I noticed that you didn't use the term "New Formalism" in your response. DG: I've never cared for the name, though it has become the standard term. I had no interest in making rhyme and meter the dominant aesthetic. What I fought for—and one really did have to fight back then—was for the poet's freedom to use whatever style he or she felt was right for the poem. I can't imagine a poet who wouldn't want to have all the possibilities of the language available, especially the powerful enchantments of meter, rhyme, and narrative. I never saw the movement as a rejection of Modernism. Why throw away the greatest period of American poetry? What interested me, and many of the other so-called New Formalists, was how to combine the legacy of Modernism with neglected resources of traditional literature and also how to combine the intensity of high art with the enormous energy of popular arts like film and music. Our readers experienced and enjoyed all of these things together. Poetry needed to reflect that cultural reality.

MJ: Did New Formalism produce any significant writers—not counting you, of course?
DG: The movement produced—or perhaps the better word is attracted—a cluster of interesting poets and critics. Any movement that includes poetic talents as distinguished and diverse as David Mason, Gjertrud Schnackenberg, Tom Disch, Vikram Seth, Timothy Steele, Mary Jo Salter, A. E. Stallings, Christian Wiman, and Marilyn Nelson, to name only a few, needs to be taken seriously. Please understand that I am not talking about a group of poets sitting together in a bunker plotting a literary takeover. I'm describing a zeitgeist, a broad-based change of sensibility affecting a generation of younger poets dissatisfied with the literary status quo in the 1970s. Most of these poets didn't even know about each other at first. Mark Jarman and Robert McDowell, the editors of *The Reaper*, were trying to reinvent the narrative poem before they ever knew about Vikram Seth, Frederick Turner, Brad Leithauser, Andrew Hudgins, David Mason, or R. S. Gwynn trying to do it elsewhere.

New Formalism was a generational change in sensibility, not a cabal. Of course, as these writers began to be published (and attacked), they discovered one another. New magazines and small presses sprang up to publish the work that the mainstream was rejecting—just as they did in early Modernism. Soon there were new conferences, such as West Chester and Sewanee, where these young poets actually met one another. I should point out that not all of these poets necessarily liked one another or even agreed with one another.

MJ: How did you fit into this history?
DG: As a poet, I simply tried to write as well as I could. As a critic, I tried to clarify the larger issues, and to bring some recognition to younger writers. I also cofounded the West Chester Poetry Conference so that there would be a place for these poets to gather and discuss their work and ideas. I was praised, vilified, marginalized, and canonized, but I was not ignored.

MJ: How would you describe your current aesthetic?
DG: I'm not sure I have an aesthetic as such—at least no abstract theory of how to write a poem. Inspiration is mostly an involuntary process. When poems arrive, I try to let them take the shapes that they themselves suggest. I want my poems to be musical, moving, and memorable. I also try to make them compressed and concise. I rely more on intuition than on any preconceived ideas. I am actually happiest when the poem unfolds in ways that surprise me. My best poems have mostly taken forms that I would never have predicted.

MJ: Some of that sounds a bit like an aesthetic.
DG: Well, I do keep certain things in mind when writing a poem. But they seem utterly remote from what literary theorists discuss nowadays when they mention aesthetics. Let me offer just two assumptions in my idiosyncratic poetics. First, I believe that a poem must enchant before it communicates. The physical sound and verbal rhythm of a poem needs to arrest the reader's attention and create a moment of imaginative openness and emotional vulnerability. This enchantment is what allows poetry to communicate so deeply. Without it, the language remains narrowly functional and prosaic. My second assumption is that a good poem is a sort of dance between the text and subtext. The surface of the poem should powerfully capture the reader's conscious attention so that the subtext is free to speak to the reader's intuition and imagination. These two notions are fundamental to my poetic practice.

MJ: Do you write mostly in traditional forms?
DG: My poems tend to fall almost equally into three categories—one-third

in free verse, one-third in unrhymed meter, and one-third in rhyme. I like that sort of stylistic diversity. (Many writers I admire, such as Wallace Stevens, W. H. Auden, Elizabeth Bishop, Philip Larkin, Weldon Kees, and Donald Justice also work in a wide range of forms.) So you can say that a majority of my poems are formal, but I rarely use "traditional" forms. I like to invent my own stanzas or patterns. I also tend to experiment with different meters or mix free and formal verse. I am very interested in the physical sound of the line. I try to make each poem different from the poems around it. Interestingly, critics *never* seem to notice what I'm doing. But the purpose of poetic technique isn't to be noticed; it is to be felt.

MJ: Has your sense of what makes a poem changed over the years?
DG: Yes, it has. I've slowly learned a few things that I didn't know when I started out. I now cut out a great deal of what I once would have left in a poem. Poems shouldn't tell you too much. They are often stronger by suggesting things they decline to state overtly. Most contemporary poetry is too long, too cluttered, and too prosaic. There's not enough music or mystery. The poets don't seem to trust the intelligence of their readers. They tell us everything in numbing detail. This strikes me as very academic. These poems lecture us as if we were students—and not particularly bright ones. I prefer poems that collaborate with their readers and treat them as equals, even as intimates.

MJ: What do you mean by collaborating with a reader who is an intimate?
DG: It's not just about your attitude to the reader. It's about your sense of the art itself. Let me offer a metaphor. Creating a poem is like building a room, sometimes with multiple entrances, into which you invite the reader. The room has a strong design and a tangible atmosphere, but it is only partially furnished. There are, in fact, some essential elements that have been left out which the reader must furnish from his or her own life. One reason that reading poetry is universally acknowledged as a more intense experience than fiction is that poetry compels—or entices—us to complete the text from our own memory and imagination. (Fiction gives us, by contrast, a more completely realized imaginary world through which we journey via the narrative.) A successful poem first entices the reader to enter an imaginary space and then creates the urgency to collaborate with the author in completing it.

MJ: When we spoke last year, you said you wanted your poems to be useful. How do you define a poem's utility?

DG: I don't believe that poetry needs to be utilitarian in any narrow sense. I began, in fact, as someone who believed in art for art's sake. My early heroes were Jorge Luis Borges, Vladimir Nabokov, Paul Valéry, and Oscar Wilde. I still feel that art needs no justification beyond the joy and splendor of its own existence. I dislike art that crudely preaches some social, political, or theological message. But over the years I have come to appreciate that one of the powers of art is that it can be applied to human uses that the creators never intended. Samuel Barber's *Adagio for Strings*, for instance, has been used in all sorts of contexts that would have surprised the composer, but those uses all have human meaning. My poems have been used to teach public speaking, as texts for music, or as subjects for state English exams. Ministers have employed them in sermons. Critics have used them to illustrate various aesthetic and cultural assumptions. I never imagined those uses, but they are all valid. The mayor of New York recently read—to my astonishment—a Rilke translation of mine at a 9/11 memorial service. Once you publish a poem, it exists as an independent object. You no longer control what it does. If you're lucky, the culture puts it to work.

MJ: In addition to your own poetry, you've done a significant amount of translation from multiple languages, including German, Italian, Latin, and Romanian. Do you recommend serving as a translator to other poets?
DG: Translation should be part of any poet's education. Poetry is an international art. If you know only the poetry of your own country (or your own era), you know very little about the art.

MJ: How has translating other poets' work affected your own writing?
DG: I've done poetic translation since I first began to write seriously, so it greatly affected my development as a writer. My earliest translations were mostly from German—Rainer Maria Rilke, Georg Trakl, Gottfried Benn. Then I concentrated mostly on Italian writers, such as Eugenio Montale, Mario Luzi, Valerio Magrelli, among others. These are all Modernists, and their hermetic styles influenced my sense of how a poem spoke. That immersion in European Modernism (with its roots in Symbolism) is one reason why my poetry is so different from many of the other New Formalists. Mine is essentially postmodernist in that it tries to combine the intensity and integrity of Modernist poetry with the sensual appeal and musical power of meter and rhyme. Even my sense of narrative poetry was shaped by Modernism. My narratives have strong story lines, but they are also elliptical and elusive, communicating important things only through

their subtexts. Seneca's influence came much later and was more specific. I began translating Seneca's *Hercules Furens* just as I was starting to write my first libretto. I learned a lot about poetic tragedy—which is what much opera essentially is—from translating that dark, neglected classic, which influenced both Dante and Eliot.

MJ: So translation had a strong impact on your own poetry?
DG: Yes, but let me also say something no one ever mentions. There is a danger in doing too much translation. When you translate, you always know where you are going. The original poem provides you with a map. But writing your own poems is a far more mysterious process. The poem is invisible until you write it down. There is no original, only impulse and intuition. It's hard to make the transition from translation back into original work.

MJ: You are also well-known for your criticism, particularly your 1991 essay "Can Poetry Matter?" Did your fame from this essay overshadow your poetry at the time?
DG: Yes, without question the fame of this essay—which was international—overshadowed my reputation as a poet for nearly a decade. I was suddenly seen as poetry's most iconoclastic critic, "the guardian of standards," as the *New York Times* once called me. Contemporary literary life is so specialized that a writer is expected to do only one thing well. I have always seen myself working in the tradition of the poet-critic, which has been important to American letters—from Edgar Allan Poe to T. S. Eliot, Ezra Pound, Kenneth Rexroth, Louise Bogan, and Randall Jarrell.

MJ: Did you resent your poetry being ignored and sometimes even attacked because of your critical notoriety?
DG: I try to accept the good and the bad with equanimity. As Oscar Wilde observed, "The only thing worse than being talked about is not being talked about." I have been lucky to have enjoyed a degree of celebrity across my career, and the experience has taught me a lot about the nature of contemporary fame. Notoriety requires you to be simplified, usually into a neat and tidy headline. First, I was widely discussed as the "businessman-poet." Then I became notorious as the ringleader of the New Formalists. Soon thereafter I became famous as the literary maverick who wrote "Can Poetry Matter?" Then I became a public figure as the champion of arts and literacy who ran the National Endowment for the Arts. Each of these reputations contained an element of truth and a simplification. But it's better to

be noticed than ignored, and properly used, fame gives you the freedom to pursue your interests as a writer.

There is also a very real burden to fame. You're besieged daily by people, mostly strangers, who want things. I hear constantly from journalists, poets, students, teachers, editors, fundraisers, job seekers, artists, activists, officials, and occasionally lunatics—who ask for my help.

MJ: People think of a poet working alone, in solitude. While you have certainly done that in writing your poems, you have also engaged in a considerable number of collaborations with other artists, especially composers.
DG: Writing is hard, lonely work. It demands solitude and sacrifice. I haven't taught for a living. I have either written at night while holding a full-time job or I have supported my family as a full-time writer. My daily life often becomes very private and reclusive. That's why I've welcomed the chance to collaborate with other artists. It breaks the solitude and brings a different sort of energy into my daily life. I've also made some very close friends this way. I've worked with composers, actors, choreographers, visual artists, filmmakers, and printers.

MJ: How are these collaborations different from solitary creation?
DG: They differ in at least two ways. First of all, there are certain artistic forms that are necessarily collaborative—opera, theater, song, film, and the book arts. If you want to work in them, you'll need partners. Second, when you are working in collaboration, you usually have a very tangible sense of how your words will be used and experienced. Writing a poem to be set to music opens different creative possibilities and responsibilities from one written for the page. There is also a give-and-take in the collaborative creative process as the work takes its final shape. For me, collaboration has not been a merely incidental activity. From the start I wanted to expand the possibilities of poetry beyond the narrow role it occupies in contemporary culture.

MJ: You worked with the composer Alva Henderson on *Nosferatu*. What was the collaboration like?
DG: Alva and I worked very well together. It took us a while to agree on an operatic subject. He had some good ideas, but they weren't right for me. I needed a subject I could inhabit imaginatively in order to produce a text that was truly poetic and not simply workmanlike. Once we settled on *Nosferatu*, which was based, of course, on F. W. Murnau's 1922 silent film, I prepared a complete scenario—a detailed scene-by-scene prose summary that also

proposed the various arias, duets, and ensembles. Alva helped focus this summary, and then the hard part began—writing the verse. I wanted to create a libretto that could stand independently as a poetic text but would work equally well with music. I drafted the libretto out of sequence. When inspiration came for an aria, I wrote it as a poem and then built the scene around it. I tended to send Alva texts half a scene at a time—a key aria or duet and the text leading up to it. Curiously, this odd system worked perfectly for his creative process since he likes to compose the central musical ideas of a scene and then develop the entire scene.

MJ: So the opera was actually written and composed out of sequence?
DG: Yes, and we also did something odd, perhaps even unique, in developing the final work. We premiered it one scene or aria at a time around the country—usually in coordination with one of my readings or residencies. By the time we did the actual staged premiere at Rimrock Opera in 2004, we had done a dozen showcases around the country, including a spectacular concert version at the Western Slope Music Festival in Colorado. This allowed the work to be heard by diverse audiences around the country—something rare in contemporary opera.

MJ: You've commented upon the libretto's yet unrealized literary potential in English. What stands in the way, and what would this realization look like?
DG: Opera is not a native form to the English-speaking world, which experienced opera for centuries in foreign languages, mostly Italian. English-language opera is a tradition only slightly more than a century old, and it was initially founded on the dubious assumption that the libretto was of secondary importance or, to put the matter more clearly, that great opera could be built on creaky theater and lousy lyrics. Opera isn't a symphonic art. It's musical theater. A powerful and original dramatic structure and memorable and moving lyrics are essential to the total impact. The best American operas, which are as dissimilar as *Porgy and Bess, Four Saints in Three Acts,* and *Nixon in China,* have also been beautifully crafted literary works. And some modern operas with gorgeous music such as *The Tender Land* and *Midsummer Marriage* sink from their awkward and stilted libretti. A great libretto, in English or any other language, should present a powerful story concisely with commanding characters, moving situations, and memorable words. The lyrics should be compelling without the music and irresistible with it. Of course, a libretto can be written in either prose or verse, but it is a historical fact that nearly all of the great operas have poetic

texts. My point is really quite simple. The literary elements of opera need to be taken as seriously as the music.

MJ: Who are your literary heroes in opera?

DG: Lorenzo da Ponte, Felice Romani, Hugo von Hofmannsthal, Bertolt Brecht, and W. H. Auden. They constitute a major poetic tradition. I also admire W. S. Gilbert. He wrote operetta rather than opera, but his lyrics are works of comic genius.

MJ: You have an interest in poetic theater and have been involved in two projects, a production of your translation of Seneca's Roman tragedy *The Madness of Hercules* and a full-length dance-theater piece based on your poem "Counting the Children." I'm particularly curious about poetry and dance. How did dancers perform your poem?

DG: "Counting the Children" astonished me as a piece of dance theater. Every line of my long poem was spoken by one of the dancers or sung by a chorus. The poem's narrator, Mr. Choi, was played simultaneously by two dancers, one male, the other female. The male dancer spoke the lines while his partner danced them to an Asian-influenced jazz score. The total effect was similar to the ritualized, mythic theater W. B. Yeats had hoped for in his *Plays for Dancers.* "Counting the Children" is a dark and complex poem, steeped in loss, dream, and anxiety, and the choreographer Mark Ruhala fashioned a startling full-length work. The audience was both shocked and deeply engaged by it. To everyone's surprise, all the performances sold out, and the run was extended.

MJ: Was this a collaboration between you and the dance company, though different than the type of collaboration between you and Alva Henderson in that I assume you didn't write "Counting the Children" with a dance performance in mind?

DG: I had never thought of the work in theatrical terms. It was conceived only as a poem—a sort of experiment in mixing the lyric and narrative modes. The idea for the dance work came entirely from Mark Ruhala and his company after the poem was published. As soon as he mentioned the idea, however, I realized what had attracted him—the two extended sequences with the dead woman's collection of injured dolls.

I was surprised that they wanted to use every line of my text—the poem is 165 lines long. I suggested they cut it, but Mark insisted that using the complete text would provide creative discipline for the music and choreography.

And he was right. The words gave the final work a richer texture—providing the pleasures of both dance and poetic theater.

Probably one reason the piece worked so well was that I stayed out of the creative development until the dress rehearsals. The creative team made the work fully their own as a piece of dance theater. I made only one significant suggestion, which they graciously adopted. Otherwise, I just answered the dancers' questions about the text. The single most interesting conversation I've ever had about my poetry was with those dancers. None of them were literary people, but they had tremendous intuitive intelligence. They had to become my characters and had thought deeply about those fictive identities. I learned many things about my poem from them.

MJ: In addition to dancers performing your poetry, composers have set your poems to music. Were you a part of this process?
DG: When composers set my poems to music, I stay out of the process. They need to make the words their own. That often means transformations of emotion, mood, or tempo that differ from my own private sense. Whenever I first hear a new musical setting of my poem, I'm shocked. The words are the same, but the emotional subtext is usually very different. I have to approach the song as something different from my original poem. That takes a couple of hearings.

MJ: In 2007 the National Opera Association chose *Tony Caruso's Final Broadcast* as the best new American chamber opera. What can you tell me about this project?
DG: *Tony Caruso's Final Broadcast* could hardly be more different from its predecessor. Despite its supernatural theme, *Nosferatu* is essentially a work of psychological realism—a redemptive tragedy in the tradition of Wagner and Hofmannsthal. *Tony Caruso's Final Broadcast* has a non-linear and experimental form—ten short scenes that alternate between past and present, reality and vision. The opera begins in realism but ends in visionary transformation. Parts of it are satiric. *Tony Caruso* contains some of the funniest verse I've ever written and also some of the saddest. The opera moves so quickly, and Paul Salerni's music has such lyric momentum that the audience is swept along, despite its innovative form and mysterious qualities.

MJ: In what ways have you performed your work, alone or in collaboration with others?

DG: Performance is an essential concept to me. I write my poems equally to be spoken aloud and to be read on the page. I want the poem to work both ways. That is how most poets, at least since the late Renaissance, have understood the art—as an auditory or musical form that reveals additional meaning when apprehended visually in print. When I write, I do much of the composition off the page, working over the lines and stanzas aloud. I may work over lines aloud for half an hour before I write anything down. For that reason I find poetry readings very natural affairs. The poems need to be spoken and heard.

MJ: You often also bring music into your poetry readings.
DG: There is nothing sacred about the format of the poetry reading. I believe in mixing the arts. I especially love to combine poetry and music. An audience will hear poems better if they have just been listening to music. They listen less analytically but with greater emotional and intuitive openness. I have done poetry readings with both Chico Hamilton's and Helen Sung's jazz ensembles. I have also read with numerous classical groups. If I give a reading at a school with a good vocal department, I often plan a short recital of songs based on my poems midway through my performance.

MJ: In *Disappearing Ink: Poetry at the End of Print Culture* (2004), you wrote about the differing effects of poetry reading on poets like Robinson Jeffers, who began giving public readings in late middle age, and a poet whose first experience with publication was spoken. How has the spoken medium affected your work?
DG: When you hear recordings of the great American Modernists, you can hear how uncomfortable most of them are reciting their work in public. Stevens, Jeffers, Williams, Moore, and even Cummings were quite awful as readers. Only Frost and Eliot seem confident and natural. These writers grew up in a typographical culture where literature was composed, published, transmitted, and preserved silently on the page. My generation grew up with radio, recordings, television, phones, talking films, and tape recorders. For us, language, even literary language, is as much auditory as written. I first "read" *Paradise Lost* by listening to the old Argo LPs—an enthralling experience that brought me into the heart of this work composed by a blind poet. I read books voraciously, but I also encounter new poetry and fiction by hearing it aloud—not just at readings but also on the radio, audiobooks, recordings, and online. This changes how one conceives the medium.

MJ: What untested inter-arts collaborations still remain for you?
DG: Well, first of all, I want to do more opera. Writing two libretti only scratches the surface of the medium. What I especially want to create is opera as living, surprising musical theater rather than opera as a stiff, staged oratorio. I think that means chamber opera with a small cast and orchestra where every word can be heard. I would also like to do theatrical works that incorporate poetry, music, and dance. Film would be interesting to try, but the expense of the medium makes it difficult to do with sufficient freedom. We did a number of short literary films while I was at the NEA, and they suggested some interesting possibilities. A screenwriter has taken two of my poems and developed them into short films. I'll be interested to see if they ever get produced.

MJ: Which are you most eager to undertake?
DG: I am most eager to work with artists I admire unreservedly. Collaboration depends upon talent—the pairing of two talents that inspire each other. Morten Lauridsen, who seems to me one of the greatest living composers, wants to create a work together. That is very exciting. Helen Sung and I are going to write a jazz song cycle. The composer William Bolcolm has suggested doing a musical setting of my narrative poem "Haunted" for a pianist and an actor. Lori Laitman is writing a song cycle using my translations of Montale's love poems. Paul Salerni and I have sketched out a dance opera. I also have a third opera subject in mind, but it is still in the early stages. But, of course, the important thing is to keep writing poems.

MJ: You've just finished your fourth collection of poetry. When will it be published, and have you chosen a title?
DG: Yes, my new book is now finished. It is called *Pity the Beautiful.* Graywolf Press will publish it next spring. I lost seven years as a writer by running the National Endowment for the Arts. It was an important thing to undertake for the country, but it came at a personal price. I am a very slow and self-critical poet. I often worried I would never have another collection. I am grateful to the Muse that she didn't desert me.

A Conversation with Dana Gioia

Erika Koss / 2012

From *Image 73* (2012): 154–76. Reprinted by permission of Erika Koss.

Erika Koss: I once heard you say that if you could only have one art form, it would be music. Why?

Dana Gioia: I could give you reasons, but that would suggest that my response is rational. It isn't. My choice of music is simply a deep emotional preference. I like the physicality of music. It is a strange art—not only profoundly beautiful, but also communal, portable, invisible, and repeatable. Its most common form is song, a universal human art that also includes poetry.

EK: What does it mean to be a poet in a post-literate world? Or to be a librettist in an age where opera is a struggling art form?

DG: It doesn't bother me much. I wasn't drawn to poetry or opera because of their popularity. It was their beauty and excitement that drew me. Of course, I would like these arts to have larger audiences, but the value of an art isn't in the size of its audience. It's in the truth and splendor of its existence.

All that being said, let me observe that a post-print world is not a bad place for poetry. Poetry is an art that predates writing. It's essentially an auditory art. A poet today has the potential to speak directly to an audience—through public readings, radio broadcasts, recordings, and the Internet. Most people may not want to read poetry, but they do like to hear good poems recited well. I've always written mostly for the ear, and I find large and responsive audiences all over the country. The current cultural situation is tough on novelists and critics, but it isn't all that bad for poets.

EK: Duke Ellington objected to his music being labeled jazz, since he just considered it music. This led me to wonder if you are bothered by the term "New Formalism" being applied to your poetry.

DG: I have never liked the term "New Formalism." It was coined in the 1980s as a criticism of the new poetry being written by younger poets that employed rhyme, meter, and narrative. I understand the necessity of labels in a crowded and complex culture, but labels always entail an element of simplification, especially when the terms offer an easy dichotomy.

I have always written both in form and free verse. It seems self-evident to me that a poet should be free to use whatever techniques the poem demands. My work falls almost evenly into thirds—one-third of it is written in free verse, one-third in rhyme and meter, and one-third in meter without rhyme. I do believe that all good art is in some sense formal. Every element in a work of art should contribute to its overall expressive effect. That is what form means. Whether the form is regular or irregular, symmetrical or asymmetrical, is merely a means of achieving the necessary integrity of the work.

EK: But don't some of those early poems have a consciously oppositional spirit?

DG: Yes, but I didn't see myself writing in opposition to free verse. Using both free and formal verse, I wrote only in opposition to the sloppy, self-indulgent, and pretentious poetry that pervaded the 1970s. I wrote against the verbose, the narcissistic, and the tone-deaf schools of poetry. Rhyme, meter, and narrative were merely some of the techniques I explored in search of compression and expressivity.

EK: You have frequently mentioned the impact of your mother reading poetry to you as a child. You've described her reciting Poe's "Annabel Lee" from memory. What other poems did she recite?

DG: She loved the popular poets of her youth—writers such as Rudyard Kipling, Robert Service, James Whitcomb Riley, and James Greenleaf Whittier. I heard her recite chestnuts such as "Gunga Din," "Maud Muller," and "Barbara Frietchie," as well as speeches from Shakespeare's plays. The pleasure she took in these poems was contagious. She was fond of Tennyson, Longfellow, Byron, and Poe. Finally, she loved Ogden Nash. His "Tale of Custard the Dragon" was one of her favorites and remains one of mine. I read it to my boys, too. It is important to remember that my mother was a working-class Mexican American woman born in poverty. Despite what the professors would have us believe, average Americans once loved poetry.

EK: I'd like to ask you about each of your earlier books of poetry before talking about your new collection. I love the title sequence of your first book, *Daily Horoscope*. How did these poems begin, and how did they eventually become a sequence?

DG: Title tells all. I was reading the horoscope column in a newspaper when I noticed how interesting the language was—second person, future tense, intimate tone, and prophetic manner. It struck me as very much like the language of the great Modernist lyric poems. Think of T. S. Eliot's "Preludes," Eugenio Montale's *Ossa di sepia*, or Hart Crane's "Voyages." Then suddenly the opening of the first poem came to me. The inspiration was so strong that over the next few weeks I filled most of a notebook with sketches. Then I had to figure out the form they should take. I could have just published a dozen or so short poems, but I felt that the poems all had a deep connection. They needed to be arranged meaningfully to suggest their affinities.

I eventually put the six best together in a sequence that addresses one protagonist through a single day from the moment in which he first wakes to a point just after he has fallen asleep at night. As I did this, the poems started to reveal things that I hadn't initially been conscious of. This is one reason why I believe that a poet works in collaboration with the language and with the unconscious. They both have things to say that at first the poet can hardly guess. These are dense and challenging poems, but I don't think I have ever written with more intense lyricality.

EK: An invisible mystery seems to permeate the sequence. You write that "In a moment's pause another world / reveals itself behind the ordinary." Lines like these seem to echo both fantasy and Christianity.

DG: It was in writing this early sequence that I started to explore what has become one of my persistent themes—the sheer mystery of our existence in which the visible and invisible worlds both press upon us. I think it was in this sequence that I stopped trying to sound smart—the great literary vice—and simply surrendered myself to the phenomenon I was trying to capture and the language that I hoped summoned it. The poems are simultaneously very mundane—describing an ordinary day—and deeply visionary. They suggest a person overwhelmed by spiritual hungers and energy who doesn't yet know how to bring them into his life.

EK: Your second collection of poetry, *The Gods of Winter*, is dedicated to your first son who died at four months. Did his death provoke a crisis of faith?

DG: No, his death simply deadened me. For several years I felt as if I existed behind a thick glass wall beyond which the rest of the world went on obliviously. I eventually discovered how many other people lived in this isolated, joyless world. I met them everywhere. I had joined a secret society no one wants to enter. But I trusted my sorrow, and it eventually led me where I needed to go. I talked to these other lost souls—most of them so much worse off than I was—and I learned a depth of compassion I had never experienced. I was broken, and only with immense pain and long suffering did I heal. I then discovered that I had become a different person—humbler, kinder, and more patient. Only then was I open to grace.

EK: You have often claimed that most of your poems aren't autobiographical. But by your own account, your elegy "Planting a Sequoia" is an exception. Did you and your brother really plant a redwood in memory of your first son with a lock of his hair and a piece of his umbilical cord wrapped in its roots—according to an old Sicilian tradition?

DG: Yes, everything in the poem is true. I left certain things out, but poetry requires excluding some details to allow the important things to emerge more clearly. My son died suddenly a few days before Christmas. We planted the sequoia on Christmas day, but to include that particular holiday seemed too much symbolism for a poem already so burdened with emotion. My sister was around, but it seemed clearer to focus on the men since the original custom of planting a tree (usually an olive or fig tree) was a father's task. When my son died, I stopped writing for nearly a year. This was the only new poem I wrote. I carried it around in my head for months before I had the strength to write it down.

EK: Is the tree still there?

DG: Yes, the tree still exists. It's over sixty feet high now and perfectly proportioned. My father tended to it till the day he died, and it reflects that care.

EK: Your third collection, *Interrogations at Noon*, begins with a poem titled "Words" and ends with the poem "Unsaid." The first poem implies that reality is greater than words. But it also affirms the importance of language "to know and remember." To me, this has always seemed one of your most distinctively Christian poems, although nothing in it is overtly religious. It seems a poem that only someone who honors the mysteries of faith could write.

DG: I hate to interpret my own poems. I see certain things, but they may not be what a reader sees. Any good poem leads a life independent of its author's narrow intentions. I began "Words" as an argument with post-modernism, which asserts that language is a social construction that has no exact relationship with reality (and indeed that reality itself is a cultural construction with no independent objective existence). This is, of course, pretentious posturing, a perfect example of what George Orwell calls "silly clever" thinking. No one believes that language has an *exact* correspondence with reality, but it is nonetheless our best tool for getting at certain truths. None of this background is essential to understanding the poem, but it was all part of my initial creative impulse. What emerged was ultimately a very Catholic sense of the relationship between language and the world.

EK: The collection begins and ends in paradox—the power of words and the power of silence. The short final poem, "Unsaid," suggests that most of what we experience remains unexpressed in language:

UNSAID

So much of what we live goes on inside—
The diaries of grief, the tongue-tied aches
Of unacknowledged love are no less real
For having passed unsaid. What we conceal
Is always more than what we dare confide
Think of the letters that we write our dead.

How would you answer a reader who thought that this poem contradicted the ideas suggested in "Words"?
DG: There are some truths that can only be expressed as paradox. Existence is not a fixed and unitary state. It is fluid and dynamic, often with opposing forces pressing on us. Poems are not so much about giving answers as about unfolding questions. A good poem argues with its author and itself. I began *Interrogations at Noon* by exploring the powers and limitations of language, but I also wanted to remember how much of what we experience is never articulated but remains private. As a poet, I have also come to believe that what one leaves unsaid is often as powerful as what one says. The hard part is, of course, making the reader actually feel what is being left unsaid.

EK: Your new book, *Pity the Beautiful*, has just been published by Gray-wolf Press. One poem, "Prayer at Winter Solstice," consists almost entirely of paradoxical statements. This seems to be a poem that only a Californian Catholic could write.

Prayer at Winter Solstice

Blessed is the road that keeps us homeless.
Blessed is the mountain that blocks our way.

Blessed are hunger and thirst, loneliness and all forms of desire.
Blessed is the labor that exhausts us without end.

Blessed are the night and the darkness that blinds us.
Blessed is the cold that teaches us to feel.

Blessed are the cat, the child, the cricket, and the crow.
Blessed is the hawk devouring the hare.

Blessed are the sinner and the saint who redeem each other.
Blessed are the dead, calm in their perfection.

Blessed is the pain that humbles us.
Blessed is the distance that bars our joy.

Blessed is this shortest day that makes us long for light.
Blessed is the love that in losing we discover.

DG: I'm not sure about the Californian part, but "Prayer at Winter Solstice" is probably the most Catholic poem I've ever written. It is not a poem for everyone. It offers a set of beatitudes that praise the suffering and renunciation necessary to make us spiritually alert. It celebrates the transformative and redemptive nature of suffering—one of the central spiritual truths of Christianity as well as one easily forgotten in our materialist consumer culture. It is also a poem about facing the hard realities of our existence. Our feel-good society tries to deny suffering—unless it can sell you a pill or product to banish it.

EK: Your poem "Special Treatments Ward" has been haunting me for days, especially lines like "Risen they are healed but not made whole" or the closing line, "And vagrant sorrow cannot bless the dead." Is it too much to say that this poem began from your continuing pain at losing your first son?
DG: This was the most difficult poem I've ever written. It began when my second son had a serious injury that required an extended stay in a

children's neurological ward where nearly every other child was dying of a brain or spinal tumor. Having lost my first son, I was entirely vulnerable to the pain and confusion of the sick children and their desperate parents. I began to write a poem about how unprepared everyone in the ward was for what they had to face. But the poem kept growing and changing. It took me sixteen years to finish. I didn't want to finish it. I wanted to forget it, but the poem demanded to be finished. So the poem is not simply about my first son or my second son, though they are both mentioned. It is about the children who died.

EK: Critics are not going to know what to do with "Haunted," your brilliant new narrative poem, whose very urbane narrator turns out to have a surprising identity. You have said that your poems often begin with a line or musical phrase. How did this long poem begin?

DG: Actually, this poem began with the first two lines:

> "I don't believe in ghosts," he said. "Such nonsense.
> But years ago I actually saw one."

As soon as I heard those two lines, the whole poem started to unfold, though it took an immense amount of work to create the narrative tone and the musical qualities I wanted. The odd thing about poems is that when the good ones come we often realize that we have been writing them in the back of our mind for years. A single line brings them into existence almost fully formed.

"Haunted" is a ghost story that turns into a love story about a mutually destructive couple, but then at the end the reader realizes that the whole tale was really about something else entirely. The real theme is quite the opposite of what it initially seems. I wanted the poem to have the narrative drive of a great short story but also rise to moments of intense lyricality. I was particularly pleased that I was able to weave humor and horror, as well as tenderness and toughness, into a continuous narrative fabric.

EK: Flannery O'Connor said that fiction is "an incarnational art." Would you broaden this statement to include poetry?

DG: All art is incarnational. Art doesn't consist of abstractions. It is embodied truth created for creatures with bodies. A poem doesn't communicate primarily through ideas. It expresses itself in sound, images, rhythms, and emotions. We experience poems holistically. They speak to us simultaneously through our minds, our hearts, our imaginations, and our physical bodies. They speak to us, in other words, as incarnated beings.

EK: Some readers may be surprised to learn that your "first literary love affair" was with Edgar Rice Burroughs, especially his John Carter of Mars novels. How old were you? And what did these books spark in you?
DG: As a boy, I loved science fiction and adventure stories. I first came across Burroughs when I was about ten. I discovered an Ace paperback of *At the Earth's Core* on the bookrack of the local drugstore. Soon my friends and I bought every book by Burroughs we could find. They were just being reissued after many years. When *A Princess of Mars* and its two sequels appeared, we knew that we would never read better novels. They were full of breathless action, lofty heroics, wild fantasy, and a rather impressive vocabulary. And there was a fetching heroine—"the incomparable Dejah Thoris." What more did a bookish boy need to attain aesthetic bliss? I eventually read forty-five of Burroughs's novels. It was the first of many literary love affairs, and I remember those books as fondly as I do my first kiss. Years later I read at least a dozen of them aloud to my sons at bedtime. They loved them as much as I did.

EK: You once listed Thomas Merton's *The Wisdom of the Desert* as one of the most important books of your life, saying it made you realize how "spiritually starved" you were during your early years in business working at General Foods. You even suggested that it eventually led you to quit your job to become a full-time writer.
DG: I picked up Merton's book on the desert saints quite by chance, and its defense of the contemplative life awakened a deep hunger in my soul. Merton described how a small group of men had abandoned the sophisticated city of Alexandria in the fourth century to live and pray in the desert—renouncing material comforts and worldly ambitions to focus on their inner lives. He made a compelling case for a life dedicated to matters that the everyday world does not understand.

It's hard to describe the force with which Merton's ideas struck me. I read his many books on the contemplative life and pondered them seriously. I recognized that I was one of those odd people who need silence and solitude (even though that would have seemed absurd to anyone observing my busy and practical daily life). I knew that I needed to remake my life. Eventually I quit business and a few years later moved back to California for a quiet rural life. Merton was not entirely responsible for those changes, but he was a catalyst. And, of course, Merton was one of the writers who made me understand I had to reconnect more meaningfully with my Catholicism.

EK: What other writers influenced you in this way?
DG: One book that has exercised a lifelong influence on me is Saint Augustine's *City of God*, which I first read as a Stanford undergraduate. It has probably shaped my adult life more than any other book except the Gospels. Augustine helped me understand the danger of letting the institutions of power—be they business, government, or academia—in which we spend our daily lives shape our values. We need to understand what it is we give to the City of Man and what we do not. I couldn't have survived my years in business as a writer had I not resisted the hunger for wealth, power, and status that pervades that world. The same was true for my years in power-mad Washington. Another writer who helped me understand these things was the Marxist philosopher and literary critic Georg Lukacs—not a name one usually sees linked with Augustine's, but he was another compelling analyst of the intellectual and moral corruptions of institutional power.

EK: Any other writers?
DG: Many other authors have been important to me. Sometimes they spoke to a particular need I felt at a point in life. Others have been lifelong companions. Many of them were poets and novelists, but to list a few of the philosophers, theologians, and thinkers, I might mention: Søren Kierkegaard, Friedrich Nietzsche, Miguel de Unamuno, Mircea Eliade, Dietrich Bonhoeffer, George Orwell, Marshall McLuhan, Jacques Maritain, and recently René Girard. I have been particularly moved by the works of Albert Schweitzer (whom no one seems to read nowadays), especially his *The Quest of the Historical Jesus* and *The Mystery of the Kingdom of God*. I generally avoid devotional works, but back in my twenties I picked up a copy of Thomas à Kempis's *The Imitation of Christ*, and for years I would pack it in my briefcase on business trips. It helped me be a little less evil.

EK: Since leaving the NEA (and being awarded the Laetare Medal by Notre Dame), you seem to be speaking more publicly about the relationship between Catholicism and the arts. What led to this change?
DG: When I was a public official, it was inappropriate for me to speak personally about a number of subjects. For example, I never made a negative remark about any living American artist. Of course, I had my private

opinions, but it was important that no one mistook those private views for public policy. I did accept numerous invitations to speak at Catholic and Christian colleges and institutions, many of which had historically felt marginalized by the NEA, but I visited them in an official capacity as cultural rather than religious institutions.

Now that I am a private citizen again, I can speak from a personal point of view. At Catholic institutions, I feel it important to remind the audiences of two facts—first, how central the arts have been historically to Catholic worship and identity; and second, how completely the church has abandoned the arts in recent times. I feel very strongly that the church needs the arts, and also that the arts need the profound traditions of spiritual awareness and practice offered by the church.

EK: What has been the effect of this divorce between the church and the arts?
DG: The schism has hurt both faith and the arts. The loss of a transcendent religious vision, a refined and vigorous sense of the sacred, and the ancient and powerful tradition of symbolism and allusion have impoverished the language of the arts. We see the result of this immense loss in the cynical irony, the low-cost nihilism, the sentimental spiritual pretentions, and the shallow novelty of so much contemporary art.

Please understand, I am not asking that all art be religious. That would be a disaster. What I am suggesting is something more subtle and complex—namely, that once you remove the religious as one of the possible modes of art, once you separate art from the long established traditions and disciplines of spirituality, you don't remove the hungers of either artists or audiences, but you satisfy them more crudely with the vague, the pretentious, and the sentimental.

EK: What is the impact on the church?
DG: The loss of a vital aesthetic sensibility in the church has not only impoverished worship. It has also weakened the church's identity in modern society and limited the ways in which it speaks to the world. The graceless architecture of most new churches, the banal and formulaic painting and sculpture, the mediocre music so indifferently performed, and the tone-deaf language of religious services reveal a Catholic Church that has not only cut itself off from culture, but also lost touch with its own great traditions of fostering beauty and creativity. You see this problem in many ways but perhaps most dramatically in the flight of artists and intellectuals from the church.

EK: Why has this happened? Does the Catholic Church view art as an unnecessary luxury? There has been such a rich tradition of sacred art.

DG: There are many reasons. The church is rightly concerned with issues of poverty, health, education, and social justice. In the US, Catholicism has always been the religion of the poor, especially poor immigrants. These are communities with huge material needs. But, to quote a relevant old phrase, "Man does not live by bread alone." Even the poorest people—perhaps especially the poor—need beauty and the transcendent. Beauty is not a luxury. It is humanity's natural response to the splendor and mystery of creation. To assume that some group doesn't need beauty is to deny their humanity.

EK: Do you consciously think of yourself as part of a tradition of Catholic writers?

DG: I am a Catholic, and I am a writer. I don't think you can separate the two identities. But I have never wanted to be "a Catholic writer" in some narrow sense. Was Evelyn Waugh a Catholic writer? Was Flannery O'Connor or Muriel Spark? Well, yes and no. They were first and foremost writers who strived for expressive intensity and imaginative power. Their Catholicism entered into their work along with their humor, violence, sexuality, and imaginative verve. The few devotional works Waugh wrote are his worst books. His merciless early comic novels, which are Catholic only in their depiction of a hopelessly fallen world, are probably his best. Anthony Burgess's *A Clockwork Orange* is a deeply Catholic novel about free will, but it is also a violent, dystopian science fiction novel about social collapse and political hypocrisy, all of which is written in an invented futuristic slang. There is something complicated going on here that cannot be simplified into faith-based writing.

I have been drawn to Catholic writers from the moment as a teenager I first read James Joyce's *Portrait of the Artist as a Young Man*. I soon began to devour the work of Waugh, Burgess, O'Connor, Graham Greene, and Brian Moore. A little later I discovered Muriel Spark. (I have read all twenty-two of her novels, most of them twice.) And let's not forget poor, doomed, marvelous John Kennedy Toole. What these writers have in common is not simply their Catholicism, but (with the exception of Greene and Moore) that they are comic writers who luxuriate in humanity's fallen nature. None of them can be construed as a devotional writer.

EK: I can't help notice that these are all prose writers. What about poets?

DG: That is the problem for a Catholic poet, isn't it? There isn't a modern poetic tradition comparable to the legacy of Catholic fiction. (And I didn't even mention half of the major novelists.) The poets constitute an odd tradition, made up mostly of converts, such as Edith Sitwell, Roy Campbell, and Allen Tate, or temporary converts such as Robert Lowell whose flamboyant Catholicism always struck me as literary posturing. This assemblage seems most notable for its eccentricity. I found little to sustain me there.

My poetic models were the great Modernists, such as Robert Frost, T. S. Eliot, Ezra Pound, Wallace Stevens, W. H. Auden, Paul Valéry, Rainer Maria Rilke, Eugenio Montale, and—much later—Robinson Jeffers. Of these poets, Rilke, Valéry, and Montale were raised Catholic, but none of them practiced the faith as adults. Stevens became a Catholic only on his deathbed. For Catholic poets I had to go back to Dante, Shakespeare, Baudelaire, and Hofmannsthal.

There was, however, one special exception. At Harvard I studied with Robert Fitzgerald, the great translator of Homer, Virgil, and Sophocles. He was deeply Catholic, and his teaching and literary example had a profound effect on me. One of the many things he showed me was the continuity of the Catholic imagination across European literature. He also helped me master prosody and versification. At Harvard I also studied with Northrop Frye, who was an ordained minister as well as professor of English. His brilliant course on myth and poetry had an enduring impact on my understanding of both literature and the Christian mythos. He was an astonishing teacher in the lecture hall.

EK: And what about your place in this tradition?

DG: I don't see myself as working in an active tradition of Catholic poets because such a tradition hardly exists in contemporary American letters. I feel deep affinities with other Catholic writers, but my deepest relationships are mostly with the dead. That will make no sense to some people, but it seems quite natural to a Catholic raised on the notion of the communion of saints. What has sustained me has been my sense of literature as an expression of the City of God, a place one has elected to enter in contradiction to the City of Man.

A poet's calling requires one to stand outside the marketplace—be it commercial or academic—and to write as well and as truthfully as one can. We don't write for the authorities—political or aesthetic. We write for the fellow citizens of our invisible city. We render unto Caesar those things that are Caesar's, but we do not render up the truth. So what is my place in this tradition? I am just another pilgrim.

EK: Whom do you write for?

DG: Let me begin by saying whom I don't write for. I don't write for poets or literary critics. I don't write for readers of any particular faith, politics, or aesthetic. It seems a grave danger to write only for people who share your own ideology—a kind of psychic laziness. I can't imagine writing just for Catholics. A religious poem, for instance, should speak to an atheist as much as a believer. It might speak differently perhaps, but it needs to transcend any system of belief and touch some common humanity. Maybe "transcend" is the wrong word. "Exceed" might be better. John Donne's "divine" poems have such an *excess* of meaning that their appeal isn't limited to Anglicans. The same is true of Dante, Hopkins, Eliot, Auden, or Dylan Thomas.

I write for other human beings who both resemble me and differ from me in ways I can't predict. I hope for readers who are alert and intelligent, though not necessarily learned. I speak to deeply felt experience rather than to higher education, though I do usually conceal a few jokes that only the erudite will catch. I still believe in what Samuel Johnson called "the common reader," who is not an unintelligent reader but one open to pleasure and surprise. I was raised among the working poor, and I know that intelligence and creativity are found in every class and race and region. A poet should entice rather than exclude.

EK: Over the years you have been put in many categories. You've been called a New Formalist poet, a California poet. Why do you think your identity as a Catholic poet has been overlooked until quite recently?

DG: Most readers are very literal, and they focus mostly on subject matter. Since I didn't write poems about the crucifixion or the Virgin Mary, it never occurred to them that I was a Catholic poet. What makes my poetry Catholic is the worldview, the sacramental use of symbols, the redemptive role of suffering, the interpenetration of the sacred and the mundane, and—crucially perhaps—the conviction that truth and beauty are interdependent. I am not drawn to the stage business of Catholicism—its pomp and circumstance. I write from the daily particulars of real life. You shouldn't have to visit the Vatican to sense the divine. It is everywhere if you know how to look.

EK: In a 2003 article in *Commonweal* you said, "American intellectual culture remains unconsciously anti-Catholic." Do you still regard this to be true?

DG: No, I don't. It has now become consciously anti-Catholic. I now regularly read the most overtly bigoted things in the press, things that no one would say about any other group. At present it seems *de rigueur* to hate

Catholics as impediments to secular progress. Robespierre felt the same way during the French Revolution. I guess we should feel grateful that our intellectual pundits don't own a guillotine.

EK: How does the Catholic vision differ from other traditions of Christianity?
DG: To answer that question would require a shelf of books. There are so many Christian traditions. But let me mention one aspect of Catholicism that affects the writer. All Christian denominations believe in original sin and humanity's fallen nature, but Catholicism emphasizes the slow and difficult nature of the personal struggle toward salvation. The notion of suddenly being "saved" feels alien to a Catholic who sees life as a pilgrimage in which each step forward can easily be followed by a fall backward from grace. For that reason the great Catholic writers characteristically write about the experience of sinners rather than saints, often people of great spiritual capacity who have lost their way. O'Connor's mass-murderer, the Misfit, is one example, as is Greene's nameless whiskey priest.

EK: Isn't this emphasis on the dark side of humanity mostly a modern aspect of Catholic literature?
DG: Think of the greatest Catholic poem ever written, Dante's *Commedia*, which was finished around 1320. Where does it begin? In the dark wood of despair where a lost sinner must confront the terrifying embodiments of his own sins. How does the poet begin his transformative journey toward grace? He descends into the darkness of hell to experience the nature of evil. That spiritual premise is profoundly Catholic. This emphasis on human weakness, spiritual failure, and evil allows the writer to explore the full range of human experience. The great theme of Catholic imaginative literature is the violent and painful struggle for redemption in a fallen world.

I am devoted to gentle books such as the *Fioretti* of Saint Francis of Assisi, but they lack the dramatic intensity of *The Power and the Glory* or "A Good Man Is Hard to Find." Catholic literature seldom feels the need to be uplifting or devotional. Instead it depicts the difficult road to salvation in a fallen world. François Mauriac's brilliant novel *Nest of Vipers* has only one secondary character who is not morally contemptible, but it profoundly explores the redemptive nature of love. These writers present life in all its rich and contradictory complexity while viewing it from the perspectives of faith. It is a potent combination. By comparison, American Protestant writing has often tried to present good people doing good things. Occasionally a masterpiece such as Marilynne Robinson's *Gilead* appears, but it is a harder task to realize.

EK: Except for Dante, you've talked about fiction. What about Catholic poetry?

DG: Dante is not an exception. The great Catholic poets tend to wrestle with the darker spiritual emotions—guilt, doubt, and despair. For every great joyous poem Gerard Manley Hopkins wrote, there is a corresponding dark one. That's why I think of Baudelaire as an essentially Catholic poet. He saw himself as a man who was damned by his own sins. All he had left at a certain point was to revel in his own damnation. Catholic poetry ponders the possibility of damnation. But while it rejects the sort of sentimentality that vitiates so much religious poetry, it also opens itself to the immanence of grace. One sees this in the best Catholic poetry—in Hopkins, for instance, or Mario Luzi, the Italian Modernist whom I consider the greatest Catholic poet of the twentieth century. Not the easiest, by any means, but a religious poet of international stature. He is hardly read in America and never—in my experience—by Catholics.

EK: After avoiding academic employment for years, you have just accepted a half-time position at the University of Southern California as the first Judge Widney Professor of Poetry and Public Culture. What was your first semester like at USC?

DG: I liked USC a great deal. It has the strongest collection of arts programs of any university in the country, and it is full of abundantly creative people. The place is also strikingly optimistic and confident about the future—a rare thing at the moment for a university. It was also wonderful to be back in my old hometown.

I taught two courses—an undergraduate survey of modern American poetry and a graduate seminar on "Words and Music" at USC's Thornton School of Music. The seminar explored material that lies outside the conventional scope of musical study—the relationship between poetry and music in opera, song, worship, and theater. It was a challenge to put the material together in a coherent form, especially since my students were singers, composers, and instrumentalists who mostly lacked any literary education. I enjoyed exploring the conjunction of the two arts.

EK: What are your plans for the future?

DG: After eight years in Washington, I want a quieter life. I want to return to writing poetry and essays. I will be teaching each fall at USC, and that will be my public life, which will be active and engaged. But the rest of the year I hope to hide in Sonoma County. I like to divide the day into writing and manual labor. I have twenty hilly acres of oaks, redwoods, and madrones, and there is always work to do. I'm trying to restore the landscape to its natural state and protect the native species. No one really cares about this goal but me. My neighbors think I should tear out the trees and plant grapes. But I prefer the place the way God landscaped it.

Dana Gioia, Poet

Michael Passafiume / 2015

From *Lunch Ticket* (Winter/Spring 2015). Reprinted by permission of Michael Passafiume.

Michael Passafiume: How would you describe the state of poetry today in relation to print versus electronic publishing?

Dana Gioia: The state of poetry in print and electronic media is oddly similar. A huge amount of poetry constantly appears in both media, but the audience is small and increasingly fragmented. The Internet makes poetry more easily accessible, but it hasn't grown the readership. I love the convenience of the Internet. If I become interested in a poet, I can usually find something instantly on the web. That's nice, but in such cases the poet gets neither sales nor royalties. That's not so nice.

MP: In "Can Poetry Matter?" you called poetry "a modestly upwardly mobile, middle-class profession—not as lucrative as waste management or dermatology but several big steps above the squalor of bohemia." That was written in 1991. Has your view on the profession of poetry since altered?

DG: I was, of course, talking about the academic profession of creative writing. Over the past twenty years things have changed but not for the better. Like many other middle-class professions, the university creative writing trade has suffered significant damage. Nowadays there are virtually no new full-time jobs. There is also a generational split between the older tenured faculty, who are comparatively well-paid, and younger people, who lack full-time employment, job security, and benefits.

The situation for writers is actually worse than for most other fields. English departments need lots of graduate students to teach freshman composition courses, so for the past three decades they have deliberately admitted far more students than can ever be placed in permanent jobs.

These young writers and scholars are openly exploited with poor pay and little likelihood of career advancement. It is a shameful situation. Academia has created a lost generation.

MP: In the title essay of your book *Disappearing Ink*, you said: "Finally, there has been a decline in the quality and seriousness of poetry reviewing itself. . . . Consequently, the reader seriously interested in following contemporary poetry finds that criticism now comes mainly in four varieties: invisible, incomprehensible, inaccessible, and insincere."

And in "Can Poetry Matter?" you again turned your sights on the topic of poetry reviewing: "Several dozen journals now exist that print only verse. They don't publish literary reviews, just page after page of freshly minted poems. The heart sinks to see so many poems crammed so tightly together, like downcast immigrants in steerage."

Today, unless it's a collection by a well-known, well-regarded poet ("well" being relative), you might find coverage about a new book of poetry in the *New York Review of Books* or the *Cortland Review*, but coverage will likely be scarce in publications such as the *New York Times* or the *Los Angeles Times*. Do reviews matter to anyone beyond the narrow scope of literary scholars and creative writers?

DG: Literature does not exist in a cultural vacuum. Criticism creates the conversation about literature that informs and enlarges the audience. When criticism is healthy, literature becomes more relevant and vital. Reviews give us the news of literature. These reviews matter greatly when they are intelligent, well-written, and honest. When I finish a piece by a critic like Clive James or Adam Kirsch, I not only feel more alert and informed; their writing whets my appetite for poetry.

Reading a first-rate critic, we enjoy the privilege of following a fellow reader's mind and emotions as he or she engages in a literary work. Their efforts amplify and refine our ability to read the work. Unfortunately, so many reviews nowadays feel tedious and untrustworthy—full of bland approbation and generic blather. Those reviews don't matter because they don't offer much that's useful to the reader.

And, at least in my case, they dull my appetite for the art.

MP: You told me that a poem should be personal, but it shouldn't be autobiographical. A poem is about us . . . a common space both of us can occupy. You should feel as much ownership of it as I do. I'm a poet whose work is highly autobiographical and whose style often pitches a tent in the confessional camp. Even so, I strive to engage a reader on multiple levels: I want them to learn about me, but I also want them to learn something about themselves, to experience that Zen-like moment of "Hey, I've been where this guy's been before; I've had those same feelings!"

What's your yardstick for transforming "this is about me" to "this is about us"?

DG: There are two ways of answering this question—first from the reader's perspective, then from the author's.

As a reader of poetry, I worry that contemporary poetry has become too mired in needless private details. I often come across poems that would be twice as good if they were half the length. It's not merely a matter of lost intensity. It's about leaving some room in the poem for the reader to bring his or her own life. Prose can gain by the slow accumulation of detail, but poetry usually loses its energy and edge. A poem should evoke memory and emotion, not just catalogue them.

As a writer, I try to make my poems personal but not exhaustively auto-biographical. What I leave out can be as important as what I include. I want to invite the reader to bring his or her own life into the poem. In fact, I've come to believe that this need for the reader to "complete" the poem is part of the particular frisson of poetry. That is why poetry is a bit harder to read than prose. We need to do part of the imaginative work, and that effort brings us deeper into the text. For that reason, I try to cut out any detail that doesn't seem necessary, and then I cut some more.

MP: In a lecture you gave to Antioch students last year on "The Poetic Line," you claimed that the line is the key factor that separates poetry from other forms of literature. You also said that "in a poem, the microcosm is the macrocosm."

DG: The most obvious difference between prose and verse is lineation. In art, obvious elements are always important—although that is often what experts ignore. Poetic technique consists mostly of exploiting the expressive possibilities of lineation as a formal principle to communicate and intensify meaning. Formal verse does it in auditory ways; free verse in syntactic or visual ways. The line is like the frame on a painting. It shows us where to pay attention.

Now on to your second question. One of the interesting things about poetry is that one can take a line or two—say from Yeats or Eliot or Dickinson—and it has the weird quality of recapitulating the power of the entire poem. "I will show you fear in a handful of dust." "The Soul selects her own Society—/ Then—shuts the Door." "The ceremony of innocence is drowned."

A few words have the ability to evoke the larger structure of meaning and music. That is why people quote poetry in a way that they don't quote fiction or drama. This social practice recognizes that a special power of poetry is its quotability. Offer a few lines from a great poem, and you already create a heightened state of attention in the audience.

MP: Taking into account today's reading audience, what is the value of rhyme and rhyme schemes to creative writing students?
DG: Rhyme is a powerful and perennially popular technique. Over the past thirty years it has become even more popular with the rise of hip-hop. Rhyme may also be one of the obvious ways in which to expand the audience for poetry since it appeals to the ordinary reader. Any aspiring poet should learn how to write in rhyme. Even if they don't find the technique useful for their later work, it improves their eye and ear.

There is also something that I've seen again and again among young writers. If you make writing students learn a dozen different verse forms—not just rhyme and meter but even different types of free verse—they are astonished to discover that they have a particular talent for some technique they've never tried before. The forms allow them to discover things about their own imagination. At the start no writer really knows what he or she does best. By learning the craft of writing they learn about themselves.

MP: I've seen you give readings and read your work. Rhyming seems to come natural to you. Is that a fair assumption? What about it do you enjoy? How do you avoid the dreaded "chime effect?"
DG: I have complicated feelings about rhyme. Over the years I've noticed that about a third of my poems rhyme—exactly the same proportion that are in free verse. I find it an intoxicating, mysterious, and maddening technique. Used well, rhyme offers pleasure and musicality to a poem in ways that most people can immediately apprehend. The trick is figuring out when a poem wants to be rhymed. As a new poem starts to emerge in one's imagination, what shape does it want to take? Rhyme moves a poem from conversational speech towards song. That is not always the right direction.

For me, rhymes either come at once or they take forever. I'm delighted that you find my rhymes so natural. It takes hard work to make them seem effortless. When I hear people talk about "imposing" a form or rhyme on a poem, it seems to me that they have the process backwards. You can't impose a rhyme on a line without making it sound false or awkward. You have to lure the rhyme out of the words. That usually means revising the whole line, not just the final words. Richard Wilbur once told me that a poet rhymes lines, not words. That observation struck me as right.

MP: Suppose that you have a day or two, unfettered from social or work obligations, and you want to get some writing done. What is your process?
DG: My process is terrible. I usually have trouble getting started. I waste hours doing everything except the task at hand. I do the dishes. I go outside and prune trees. I answer letters. I drink lots of coffee. Finally, I get so angry at myself that I become depressed. I boil in self-contempt. About half an hour later, I start writing. I'm sure if I had an analyst, he or she would have a great deal to say about my need for psychic disturbance.

I should add that every now and then a poem just comes in the window and lands on the page. In those cases, it seems that I have been writing it for years in the back of my mind. On those days the dishes sit in the sink.

MP: Do you ever tire of poetry—either reading or writing it?
DG: I honestly love reading poetry—good poetry. What happens, however, is that after one gets bombarded by bad poetry, it just kills the appetite. I remember Elizabeth Bishop telling me that after reading some literary journals, she didn't want to look at another poem for months. In order to read poetry well, you need to be open and vulnerable. That's why bad poetry is so excruciating.

MP: Speaking of reading, what occupies space these days on your nightstand or iPad?
DG: Reading is a great and constant pleasure in my life. I can't recall a time in my life that I didn't read for pleasure. I still read a great deal of fiction—at least one novel or book of short stories a week. The trouble is that I often feel I've read most of the books I'm likely to love. So I reread a great deal. This past year I've reread four novels by Friedrich Durrenmatt as well as much of Chekhov. Last night I finished *Dear Committee Members* by Julie Schumacher, a short novel that consists entirely of letters of recommendation by a teacher of creative writing. It was very witty and at times quite touching. The best new novel I've read lately is Ben Lerner's *Leaving the Atocha Station*. It is in some ways a conventional *Bildungsroman* about a young poet trying to find himself on a fellowship to Spain, but Lerner's prose has remarkable richness and bite. He portrays the delusions of a young male artist with merciless accuracy. Lerner is also a poet. His verse is good, but fiction is his true métier.

For poetry, the best new book I've read is J. Allyn Rosser's *Mimi's Trapeze*. I'm still not crazy about the title, but the poems both moved and fascinated me. Rosser's poetry is smart and clever, but her work seethes with such quiet emotion that the effect is deeply emotional. I don't understand why Rosser isn't on everyone's list of the best younger poets.

MP: If time travel becomes a reality tomorrow, where will you go?
DG: I would go back to December 1987 and try to prevent the death of my first son.

MP: Do you write for an audience or only for yourself?
DG: I suppose a poet might write only for oneself, but that situation doesn't appeal to me. A poem without readers seems a diminished thing. I have always written for an audience—but not the small, cantankerous audience that exists for contemporary poetry. I write for the sort of person who reads novels, listens to jazz, watches old movies. These people don't pay much attention to poetry. But it's my experience that they like good poems when they encounter them. It's not a bad thing for poetry to compete with fiction or film. I've always assumed that I would have to create my readership as I went along.

MP: What advice would you give a fledgling writer pertaining to the craft of poetry?
DG: Love the art. Be passionate. Immerse yourself in it for hours every day—reading, writing, memorizing, reciting. Learn poems by heart. Bring them into the center of your being. Take pleasure in mastering technique. Study great poems and not-so-great poems, so that you can tell the difference. If you don't love poetry so much that all this labor seems like fun, then try something else. Fame and fortune are unlikely outcomes for the poet. The main reward is doing work you love.

An Interview with Dana Gioia

Mia Herman / 2016

From *Tethered by Letters* (https://tetheredbyletters.com/?s=dana+gioia).
Reprinted by permission of Dana Gioia and Mia Herman.

Mia Herman: How would you say your writing career began?

Dana Gioia: I was a dreamy kid. Both my parents worked, so I was left alone much of time. I lived in an apartment. There weren't any other kids around except for a few cousins. I read. I played records. I fiddled at the piano my dead uncle had left us. I wanted to hang around music, art, literature, but I didn't know what that meant back then. Art seemed to exist in a different world from my ugly urban neighborhood. But my destiny was already settled. Something was unfolding inside me. I was doomed to be an artist.

MH: Was there a certain event, person, or creative impulse that guided you to forge your own literary path?

DG: My mother used to read or recite poems to me. They were not poems that today's critics would celebrate. They were verses she had learned in school—Poe, Whittier, Longfellow, Riley, Kipling, Tennyson. I loved the sound of them. I found poetry intoxicating, though I never imagined myself writing a poem. But I always associated poetry with pleasure and an exhilarating sense of heightened consciousness.

I assumed I'd be a musician. I played piano, clarinet, and saxophone. I composed lots of amateurish music. I read poetry, but not in any serious way. Then at 19 I suddenly found myself drawn into the art. It surprised me, but I went with the impulse. In a few months I knew that this was what I had to do with my life. I also knew that I had much to learn. I've spent the rest of my life as a student of the art.

This is what happens in the lives of poets. You don't choose to be a poet. The art chooses you.

MH: What can you tell us about your creative process? Is there a daily routine you follow?
DG: I write according to a simple, five-step plan—anxiety, delay, avoidance, despair, and then a little work. Each night I plan to reform my terrible habits. The next morning I go through the same process. But things get done.

I can write prose on demand. But poetic inspiration is a mostly involuntary process. A poem either comes or it doesn't. When poems arrive, I try to let them take the shape they want. I never choose a topic in advance, though my poems often have a clear subject. Nor do I choose a form, though many of my poems use meter, rhyme, and stanza patterns. A phrase or line comes into my head along with a powerful rush of feeling. Writing the poem is my way of figuring exactly what this impulse is telling me. I don't will a poem into being. I unravel it.

MH: How does that process work in practical terms?
DG: My poems develop slowly. I write the first draft in a sort of trance. I don't try to impose any design on the poem. I just let it come in whatever way it wants. I usually draft between one and three pages of fragments before the rush of inspiration runs out. I then put the poem down for a day or two. When I return to it, I look at the draft to decide what shape the language suggests. Does it want to be in free verse or meter? Does it want to rhyme? Then the process of revision begins.

MH: How much revision does it take to finish a poem?
DG: An easy poem takes fifteen drafts, a hard one takes fifty. I sometimes work on a poem for years before it's finished. I get some of my best ideas in revision. I am happiest when the poem unfolds in ways that surprise me. My best poems have mostly taken forms that I would never have predicted in the first draft.

MH: Your book, *99 Poems: New & Selected*, was just published by Graywolf Press. How is this book different from your others?
DG: *99 Poems* surveys my whole career as a poet. It presents my best work from the last thirty years. Few people really know the range of my work because I've published my books at such long intervals—only four volumes since 1986.

MH: How did you choose what to include?

DG: I tried to make my *Selected Poems* selective. Most selected volumes are too long. They include too much work for the average reader. I cut over half of my poems. I also gave *99 Poems* a unique organization. I dislike the weird way in which new and selected volumes are organized—usually with the new poems up front followed by the earlier work in chronological order. I find that distracting. Most readers don't care much about the chronology of a poet's work. That is for scholars to ponder. The common reader wants to appreciate the individual poems. I decided to arrange *99 Poems* around seven themes—Mystery, Place, Remembrance, Imagination, Story, Song, and Love.

MH: Can you discuss the themes and topics that interest and inspire you most?

DG: I write about the ideas and experience that emerge from my life. Some people write poems about the epistemology of perception or the unified field theory. I write about love and death, time and nature. I'm fascinated by what Yeats referred to as "the supreme theme of Art and Song." I like to write about the difficult lives of artists and thinkers.

But let me repeat that for me writing poems is not a voluntary process. I write the poems that life and the Muse give me.

MH: What would you say is the most important element for crafting a poem?

DG: Creating a magic spell of heightened attention and sensitivity in the reader. All poetic technique is about creating that sense of enchantment. If the poem doesn't cast that spell, it's just ordinary language.

MH: Your essay titled "Can Poetry Matter?" created an international discussion about the role of poetry in contemporary culture. (And it became the title essay of your critical collection that was a finalist for the National Book Critics Circle Award.) If there were one main point you could have your readers take away, what would it be?

DG: The essay makes a long, careful argument about the current state of poetry—to demonstrate how marginal it has become in our society. The essay also contains a number of positive ideas about reviving poetry's popularity. If I had to pick one point from the piece, it would be the conviction that we can increase the audience for poetry.

MH: What advice might you give to writers who are just starting their careers?

DG: Love the art. Immerse yourself in it. Read as much as possible. Memorize poems that move or delight you. Search out friendships with other writers. Create your own community of writers. It doesn't have to be large—two or three people will sustain you. Write or revise every day, even if only for an hour. Don't postpone writing until some mythical moment arrives. Poetry begins in your real life or not at all. Poetry is not a career. It is a vocation, a dedication. It will transform your life, if you let it.

Interview with Dana Gioia

John Cusatis / 2016

From *DLB: Twenty-First-Century American Poets*, vol. 380 (2017): 327–33.
Reprinted by permission of John Cusatis.

John Cusatis: You are credited with being a major figure in the widespread revival of form in American poetry. Can you trace the development of this revival and its continuing impact on twenty-first-century poetry?

Dana Gioia: When I began writing poetry in the mid-1970s, there existed a general hostility toward rhyme, meter, and narrative in the literary world. Sometimes form was openly attacked; mostly it was just marginalized as stylistically retrograde. Some older poets, such as Richard Wilbur and Anthony Hecht, still published formal verse, but most of the influential elders, including Donald Hall, W. S. Merwin, Anne Sexton, Philip Levine, and Adrienne Rich had publicly converted to free verse. Not surprisingly, almost all younger poets rejected form and narrative. They saw themselves as champions of a Modernist tradition that privileged free verse and the lyric mode.

As a poet, I felt equally drawn to both free and formal poetry. Each mode provided different insights and pleasures. It seemed silly not to use all of the resources the art provided. My motivation was less ideological than erotic. I was spellbound by the pleasure of shaping language. I was particularly attracted by the physicality of meter.

As soon as I began publishing formal poems, my work was attacked. In response, I felt the need to articulate my poetics, so I wrote several essays, such as "Notes on the New Formalism" and "The Dilemma of the Long Poem." Other poets did the same. These pieces generated a huge amount of controversy—often more smoke than fire. The ongoing public debate came to be known as the "Poetry Wars."

Literary movements are always temporary. They last a decade or so, and then they either die or merge into the mainstream. The best "New Formalist" poets gradually became mainstream figures. There was no dramatic climax to the so-called "Poetry Wars," only slow assimilation and change. Free and formal verse gradually ceased to be considered polar opposites. Form became one of the available styles of contemporary practice. Today one finds poems in rhyme and meter in most literary magazines. New Formalism became so successful that it no longer needed to exist.

Actually, it feels strange to talk about these events—historical episodes from a previous century. At the time I was immersed in the unfolding drama of it all. Everything was so public and contentious. It was a very complicated coming-of-age for a writer. Now it feels so distant, as if it had happened to someone else. I have had so many different lives in the meantime.

JC: In your 2002 preface to the Tenth Anniversary Edition of *Can Poetry Matter?* you wrote that in the decade following the publication of your landmark title essay, "The state of American poetry has changed radically." More than another decade has passed since this reassessment. How does the state of contemporary poetry appear to you now, both in the quality of the work produced and the popular and critical attention given to that work?

DG: Two of the most important changes in American poetry over the past quarter-century have been the creation of a huge nonacademic literary culture and the revival of poetry as an auditory art. These developments have both expanded the art and diversified the sorts of artists who practice it.

While university-based poetry programs have remained mostly unchanged (though slightly more diverse in their participants), nonacademic literary activity has grown exponentially. There are now thousands of venues—bookstores, libraries, cafés, pubs, galleries, and community centers—where poetry is performed and discussed. There are also innumerable independent presses, small magazines, websites, online journals, radio shows, fine presses, and podcasts to publish and present it. There has even been an explosion of civic offices for poets—state, county, and town laureateships.

Young poets no longer depend solely on the university for employment and validation. This growing trend has been accelerated by the collapse of the academic job market. Younger writers are now less likely to be teachers. In response, they have created an alternative literary culture in the cities and even suburbs where they live. This is the new bohemia—vital, inclusive, democratic, economically mixed, and geographically dispersed.

Historical bohemias were concentrated in a few urban neighborhoods. The new bohemia is both everywhere and nowhere, linked only by technology and common purpose.

In the new bohemia, poetry is mostly oral and performative. The most common form of publication for today's poet is the poetry reading, either real or electronic. Print remains foundational; book publication still validates the poet. But the printed page has gradually become a secondary means of reaching new readers. Most poetry "readers" now want to hear a poet before they buy a book.

JC: In *Can Poetry Matter?* you discuss "critical boosterism" regarding the tendency for creative-writing colleagues to help one another build literary reputations by publishing only positive reviews. In the mid-twentieth century, tough poet-critics such as Yvor Winters or Randall Jarrell could singlehandedly damage a poet's reputation. Can you comment on the politics of literary reputation? What do you believe ultimately secures a writer's place in the American literary tradition?

DG: How poets achieve posterity is a complicated question. Let me suggest two basic forces that are at work above and beyond questions of literary quality. First, do a significant number of people continue to read the work? Second, do readers (especially the teachers and critics) have some larger context in which to place the work?

I am just old enough to have seen famous poets sink into obscurity. Some deserved the fate; others, I felt, did not. In both cases, their decline in reputation came from their failure to sustain any posthumous readership beyond their scholarly advocates. For example, the Fugitive poets, still the subject of considerable scholarship, have all disappeared from the canon, even the very fine John Crowe Ransom. People still publish articles and books about Allen Tate and Robert Penn Warren, but they have no general readership.

I have also seen unfashionable poets revived because their work suddenly seems relevant to some new cultural development. Edna St. Vincent Millay, for instance, vanished from anthologies and curricula because her formal and self-dramatizing autobiographical sensibility seemed old-fashioned and sentimental to Modernists. Half a century later she was revived by feminists and formalists. (It helps to have more than one group championing a poet's work, even if they praise different things.) Posterity isn't just about quality. Many fine poets are forgotten. Readers need a context in which to perceive the particular qualities of a poet.

JC: Speaking of reputations, I note that in 1987, the year of Robinson Jeffers's centennial, you wrote, "No major poet has been treated worse by posterity than Robinson Jeffers." Has this neglect subsequently been remedied? In what ways do you feel Jeffers's spirit may linger among the work of twenty-first-century poets?

DG: There has been a slow but significant revival of Robinson Jeffers over the past thirty years. All of his work is now in print, including three thousand pages of letters. There have been new biographies, a new bibliography, assorted critical studies, and an active scholarly society. There are also regular conferences and festivals. Meanwhile, in creative terms, Jeffers's work continues to haunt West Coast poets, writers, and photographers—especially naturalists. The impact isn't merely literary. In the West, nature writing and photography is political art.

Most of Jeffers's readership, however, remains outside the English Department. He has always had more influence among scientists, naturalists, and artists than among professors of literature. Jeffers fits neither into the standard academic views of Modernism nor into the poetics of personality identity. There is a scientific objectivity in Jeffers's poetry at odds with any aesthetic of confessional lyricism.

Jeffers's continuing influence is felt most strongly among environmentalists. He is the poetic prophet of global ecology. He understood how mindlessly humanity has misused Nature, and he wrote presciently from a global perspective. No other Modernist seriously explored the issue that most people now consider humanity's greatest challenge.

JC: As a major poet, critic, and cultural force of the late-twentieth and twenty-first centuries, what literary achievements of yours do you consider most satisfying?

DG: Most satisfying? In general terms, I'm proud to have engaged and expanded the audience for poetry. I tried to do this as an artist, a critic, and a cultural leader.

JC: Can you elaborate by providing some specific accomplishments, first, as a poet?

DG: As a poet, I developed a contemporary idiom, musical but very close to speech, which could shift from formal to free verse. I tried to reconcile different modes. That fusion allowed me to write in a variety of styles and genres—including longer narratives and even poetic drama for the stage and opera—without ever losing my individual voice. I'm proud of the diversity of my poems, though that is precisely the quality that confuses some critics who equate stylistic consistency with poetic sincerity.

JC: How about as a critic?
DG: As a critic, I wrote as a public intellectual in a clear and accessible style that addressed the intelligent common reader as well as the literati. I like to think that my essays and anthologies enlarged the audience for poetry as well as restored or established the reputations for neglected writers, such as Weldon Kees, Robinson Jeffers, Kay Ryan, and Ted Kooser.

JC: What about your career in public life?
DG: As a Chairman of the National Endowment for the Arts, I helped create public programs that brought millions of young people into fiction, poetry, and theater. That effort cost me nearly ten years of my writing life, but it gave me deep personal satisfaction. It also demonstrated that our country doesn't have to accept the notion of cultural decline. Of all the public programs, my favorite is Poetry Out Loud, the national high-school poetry recitation competition—now in its eleventh year. Over three million teenagers have participated. Poetry Out Loud has brought a new generation of Americans into poetry.

As a former federal bureaucrat, I was also proud to get out of Washington alive and return to poetry.

JC: In *Disappearing Ink* you noted that we were witnessing "the first generation of young intellectuals who are not willing to immerse themselves in the world of books." Now that you are a teacher, what changes have you noticed in how your students approach the study of literature versus your own habits as a student?
DG: Among college students today the demise of print culture has been almost absolute. They now use print as a secondary medium, acquiring their information electronically on screens. But no medium is content-neutral. Different media foster different sorts of communication. Students raised on screens are not easily able to read extended texts. They live in a lyric universe of short, sudden bursts of information, usually reinforced with images and background sound.

Bright, artistic undergraduates now tell me that they have never been able to finish a novel. Book-length narrative with its meticulous social and psychological detail is just too boring—which is to say *too difficult*—for many young readers. The new generation's total absorption in electronic media also traps them in the present tense with very limited knowledge of the past. Of course, the new media trains their intelligence in other ways. For example, it gives students extraordinary visual sophistication and aural dexterity.

Oddly, this cultural situation puts poetry at an advantage because it is short, evocative, and musical. Students respond to poetry, especially when they hear it aloud before they see it on the page. Through hip-hop and rock lyrics, they have considerable expertise in hearing poetry. Musical language is part of their daily experience.

It is a terrible time for the humanities, but not all that bad for poets. As Rome collapses, we get to strum our lyres to serenade the Ostrogoths. Who knows? The apocalypse could be an interesting gig. The end of one civilization marks the beginning of another. I'm curious to see the future.

JC: As a writer of many literary essays that have made an indelible impression on modern letters, and a proponent of the genre, what pieces do you consider among the most important literary essays of the past?

DG: The essay is the most direct and immediate way to shape literary culture. Critical books consolidate literary opinion, but essays provoke changes in sensibility and perspective. It's not merely that an essay can be read more easily. The essay form also requires a writer to concentrate and focus the argument. One reason academic criticism has become so remote from general literary culture is that the university bases its reward system on the publication of full-length monographs. Ideas that might have animated a fine essay are inflated into overlong and repetitious books.

What are some of my personal classics? As a teenager, I read Susan Sontag's *Against Interpretation* along with W. H. Auden's *The Dyer's Hand*. Sontag's title essay became a model for the sort of piece I wanted to write—tightly argued, sharply phrased, savvy but accessible. A few years later I read James Baldwin's *Notes of a Native Son*, which displayed even more of that electrifying energy. Meanwhile, Auden's more casual and aphoristic essays, such as "Reading" and "Writing," showed how an associative style could make connections that more closely reasoned prose could not. I found the same idiosyncratic energy, much amplified, in Ezra Pound whose powerful, telegraphic style now seems prophetic of streamlined twenty-first-century prose. Pieces like "A Retrospect" or "How to Read" remain perpetually useful. I admire the drier style of T. S. Eliot. His best pieces are generally his shortest and least formal. His brief note "Reflections on *Vers Libre*," for example, continues to influence contemporary poetic practice.

No one reads Anne Stevenson much in the US, but I find her essays, such as "Writing like a Woman," clarifying. She is part of an older generation in which many poets brought their full imaginative power into prose. I remember my thrill in grad school of taking new issues of quarterlies from the library shelf and reading essays by writers like Donald Hall, Cynthia Ozick, or Wendell Berry. Hall's "Poetry and Ambition," Ozick's "Against Modernity," and Berry's "The Specialization of Poetry" each condense the intellectual energy of a book into a dozen pages. All these writers were public intellectuals writing for a broad but mixed audience. I knew early that they were my people.

Two other critics I especially admire are Clive James and Adam Kirsch. James can't write a page without giving the reader a tangible sense of poetry's relation to real life. Kirsch has a relentless intelligence that gets to the heart of every writer he examines.

JC: Your 2012 collection, *Pity the Beautiful*, contains scattered references to a declining spirituality: the shopping mall as a temple, a crippled saint, a doubting monk, gods "no longer divine." Do these references reflect a criticism or a lament of twenty-first-century values, and, if so, can you elaborate on the subject?

DG: Contemporary America is besotted by a culture of material acquisition and the conspicuous display of wealth, of constant distraction and superficial novelty. Neither our secular nor religious ideals can hold their own against the global marketplace and its nonstop entertainment environment. Our culture has lost its ability to speak to what is best in us as a society. Our public values are now wealth, celebrity, fashion, and excessive consumption—all haunted by a reckless infatuation with violence.

You can make a good diagnosis of a culture by the people it celebrates. When I was a child, there were famous scientists, poets, humanitarians, doctors, scholars, and even a few saints. Even school kids knew that Dr. Albert Schweitzer, one of the most brilliant men of his generation, labored in poverty in equatorial Africa to provide free medical care. Nowadays, our celebrities are entertainment figures, sports stars, and the flamboyant super-rich, with a few politicians (most of them wealthy, too) to recognize the importance of sheer power. Even the visual arts have become a form of tax-deferred financial speculation.

Contemporary society is alienated and detached from itself. A decadent sense of materialism pervades contemporary thinking on both the right and the left—a shared assumption that more stuff, more money, more physical pleasure will make people happier and society more just. Is it any wonder that people have retreated into private worlds where they are sedated by a constant and addictive stream of electronic entertainment? They need these digital narcotics because they can't bear the reality they find around them—the chaotic clutter of our cities and our despoliation of nature.

So to answer your question—yes, my newer poems reflect a critique of our time and culture. The reason you have to ask is that I don't editorialize in my poems. The views are implicit rather than explicit. My sorrow for society's failures and our destruction of the natural world pervades every poem I write. I want the reader to feel the crisis from the inside and to be forced to articulate the ideas individually.

JC: You have speculated that the new post-print culture has not only changed the way that poetry is presented but also how it is written. Writing the new poems in your latest volume, *99 Poems: New & Selected*, were you conscious of a listening audience? If so, how did it affect the poems?

DG: With one exception, every poem in my last two books was written so that it could be heard aloud as well as read silently on the page. My method is not an original theory. This was the way in which Shakespeare, Blake, Frost, or Baudelaire conceived their poetry—speech raised to the level of song. There are things that become most tangible when the poem is heard, and other aspects that reveal themselves on the page. I like poems that seem simple until you reread them. I like to catch the reader coming and going.

JC: Which poem was the exception?

DG: It was "Title Index to My Next Book of Poems," an intricately disguised postmodern narrative that had to be seen on the page. It is impossible to read aloud without losing its essential *esprit*. So naturally someone immediately asked me to record it!

JC: Many of the poems in *99 Poems: New & Selected* contain references to time slipping away and taking the thing people value with it. How does poetry serve as a "spiritual resource," to borrow a term you use in *Disappearing Ink*, in the face of the erosive nature of time?

DG: Time and mortality are inescapable themes for poetry. If we were immortal, like the Olympian gods living outside time, we wouldn't need art to intensify and commemorate our existence. We would have existence itself, endless and unselfconscious. But humanity needs poetry to articulate what it means to be alive and mortal.

Poetry is our most concise, moving, and memorable way of using language to express our existence in this astonishing world where we move through time toward our own extinction. Like all art, poetry makes us more alert and attentive to the mystery of our own lives. Mortality makes every moment precious and unrepeatable. If it is good enough, poetry captures those moments in a way that makes them repeatable and enduring. Since we aren't gods, we need to write as if we were.

The California Imagination: Dana Gioia

Maggie Paul / 2017

From *Catamaran Literary Reader* 5.2 (Summer 2017): 81–89. Reprinted by permission of Maggie Paul.

Maggie Paul: You are a native Californian who has written about the literary heritage of the state. Did that affect your reaction to being named the tenth California Poet Laureate, and did the appointment come as a surprise or was it something you were expecting?

Dana Gioia: I was delighted and surprised to be chosen laureate. It was a great honor to be recognized by my native state. I didn't expect it.

MP: What have you been doing as laureate?

DG: The laureate's official duties are minimal—just a few readings a year. I wanted to do something more ambitious in order to reach beyond the urban cultural centers. Los Angeles, San Francisco, and Berkeley dominate our literary scene. Why not visit all of the state's fifty-eight counties, most of which are small and rural? California is immense, almost half the size of Western Europe. I thought it would be fun. So far I've visited thirty-five counties.

We've put together a different event in each county—combining my visit with local talent. We invite the town or county laureates to read with me. We also invite the high school students who have won the local Poetry Out Loud competitions. Sometimes the events get very large. In Ukiah we had six past and present laureates as well as the high school recitation champ. In Lakeport we had five laureates. My visit creates a chance for the local literati to gather.

MP: Can you tell us how your parents came to settle in California?

DG: My father arrived in LA in the Depression when his immigrant family was wiped out in Detroit. My grandfather packed everyone in an old car and drove west to start over. He liked California because the weather and landscape reminded him of Sicily. They chose Hawthorne because that was a place poor people lived. Eventually his whole clan followed. I had a hundred relations in or around Hawthorne.

My mother, Dorothy Ortiz, was born in Hawthorne. The Mexican side of my family has been in the US since 1900. The Ortiz men were vaqueros from Sonora and Chihuahua. After my great-grandfather, Jesús Ortiz, was murdered on the Wyoming frontier, my grandfather rode the cattle drives for a few years and then drifted into Los Angeles. The family became assimilated but remained poor.

MP: What was it like to be a child from two different cultures in Los Angeles in the 1950s and 1960s?

DG: It was odd. My father was the only person in his family who had married a non-Sicilian. I was always conscious that I was different. The experience didn't traumatize me, but it made me very sensitive to ethnicity—how cultures differ in even the simplest things. I'm still fascinated by immigrant family histories.

MP: What was it like in Hawthorne when you grew up?

DG: I was raised in a cluster of stucco apartments occupied by my Sicilian relations—grandparents, uncles, aunts, cousins. It was an urban peasant village speaking a Sicilian dialect in the middle of Los Angeles. The neighborhood was pretty bleak. Our apartment faced the garbage dumpsters behind a Chinese restaurant and a liquor store.

The whole family went to the same parish church, except my atheist uncle who never entered a church except for a funeral. My cousins and I walked together to the local parochial school. Hawthorne was mostly Mexican. The only Anglos I knew were Dust Bowl Okies. (I've been told recently not to say *Okie*, but these people proudly used the term to describe themselves.) My mother's family was scattered in nearby towns, though one of her brothers, a merchant marine, shared my room when he was on shore.

My dad's family spoke a Sicilian dialect. My mother knew no Italian so we spoke English at home—not always grammatically. The neighborhood spoke Spanish. The schools taught in English. And the Church still worshipped in Latin. My polyglot childhood was good training for life in California.

We were all poor, but we were together. I can't imagine a better way to grow up.

MP: Some writers resent being closely associated with their geographical homes. They feel it makes them appear regional or provincial. You seem proud of your California identity.
DG: Life doesn't occur as an abstraction. Each person's life happens in real time and specific places. The best writing usually emerges from that reality.
The problem for most writers is that they read things written in London or Paris, Vienna or New York, but that isn't where they live. Literature seems like an art that happens somewhere else. They worry that no one will take their actual lives—far from any cultural capital—seriously. Consciously or not, these writers begin to marginalize their own existence. That is a fatal mistake. Imagine if Faulkner or Joyce, Austen or Achebe felt their home landscapes were not worth writing about?
California shaped my imagination—the landscape, the cities, the rich demographics, the cultural energy. It was a fantastic place for a poet to be born. The challenge was to figure out what to do with all its weird and wonderful diversity. That's the hard part. Los Angeles in particular has never been fully assimilated into poetry, but what a subject!

MP: Several of your poems such as "California Hills in August," "California Requiem," "The Freeways Considered as Earth Gods," or "Becoming a Redwood" are tributes to your state. One of the many qualities of these "love poems" to California is their honesty; they embrace both the beauty and difficulties of the Golden State rather than idealizing it.
DG: One purpose of poetry is to allow us to see and bear the truth. The poet needs to reconcile our imagination with the world we actually live in—which is so often disturbing or confusing. Even in the best of times and places, there is always a distance between our inner and outer reality. In our beautiful but despoiled state, the distance is enormous. That gap is where a poem needs to begin.

MP: In *California Poetry: From the Gold Rush to the Present,* you assert, "No single quality characterizes all, or even most California writing." Like the landscape itself, California's literature is diverse and should be seen as "its own distinct imaginative enterprise." Can you describe an "underlying worldview" of the varied poets you included in the anthology?
DG: I reject the narrow stereotypes that have been used to describe

California writing. Critics or journalists, especially from the Northeast, often assume that all California poets are Beats and rebels. How does that stale and secondhand opinion account for Robinson Jeffers, Yvor Winters, Kay Ryan, Josephine Miles, or Shirley Geok-lin Lim? We need engaged criticism not clichés. A description of California poetry needs to start by actually reading and thinking about the poetry that has been written here.

California has a different history and geography from the Eastern United States. We were originally a Spanish colony. We face Asia and the Pacific Rim. We merge into Central America. Our population has been diverse from earliest history, even before the Spaniards arrived, when over a hundred native languages were spoken. The first colonial settlers were Spanish Catholics, not English Puritans. The first Anglos were sailors, soldiers, and prospectors, not families and farmers. California has always been different.

MP: How have those differences influenced the poetry?

DG: California poetry does not share a single theme or style. Its underlying character come from its particular perspective on the world. California poets tend to have a reverence for the natural landscape combined with an anxiety about its current human despoliation and colonial past. California writers also tend to see themselves as existing outside history. The place remains a sort of *tabula rasa* on which artists project their own dreams and nightmares. That is one reason why our writers are so frequently drawn to myth, religion, and philosophy, often borrowed from outside Western culture.

Our major poets also tend to be visionaries or dissenters. California poets usually see themselves in opposition to some cultural or political authority located elsewhere—Europe, Washington, New York. This defiant or sometimes sly contrarian stance is what unifies poets whose styles have nothing in common—Rexroth, Jeffers, Winters, Ryan, Snyder, Reed, Herrera, Addonizio, Bukowski. We are all contrarians.

MP: Does New Formalism fall into this category of contrarianism?

DG: If California poetry is oppositional, then it tends to move against the mainstream consensus of the moment. Just as the Beats reacted to the formalist academic poetry of the immediate post-war era, part of my generation reacted against the confessional, free verse poetry of the late 1970s. Many of the poets who revived form and meter either came from California or emerged there—Robert McDowell, Timothy Steele, Mark Jarman, Vikram Seth, Leslie Monsour, Kay Ryan, Kim Addonizio, and myself.

We weren't a group in any conscious sense, though some of the writers knew each other. Jarman and McDowell, for instance, met at UC Santa Cruz. Seth and Steele were friends at Stanford. We were just young poets playing with things like rhyme and narrative that had been discarded by the older generation. It was surprising how annoyed the literary world got at our dissenting views.

MP: When was the first time you read the work of Robinson Jeffers? How were you introduced to his poetry?

DG: I was never assigned a single poem by Jeffers in my schooling—not at Stanford or Harvard, not even in high school. In college I independently read Jeffers's play, *The Tower Beyond Tragedy*, because I was interested in Greek tragedy. I liked the play, but it made no deep impression. Today it strikes me as amazing that only a decade after his death, Jeffers had totally vanished from literary consciousness, even in California.

The event that had a profound impact was the Broadway revival of Jeffers's *Medea* with Zoe Caldwell and Judith Anderson in 1982. I was unprepared for the play's enormous power. Leaving the theater, I told my wife, "No one writes this well just once." I began reading through Jeffers's works and encountered a great American poet who had been written out of literary history. As a Californian working in New York, I also discovered a poet who captured the magnificence of my native landscape. A few years later I seized the opportunity to review *Rock and Hawk*, Robert Hass's edition of Jeffers's selected poems in the *Nation* and wrote the essay reprinted in *Can Poetry Matter?* Since then I have done my best to champion California's greatest poet.

MP: Jeffers attended USC where you currently teach each fall semester. When you were offered the Judge Widney Chair of Poetry and Public Culture at USC, did you think of Jeffers?

DG: Yes, I did remember Jeffers, but other memories were more important. The University of Southern California was a place I'd often visited in high school to compete in debate tournaments and attend concerts. My friends and I were young musicians. We couldn't afford seats at the LA Philharmonic or visiting opera companies. USC's Thornton School of Music, which was already a world-class institution, let us into concerts, operas, and recitals for free. I'd never forgotten the school's generosity to a bunch of scruffy teenagers.

I've tried to make Jeffers more visible at USC. He is our greatest literary alumnus. I've sponsored two big conferences. I also teach him in my undergraduate poetry course. At last year's conference a dozen of my students performed Jeffers poems from memory.

MP: In his book, *Robinson Jeffers: Poet and Prophet,* James Karman refers to Jeffers as an anti-Modernist whose poems differed in content and form from those of his contemporaries. His work reveals a reverence for earlier forms and traditions, including narrative verse and poetic drama. Might you also be considered an anti-modern modernist?
DG: That's an interesting but complicated question since it depends on how you define "modernism." Karman and I are probably in agreements, but we are using the term "modernism" in different ways. Let me explain my view.

I consider Jeffers a Modernist, but a different sort from T. S. Eliot or Ezra Pound. There is a modernism of style and a modernism of content. Jeffers's vision and content were modernist rather than his style, though his style was innovative. In this sense, he resembles some other key modern writers such as D. H. Lawrence, Eugene O'Neill, and Robert Frost (in his narratives). Jeffers's vision grew directly out of modern science and philosophy. His poetry was shocking to his early readers.

MP: Did Modernism influence you?
DG: I grew up on the "High Modernists," not only Eliot, Pound, and Stevens in English but Eugenio Montale, Paul Valéry, and Rainer Maria Rilke. These were formative authors for me. I would've loved to follow them. The problem was that their style and concerns belonged to the past. By the time I started writing, Modernism had been exhausted. All the major Modernist poets were dead. I loved my literary grandparents, but I didn't want to dress like them.

I had to develop another mode of writing that reflected my time and place. My life experience differed from the milieu of these exquisite mandarins. I was a working-class Catholic from California with roots in Mexico and Sicily. I had assimilated the Modernist tradition, but it wouldn't work for me unless I transformed it. I had to create my own brand of postmodernism.

MP: So what did you salvage from Modernism?
DG: From the Symbolist side of Modernism (especially Stevens, Rilke, and Montale) I learned the power of sound. So much of the meaning in early Modernist poetry is carried by its music. By contrast, the sound of 1970s American free verse seemed very boring. I wanted to create poetry with

compelling physical sound like the work of Stevens and Cummings (or a century earlier Dickinson). Sometimes I used meter or rhyme, sometimes just the word music of free verse.

From Frost, I learned how to create a poem that seems to unfold directly on the surface but contains a subtext that moves in a different direction—a poem that quietly argues with itself. One sometimes finds this quality in Symbolist poetry, but Frost does it in a tougher and more mischievous way.

My debt to Symbolism and High Modernism made me different from most of the New Formalists. My practice grew out of Modernism. I wasn't reacting against it. And, yes, I learned one other thing from the Modernists—the futility of imitating them. I had to make it new.

MP: Can you speak about the genius of another California poet, the former US Poet Laureate, Kay Ryan? Her brilliant work is reminiscent of Emily Dickinson's—so quick-witted, concise, and universal, using the fewest words possible to turn our preconceived notions inside out. I believe you were one of her earliest readers.

DG: In 1994 I came across Ryan's *Flamingo Watching* in a pile of new small press books. I had never heard of her. She had not yet appeared in the *New Yorker*. It was a wonderfully odd and entirely fresh book. I wasn't quite sure how to read the poems. But I kept the volume on my desk for months and kept dipping into it. As I slowly learned how to read her tightly packed poems, I realized that she wasn't merely good; she was fabulous! I showed her poems to several other writers who seemed indifferent. I decided to write a short essay on her work. It turned out to be the first essay anyone had ever done.

It is important to champion the work of new or neglected writers. I started putting Ryan into my anthologies and convinced a few other editors to do likewise. I introduced the Librarian of Congress to her work. Gradually, the rest of the world caught on. Things happened. Now it is a truth universally acknowledged that Ryan is one of the best poets writing in English.

MP: The legacy of William Everson is especially prominent in Santa Cruz. He taught at UC Santa Cruz in the 1970s and 1980s, and he lived for many years in a cabin north of the city. You have praised his accomplishments as a poet, critic, fine press printer, and Jeffers advocate. What about his work in particular appeals to you?

DG: Everson was a man of passionate dedication and varied accomplishment. He was also one of the most interesting Catholic poets in American literature. If I had to pick one thing that Everson did supremely well, I would choose his criticism. I don't know any American poets except Ralph Waldo Emerson or Ezra Pound who wrote criticism of such imaginative intensity and originality. Everson's book on Jeffers, *Fragments of an Older Fury*, is stunning. It's hard to think of anything that matches its tempestuous advocacy. His *Archetype West: The Pacific Coast as a Literary Region* (1976) and its "sequel," *Birth of a Poet: The Santa Cruz Meditations* (1982), are the best books ever written on the idea of West Coast literature. I'm sorry to describe him solely in superlatives, but only excess will suffice for Everson.

MP: You have often said that poetry is for everyone. It does not require an academic education to appreciate the power of its music and meaning.

DG: Not everyone enjoys reading poetry, but in my experience nearly everyone likes to hear a good poem well recited. The power of the art resides primarily in its orality. It's not a matter of simplicity. People respond to the dense and the mysterious if it has sufficient aural energy. Consider the popularity of Eliot, Cummings, Thomas, and Neruda, none of them simple poets.

MP: Many of your poems have an intimate conversational tone. They invite the reader in, often seeming to confide in the reader. How do you envision your reader during the act of composition?

DG: I love the kind of poem that starts as ordinary speech but quietly changes into a lyric without the reader noticing exactly how or when. Frost, Bishop, and Larkin are masters of this mode.

I never worry about the reader as a poem begins, but when I finish a poem for publication, I always remember that another human being will read it. Recognizing the reader doesn't mean making the poem easier. It's often just the opposite. I cut things out. I explain less. Why? Because all of my readers have spent their entire lives on the same planet as I have. Their minds are stocked with similar knowledge and experience. I want them to bring their life experience into my poems. I want their imagination and memories to collaborate with mine. I always treat my reader as an equal.

Seeing the reader as an equal also makes me avoid certain things. I hate poems that lecture the reader. Or poems that nag. I particularly dislike poems that become self-advertisements for the poet's own moral perfection. I'm a screwed-up person full of contradictions—just like my readers.

MP: Do you sometimes think of poetry as a way of sharing some secret, insight or story with the reader?

DG: Yes, I say things in poems I would never say in person to anyone except my confessor. I also write narrative poems because there are some truths that we can only tell one another as jokes or stories.

MP: Elizabeth Bishop was your teacher at Harvard. Was your poetry influenced by her work? "Nothing Is Lost" brings to mind her famous villanelle. What was it you learned from her?

DG: "Nothing is Lost" was actually written before Bishop's villanelle was published or at least before I read it. The connection you feel shows how powerfully her poem now owns the verb *lose*. My poem was originally part of a sequence called "Daily Horoscope," which played with the rhetoric of newspaper horoscope columns (second person, present and future tense, prophetic tone). Two other poems in that sequence, "Beware of Things in Duplicate" and "Do Not Expect," were reprinted in *99 Poems*.

Bishop influenced my poetry only slightly, but she had a major impact on how I understood poetry. She pulled me away from abstract theories and made me pay attention to the surface of the poem. She made us understand every word, image, or detail in the poems she assigned. If there was a flower or bird in the poem, she asked us to look it up. She told us to visit the Boston buildings that appeared in Robert Lowell's poems. She didn't want us to analyze poems; she required us to memorize one each week. Bishop made me understand that the surface of a poem was the poem. That insight changed me as both a poet and a critic.

MP: Are there East Coast poets whom you consider important influences on your work?

DG: I've never cared where a poet came from. Only the poetry matters. The poets who shaped me came from everywhere. To name just the Americans—Eliot, Stevens, Frost, Pound, Cummings, Hughes, Millay, Bishop, Weldon Kees, Theodore Roethke, Randall Jarrell, Richard Wilbur, Anthony Hecht, Anne Sexton, Donald Justice. I should also name Auden, who died an American citizen. He has always been a huge influence on me, not simply as a poet but also as a moral conscience.

Influence is a fluid thing. Sometimes a poet teaches you one small but useful trick, sometimes they change your life. If I were asked what American poets had been the most influential on my work, I would say Frost and Stevens—plus Auden, if we can count him as a Yank.

MP: Was Frost an early influence on your poetry?

DG: Not an early one. Frost was too plain-spoken for my modernist younger self. But when I started to write narrative poems in my midtwenties, he was decisive. I realized that he had opened up possibilities for verse narrative in his *North of Boston* (1914) that no one had pursued. This book is an unacknowledged masterpiece of American Modernism. (I believe its minimal style influenced Hemingway's fiction a decade later through their common friend Ezra Pound.) Frost's example changed everything for me. I could learn from him without in any sense copying him. He gradually became central to my sense of the art.

MP: I hear echoes of Frost in your dramatic monologue "Haunted" and in the final stanza of "The End of the World":

> I stood at the edge where the mist ascended,
> My journey done where the world ended.
> I looked downstream. There was nothing but sky,
> The sound of the water, and the water's reply.

DG: Well, certainly the idea of "The End of the World" is very Frostian—a walk through nature, though that theme was something Frost himself had borrowed from Wordsworth. When I left the urban world for rural life twenty years ago, Frost became more important—not just to writing but to seeing the world. I actually have a long un-mortared stone wall on my property. I live Frost's "Mending Wall" on a weekly basis.

Sadly, the city is constantly getting closer. California is insatiable for development. I may end my days in a suburb without ever moving.

MP: Your appreciation for classical music is evident in such poems as "Elegy for Vladimir de Pachmann," "Lives of the Great Composers," and "Marketing Department Trio." You have also written three opera libretti. Did you study classical music in school? Was playing part of your upbringing?
DG: Music was everything to me as a kid. I took piano lessons from Sister Camille Cecile in parochial school. She also gave me a weekly class in theory. It only cost a few dollars a month—God bless the nuns who serve the poor. By eighth grade I was playing Beethoven sonatas and Bartók's *Mikrokosmos*. She also got me my first symphony tickets—for free. I was no musical wunderkind, but I was proficient. I received from her the great gift of experiencing music from the inside. I soon took clarinet lessons, then picked up the tenor saxophone. I also started writing music.

MP: How long did you continue to study music?
DG: My otherwise undistinguished Catholic high school had the best concert band in Los Angeles. That was another gift. For two years our teacher was a professional trumpeter who had us play Holst, Vaughan Williams, Hindemith, and Persichetti rather than military marches or show tunes. My friends were all musicians. Los Angeles was already a great musical center. We drove all over to attend concerts, sometimes sneaking in if we couldn't afford tickets.

We also read novels and poetry, went to foreign films and museums. But music was the center of our cultural lives. When I entered college, I thought I would be a composer. Then, without warning, poetry claimed me.

MP: What is the value of creating a canon of American literature? Should there be a separate West Coast canon of poetry? Or is it better simply to open up our definition of the American canon to include all?
DG: A canon is just a reading list. We can't read everything that has been written, and nor can the young study it all. Since ancient times various teachers and writers have contrived to list what they consider the best or most useful works. All canons are provisional because there is always someone coming onto the scene with new perspectives.

Any adequate canon of American literature needs to include California writers, though many have not. There is also great value in starting from a local perspective. Once you start by listing the most interesting works written in California, you notice the importance of the Naturalist tradition—Jack London, Frank Norris, Edwin Markham, Robinson Jeffers, John Steinbeck, and later John Fante and Charles Bukowski. This starkly realistic and political tradition tends to be slighted in Ivy League histories and anthologies.

MP: Has California literature expanded the canon?
DG: Yes, but very slowly. Our state's two most innovative genres, science fiction and realist detective fiction, took over half a century to be acknowledged by academia. It happened only after those disreputable populist genres transformed both international entertainment and literary fiction. Raymond Chandler, Dashiell Hammett, Ray Bradbury, Philip K. Dick, and Octavia Butler are now canonic figures.

MP: Poems such as "Do Not Expect," "Most Journeys Come to This," "Progress Report," and "The Road" read like directives from the narrator to the reader, and to the self. Is writing a way for you to come to terms with essential lessons from your own experience?

DG: Some of my poems are conversations with myself that the reader is invited to overhear. That isn't a particularly literary notion. Everyone lives inside his or her own mind. We all constantly talk to ourselves, sometimes even out loud. That inner conversation is part of consciousness. I like poetry which imitates the shifting nature of consciousness. Not "stream of consciousness" with its avalanche of details but the essentially lyric shape of consciousness, shifting moment by moment.

I never set out initially to say anything in a poem. I follow the impulse of inspiration to see where it will lead. If I'm not surprised by what I write, the poem won't feel new to the reader.

MP: Some of your poems do the hard work of social critique, yet avoid didacticism because of your sense of humor, mastery of form, or even ironic use of cliché. The poem "Money," for example, explores vocabulary around the subject.

DG: Sometimes the most powerful way of getting at truth is by being funny. Humor entices people to listen to ideas that they would shut out if stated straightforwardly.

Music is important, too. The tougher the truth you tell the more important the pleasure principle becomes. That is one advantage of form. The musical structure provides pleasure even if the message is painful. A bitter critique like "A California Requiem," which excoriates our state's lack of respect and awareness of its natural environment, would not be bearable without its formal rhythm and rhyme. My sorrow for society's failures, its crass materialism, and its destruction of the natural world pervades every poem I write. That's why the language needs to be compelling, even beautiful.

MP: One of my favorite poems is your six-line "Unsaid." I admire its honesty, the way it captures art's attempt to express the ineffable. At the same time the poem honors the private silences in which many of us live.

Unsaid

So much of what we live goes on inside—
The diaries of grief, the tongue-tied aches
Of unacknowledged love are no less real
For having passed unsaid. What we conceal

Is always more than what we dare confide.
Think of the letters that we write our dead.

DG: In a poem, there is what you say and also what you don't say. There is always a temptation to over-explain things. I leave much unsaid in my poetry. The reader needs to fill in those silences from his or her own life. Creating that secret conversation with the reader is the purpose of the art.

"This Poem Has Had a Strange Destiny": Interview with Dana Gioia about "The Ballad of Jesús Ortiz"

John Zheng / 2019

From *Journal of Ethnic American Literature* 9 (2019): 88–93. Reprinted by permission of John Zheng.

John Zheng: What led you to write "The Ballad of Jesús Ortiz"?
Dana Gioia: That's a complicated question to answer. The poem tells a story I first heard as a child, but I didn't write the poem until I was sixty-five.

JZ: When did you first hear the story of your great-grandfather's death?
DG: I was about ten on a visit to my Mexican grandfather. He was a hard-drinking and temperamental man, extremely intelligent despite his lack of education. My mother had left home in her mid-teens to escape his violent outbursts. We visited him only on holidays. He and I had been left alone for a few minutes. He asked what grade I was in.

"Fourth," I replied.

Then he told me that he had left school when he was my age. I wasn't surprised. I knew that both of my grandfathers had only been in school a few years. I asked him why he had left.

"My dad got shot in a saloon," he replied. "My brother and I had to support the family so we became cowboys."

I was astonished. He then described his father's death and his early days on the Wyoming frontier as a *vaquero*. I never forgot his rough and violent story.

JZ: Was this conversation the origin of your poem?
DG: Yes, but it took over half a century. I never entirely trusted the details of my grandfather's story. I asked my mother about it. She told me it was true. She added that the killing had occurred around 1910 in town called Lost Cabin, Wyoming.

The story helped shape my sense of my family history, which had violent episodes, including murders, on both sides. But the episode never emerged in my imagination as a poem.

JZ: How did it emerge as a poem? Did you research it?
DG: It happened very oddly. Many years later, when I was the Chairman of the National Endowment for the Arts, I gave a speech in Casper, Wyoming, which wasn't far from Lost Cabin. In my talk I mentioned that the last member of my family who had visited the area had been shot dead in a bar and briefly told the story.

Afterwards a stern and serious woman approached and cross-examined me about the episode. She clearly thought I had made it up. She was, I learned later, the State Librarian. I gave her the facts that I knew, which she wrote down like a suspicious detective taking evidence.

JZ: What happened then?
DG: Two months later a large packet from the Wyoming State Library arrived in my office in Washington, DC. It contained photocopies of newspaper clippings and official documents concerning my great-grandfather's life and murder. Even though the documents were a hundred years old, I felt my throat tighten as I read through them. I now had the names of everyone involved as well as a description of the killing and its aftermath. I also had many facts about my great-grandfather's earlier life. I knew then I had to write about the incident.

JZ: Did the poem come quickly?
DG: No, it didn't come at all. Several times I started to write about the murder, but everything I wrote seemed lifeless and literary. For the next five years I couldn't find my way into the story.

JZ: What was the creative process that eventually led into the poem?
DG: I kept thinking about the poem. I filled a few pages with dead ends. Then one day I jotted down a couple of lines. I said them aloud, and they felt

right. As I repeated them to myself, I realized that the poem wanted to be a ballad. Slowly the poem fell into place, stanza by stanza.

JZ: Can you talk more about the language and form? What worked or didn't work in creating the poem?

DG: I wanted to write a poem that told a story but was never prosaic. The language needed to be both transparent and lyric. I tried to put a small twist—ironic or musical—in every stanza. As I got into the poem, I knew the ballad was the inevitable form for the subject. The ballad has traditionally been the form that documents the stories of the poor, especially in the Old West. The people I was writing about sang and recited ballads or *corridos.*

It was important for me to write a poem that the working-class people I came from could understand. It needed to be a poem my mother and grandfather could have understood.

JZ: Were you surprised to write a cowboy ballad?

DG: Yes, but I was also a little alarmed. Literary poets today are not supposed to write traditional ballads. I knew the form was artistically right, the best possible way to handle the subject.

There was also a new energy gained from inverting the traditional form by making the ballad about an outsider. Jesús wasn't a Western gunslinger. He was an unarmed Mexican immigrant—not the traditional protagonist for a Western ballad.

JZ: What did you want to emphasize in the poem?

DG: I wanted to tell the actual story as accurately as possible. It had to feel real. The reader needed to experience the events as Jesús Ortiz did. I trusted the story itself to do the rest. I tried to avoid moralizing. Ballads are strongest when they are most objective.

JZ: Did this poem liberate you emotionally?

DG: Writing the poem released all sorts of emotions. It felt affirming to tell a story that had gone untold for over a hundred years. I was proud to remember my great-grandfather. The stories of poor Mexican immigrants have mostly been forgotten. They have remained unsung.

JZ: Did you give much attention to the musical elements when you composed the poem?

DG: I thought about the sound and rhythm of every phrase, every line, and every stanza. Music is what creates the emotional connection. I didn't want the poem to sound contrived or academic. I wanted the lines to evoke a sung ballad—with a strong metrical beat but not too tight. I avoided the strict accentual-syllabic meters of literary ballads. Instead I alternated accentual-syllabic lines with three-stress lines. That technique made the poem sound closer to both everyday speech and folk song.

JZ: As a poet, how did you play with imagination in the ballad?
DG: It was important that the poem be true. Every name, place, and major event in the ballad is factual. I only filled in a few transitions. I focused my imagination on making the facts come alive. I didn't want the ballad to present a generic story of racial injustice. I wanted to tell the story of a real man.

JZ: What was your family's response when they read this poem about their ancestor?
DG: No one in my mother's family knew about the poem until it was published. They were surprised but grateful to see the family history presented. Most Mexican Americans feel their lives are invisible, and their family histories have been erased. My family felt vindicated to see the story told, even if it did take a hundred and six years.

JZ: How did the ballad come to be published?
DG: "The Ballad of Jesús Ortiz" had an odd debut. When I finished the poem, I didn't send it out. I just let it sit. It was published through a lucky coincidence.

The BBC was doing a radio documentary about my project as California Poet Laureate to visit all of the state's fifty-eight counties. The producer, the poet Julian May, came to my home to start the interviews. He asked if I had any new work. I showed him a few things. Then, with some hesitation, I read him the ballad. Julian asked to borrow the manuscript to reread. The next morning he announced he wanted to do a second radio program about the genesis of this poem.

JZ: So the poem first appeared on radio as a spoken work without the text?
DG: It appeared simultaneously on radio in the UK and online in the US. With the broadcast approaching, I had to publish the poem quickly. Given how slowly most journals accept and publish poetry, this posed a problem. I also wanted it published in the West. I had always been reluctant to publish

poems online, but I sent it to *Los Angeles Review of Books.* Within half an hour the editor Boris Dralyuk accepted it.

JZ: How was it received by the public?
DG: This was a great surprise. It created an immediate stir. Two other journals asked to reprint it. The BBC broadcast the second show about its genesis, first in the UK and then in the US (Interestingly, in the US, NPR censored the killer's racist outburst.) A fine press printer asked to do a special edition. It was translated into Spanish and Vietnamese. The composer Paul Salerni set it to music. Finally, the sculptor and *santero* Luis Tapia surprised me by creating "El Cantinero," a statue of Jesús Ortiz. He said that the poem had moved him so deeply that he felt compelled to carve it.

JZ: Did you ever read this poem to audiences when you toured the counties of California?
DG: I hesitated to read it in public. Not only was it long, it was also a cowboy ballad on a serious and uncomfortable subject. I waited till I started visiting towns in the Central Valley, California's agricultural belt. When I read it for the first time in public—in Yuba City—the crowd broke into applause. That started happening everywhere. People understood the importance of the story.

The poem has had a strange destiny. It was a story that had to be told. I was simply the spokesman.

Bibliography

Books

Brennan, Matthew. *Dana Gioia: A Critical Introduction*. West Chester: Story Line Press, 2012.

Foley, Jack, ed. *The "Fallen Western Star" Wars*. Oakland: Scarlet Tanager Books, 2001.

Hagstrom, Jack W. C., and Bill Morgan, eds. *Dana Gioia: A Descriptive Bibliography with Critical Essays*. Jackson: Parrish House, 2002.

Lindner, April. *Dana Gioia*. Boise: Boise State University Press, 2000. Rev. ed. 2003. Western Writers Series 143.

Peich, Michael. *Dana Gioia & Fine Press Printing: A Bibliographic Checklist*. New York: Kelly-Winterton Press, 2000.

Books with Chapters on Dana Gioia

Bauerlein, Mark, ed. *National Endowment for the Arts: A History (1965–2008)*. Washington DC: NEA, 2008.

Mcphillips, Robert. *The New Formalism: A Critical Introduction*. Expanded ed. Cincinnati: Textos Books, 2005.

Walzer, Kevin. *The Ghost of Tradition: Expansive Poetry and Postmodernism*. Ashland: Story Line Press, 1998.

Welford, Theresa Malphrus. *Transatlantic Connections: A Literary History*. Pasadena, CA: Story Line Press, 2019.

Selected Reference Articles

Austenfeld, Thomas. "The Drama of Shaping a Lyrical Moment: An Approach to the Poetry of Dana Gioia." *New Pilgrimages: Selected Papers from the IAUPE Beijing Conference in 2013*. Beijing: Tsinghua University Press, 2015. 244–58.

Bauerlein, Mark. "The Gioia Effect." *First Things*. 19 Oct. 2016. www.firstthings.com.

Clausen, Christopher. "Culture and the Subculture." *Commentary* 95.2 (1993): 75–76.

Clausen, Christopher. "Poetry Formal and Free." *Sewanee Review* 99.4 (1991): xcvii–c.

Donaghy, Michael. "Dana Gioia—Criticism and Hedonism." *The Shape of the Dance: Essays, Interviews and Digressions*. Ed. Adam O'Riordan and Maddy Paxman. London: Picador, 2009. 74–78.

Doncu, Roxana Elena. "Coaxing Words into Form: The Poetry of Dana Gioia." *Literary Form: Theories—Dynamics—Cultures, Perspectives on Literary Modelling*. Ed. Robert Matthias Erdbeer et al. Heidelberg: Heidelberg University Press, 2018. 457–76.

Foley, Jack. "The Achievement of Dana Gioia." *The Dancer and the Dance: A Book of Distinctions, Poetry in the New Century*. Los Angeles: Red Hen Press, 2008. 150–56.

Hix, H. L. "Dana Gioia's Criticism." *A Descriptive Bibliography with Critical Essays*. Ed. Jack W. C. Hagstrom and Bill Morgan. Jackson: Parrish House, 2002. 283–96.

Hren, Joshua. "Climbing to God on 'The Burning Ladder': Dana Gioia's *Via Negativa*." *Religion and the Arts* 23.1–2 (Mar 2019): 124–41.

Juster, A. M. "The Case for Dana Gioia." *CRB Digital*. 15 May 2016. www.claremont.org.

Kirsch, Adam. "The Poetry Problem: Can Poetry Matter?" *New York Sun*. 18 Sept. 2002: 1, 10.

Kramer, Hilton. "Poetry and the Silencing of Art." *New Criterion*. Feb. 1993: 4–9.

Lind, Michael. "Dana Gioia as a Literary Figure." *A Descriptive Bibliography with Critical Essays*. Ed. Jack W. C. Hagstrom and Bill Morgan. Jackson: Parrish House, 2002. 297–300.

Maio, Samuel. "Dana Gioia's Dramatic Monologues." *The Formalist* 13.1 (2002): 63–72.

Mason, David. "Dana Gioia's Case for Poetry." *Sparrow* 60 (Summer 1993): 22–28.

Mason, David. "Dana Gioia." *Encyclopedia of American Poetry: The Twentieth Century*. Ed. Eric L. Haralson. Chicago and London: Fitzroy Dearborn, 2001. 247–48.

Mason, David. "The Inner Exile of Dana Gioia." *Sewanee Review* 123.1 (Winter 2015): 133–46.

McCann, Janet. "Dana Gioia: A Contemporary Metaphysics." *Renascence* 61.3 (2009): 193–205.

McDowell, Robert. "The New Narrative Poetry." *Crosscurrents* 8.2 (1989) 30–38.

McPhillips, Robert. "Dana Gioia." *Oxford Companion to Twentieth-Century Poetry in English*. Ed. Ian Hamilton. New York and Oxford: Oxford University Press, 1994, 188.

Meyer, Bruce. "(Michael) Dana Gioia." *Dictionary of Literary Biography: New Formalist Poets*. Vol. 282. Ed. Jonathan N. Barron and Bruce Meyer. Detroit: Gale, 2003.

Oxley, William. "(Michael) Dana Gioia." *Contemporary Poets*. Ed. Thomas Riggs. 6th ed. Detroit: St. James Press, 1996. 388–89.

Russell, Peter. "Dana Gioia and the New Formalism." *Edge City Review* 1.2 (1994): 13–19.

Simpson, Louis, "On the Neglect of Poetry in the United States. *New Criterion* 10.1 (1991): 81–85.

Thwaite, Anthony. Preface. *Contemporary Poets*. Ed. Thomas Riggs. 6th ed. Detroit: St. James Press, 1996. vii–viii.

Turco, Lewis. "(Michael) Dana Gioia." *Dictionary of Literary Biography: American Poets Since World War II: Third Series*. Vol. 120. Ed. R. S. Gwynn. Detroit: Gale Research, 1992. 84–90.

Wilson, James Matthew. *The Catholic Imagination in Modern American Poetry*. Wiseblood Books, 2014.

Wilson, James Matthew. "The World of New Formalism," *The Fortunes of Poetry in an Age of Unmaking*. Wiseblood Books, 2015. 77–99.

Winchell, Mark Royden. "Dana Gioia." *Oxford Encyclopedia of American Literature*. Vol. 2. Ed. Jay Parini. New York and Oxford: Oxford University Press, 2004. 115–17.

Young, R. V. "The Place of Poetry in Twitterland." *Modern Age*. Summer 2013: 49–56.

Zheng, John. "The Art of Telling: Dana Gioia's 'The Ballad of Jesús Ortiz.'" *Valley Voices: A Literary Review* 18.2 (2018): 117–22.

Selected Reviews

Applegorth, Ann. "A Poet Reflects on Our Times." Rev. of *Pity the Beautiful*. *Catholic World Report* (June 20, 2012).

Balbo, Ned. "The Two Dana Gioias: *Pity the Beautiful*." *Italian Americana* 30.2 (Summer 2012): 227–31.

Balée, Susan. "Poems for Those Aching for Words." Rev. of *Interrogations at Noon*. *Philadelphia Inquirer*. 15 April 2001: H13–14.

Bawer, Bruce. Rev. of *Pity the Beautiful*. *The Hudson Review* 65.2 (Summer 2012): 336–39.

Bilbro, Jeffrey. "Teaching Us the Names: The Poetry of Dana Gioia." Rev. of *99 Poems*. *Books & Culture*. 7 Oct. 2016. www.booksandculture.com.

Carnell, Simon. Rev. of *The Gods of Winter*. *Times Literary Supplement* (December 27, 1991).

D'Evelyn, Thomas. "Poetry That Matters: A Plunge Into Shared Experience." Rev. of *The Gods of Winter*. *Christian Science Monitor*. 2 July 1991: 14.

Edwards, Lynnell. Rev. of *Disappearing Ink*. *American Book Review* (July/August 2005).

Foley, Jack. Rev. of *Interrogations at Noon*. *Caesura* (Spring/Summer 2001).

Greening, John. Rev. of *Pity the Beautiful*. *Times Literary Supplement* (April 19, 2013): 23.

Gwynn, R. S. Rev. of *The Gods of Winter*. *Dictionary of Library Biography Yearbook* (1991).

Haddin, Theodore. Rev. of *Pity the Beautiful*. *Poetry South* 2012: 35–37.

Haddin, Theodore. Rev. of "The Ballad of Jesús Ortiz." *Journal of Ethnic American Literature* 9 (2019): 94–96.

Haven, Cynthia L. Rev. of *Interrogations at Noon. San Francisco Magazine* (April 2001).

Jalon, Allan M. Rev. of *Interrogations at Noon. San Francisco Chronicle Book Review* (April 1, 2001).

Mason, David. Rev. of *Daily Horoscope. The Literary Review* (Spring 1988).

Massimilla, Stephen. "The Achievement of Dana Gioia." Rev. of *99 Poems. Italian Americana* 35.1 (Winter 2017): 75–79.

Mattix, Micah. "Everyman's Poet." Rev. of *Pity the Beautiful. First Things* (October 2012): 60–62.

Mattix, Micah. "Dana Gioia's Poetry." Rev. of *99 Poems. Washington Free Beacon.* 19 Mar 2016. www.freebeacon.com.

McDowell, Robert. "New Schools & Late Discoveries." Rev. of *Daily Horoscope. Hudson Review* 39.4 (Winter 1987): 673–89.

McPhillips, Robert. Rev. of *The Gods of Winter. Verse* (Summer 1992).

Meinke, Peter. Rev. of *The Gods of Winter. Sunday Sentinel* (April 19, 1992).

Middleton, David. "The Mystery of Things." Rev. of *99 Poems. Chronicles.* April 2017: 22–23.

Oxley, William. "The First Shall Be Last." Rev. of *Interrogations at Noon. Acumen* 41 (Sept 2001): 101–4.

Perloff, Marjorie. "Poetry Doesn't Matter." *American Book Review* 15.5 (Dec. 1993–Jan. 1994): 3, 5, 7, 9.

Stevenson, Anne. "The Poetry of Dana Gioia." Rev. of *The Gods of Winter. Between the Iceberg and the Ship: Selected Essays.* Ann Arbor: University of Michigan Press, 1998. 156–58.

Swarbrick, Andrew. Rev. of *The Gods of Winter. Oxford Times* (October 18, 1991).

Wilson, Frank. "Dana Gioia's Achievement Shines in *99 Poems." Philadelphia Inquirer* (July 1, 2016).

Wilson, James Matthew. "In Christ-Haunted California: Dana Gioia's *99 Poems." Catholic World Report* (April 26, 2016).

Zheng, John. The Comic Irony in Dana Gioia's *Two Epitaphs." Rev. of *Two Epitaphs. Valley Voices: A Literary Review* 19.1 (2019): 96–97.

Zheng, John. Rev. of *Jack Foley's Unmanageable Masterpiece. Journal of Ethnic American Literature* 9 (2019): 97–100.

Index

149, 166, 174–75, 200, 213–14;
on art, 10, 16, 18–19, 28–29, 32,
34–35, 37–39, 44–52, 62–64,
79, 84, 87, 101, 111–16, 119–24,
126–28, 130–31, 152–53, 155, 161,
166–67, 175, 177–78, 184, 186–87,
192, 195, 200, 204, 208–10, 213,
218–20, 228, 233; on beauty,
28, 58–59, 143, 186, 195–98; on
California poetry, 82, 223–24;
on canon, 7, 16, 18, 48, 70–71,
111, 148, 231; on Catholicism,
4, 35–36, 84, 86, 138, 142, 149,
151–53, 194, 196–99; on Catholic
Church, 4, 94, 129, 149, 151–52,
195–96, 222; on Catholic poetry,
36, 200; on character, 61–62, 66,
95, 139, 155, 169, 172, 181, 183; on
Christianity, 131, 142, 152, 191, 199;
on collaboration, 41, 63–64, 167,
174–85, 188; on criticism, 16–24,
33, 35–36, 38–39, 42–44, 56–57,
72, 83, 97, 110–18, 131, 165, 179,
203, 217–18, 224; on culture, 4, 15,
22, 28, 32–35, 38, 42–47, 51, 72,
78, 90, 99–107, 112–13, 116, 119–
24, 130, 151–53, 174, 180, 184, 191,
213, 217–19, 222–25; on the devil,
139; on displacement, 132–33; on
drama, 41, 60–64, 81, 108, 131; on
dramatic monologue, 24, 39, 94,
106, 230; on epiphany, 28, 135; on
evil, 54, 138–39, 143, 199; on fame,
9, 98, 179–80, 207; on feeling,
53, 138; on form, 9–10, 18, 27, 29,
36–37, 49–54, 60–66, 99, 101–6,
122–23, 137–38, 159–61, 165–66,
171, 174–77, 180–81, 183, 186–92,
205, 209, 212, 232, 236; on fragments in poetry, 157–58; on
General Foods, 80, 89–91, 107; on
Hawthorne, California, 3–4, 222;

on imagination, 19–20, 27, 31,
111–12, 129–30, 147, 149, 176–77,
197, 223, 228, 237; on immortality, 55; on impulse, 23, 30, 54–55,
65, 79, 91, 142, 166, 171, 179, 190,
208–9, 232; on influence, 8–12,
19–20, 23–25, 28, 33, 52, 57–58,
76, 81, 84, 88, 91–92, 100, 115, 117,
131, 166–67, 172, 178–79, 194, 215,
224, 226, 229–30; on inspirational poetry, 68; on inspiration,
75, 104, 135, 155, 166, 170–71, 176,
181, 188, 209, 232; on intelligence,
52, 87, 115, 177, 198; on intuition,
29, 31, 115, 121, 176, 179; on Irish
poetry, 39; on jazz, 56, 120, 122,
126–27, 182, 184–85, 187, 207;
on language, 4, 9, 21, 27–29,
37–41, 50, 52, 55–56, 58–59, 61,
63, 65, 67–72, 74, 77, 81, 87, 105,
108, 120, 131–32, 138, 141–42,
153–54, 164–65, 171, 175–76, 181,
184, 188–90, 195, 209–10, 212,
217, 220, 232, 236; on libretto, vi,
xxvi, 35, 60–66, 67–68, 81–82,
108, 179–81; on literary culture,
37–38, 42–43, 51–52, 72, 78, 90,
99, 102, 112, 213, 217; on loss, 52,
64, 67, 133, 142–47, 182, 195; on
lyric poetry, 26, 52, 58, 67–68,
101, 108, 132–34, 138, 145; on
meditation, 35, 120, 142; on
modernism, 14–15, 26, 28–29, 34,
41, 46–47, 49, 100, 120–21, 138,
166–67, 175–76, 178, 215, 226–27,
230; on music, 5–6, 16, 31–32, 39,
45, 51, 55, 60–66, 74–75, 81–82,
84, 91–92, 101, 103, 108, 110, 114,
121–23, 126–27, 131, 140, 153–54,
157, 164, 166–67, 176–78, 180–85,
186–87, 192, 195, 200, 205,
208, 215, 217, 225–28, 230–32,

About the Editor

John Zheng is professor of English at Mississippi Valley State University, author of *Enforced Rustication in the Chinese Cultural Revolution*, and editor of scholarly books including *African American Haiku: Cultural Visions* and *The Other World of Richard Wright: Perspectives on His Haiku* (University Press of Mississippi).

Printed in the United States
By Bookmasters